CROCHET and CREATIVE DESIGN

Also by Annette Feldman
Knit, Purl, and Design!

CROCHET
and CREATIVE DESIGN

Annette Feldman

HARPER & ROW, PUBLISHERS
New York, Evanston,
San Francisco, London

CROCHET AND CREATIVE DESIGN. Copyright © 1973 by Annette Feldman. All rights reserved. Printed in the United States of America. No part of this book may be used or reproduced in any manner whatsoever without written permission except in the case of brief quotations embodied in critical articles and reviews. For information address Harper & Row, Publishers, Inc., 10 East 53rd Street, New York, N.Y. 10022. Published simultaneously in Canada by Fitzhenry & Whiteside Limited, Toronto.

FIRST EDITION

Designed by C. Linda Dingler

Library of Congress Cataloging in Publication Data

Feldman, Annette.
  Crochet and creative design.

  1. Crocheting. I. Title.
TT820.F43 1973   746.4'3   73–4080
ISBN 0–06–011223–9

CONTENTS

1. HISTORY AND LEGEND OF THE CROCHETING ART   1

A documentary tracing the history of this fascinating one-needle art from its earliest beginnings through its stellar role as a "cottage industry," producing magnificent hand-crocheted lace during the potato famine in 1846 to help save Ireland from financial disaster, and then on to its peak of popularity today as a medium for the making of contemporary high-fashion clothing and stunning home decor.

2. CONTEMPORARY CROCHET   5

A listing of all the things that can be crocheted for everyone in the family, for the home, and for small gifts, with suggestions ranging from baby mittens to hostess coats and carpeting by the yard, and a vivid description of why more people have acquired the crocheting habit during recent years than ever before in history.

3. YOU CAN DESIGN YOUR OWN CROCHETS   10

Encouragement is offered to all who want reassurance that you can do your own crochet designing, reminding you that "beauty lies only in the eyes of the beholder," and that if a design you have in mind looks good to you, then it is a good design. You will learn here how it is possible to create completely original things of your own, or if you are a little hesitant, to start out at first by projecting just a little of yourself into an already established design by changing a stitch, a sleeve, or a neckline.

4. CROCHETER'S GUIDE   12

All techniques in crocheting are explained, many of them illustrated, and an attempt is made to answer any questions about the skill that might possibly be asked by those who are new at it, and by the more experienced. There are paragraphs on—among other things—gauge, increasing, decreasing, binding off, and making circles and squares. Guidance is offered to those who are left-handed, teaching you how to manipulate your needle and yarn with your more dextrous left hand, and how to interpret illustrations and directions for your own particular needs.

5. HOW TO DESIGN   22

Complete information on crochet designing, explaining the simple rules and mechanics involved in this creative skill, and offering easy-to-follow, step-by-step instructions to both experienced crocheters and those who have never held a hook in their hands before. Examples are given, and designs are worked out together with you, even as you read.

6. PATTERN STITCHES 35

Many beautiful pattern stitches are shown, all with clearly written directions to follow. Some are quite easy to work, others more intricate, and the patterns range from simple stitches and rich textures to shells, clusters, puffs and popcorns, delicate lacy designs and those made with two and three colors.

7. AFGHAN STITCH, OR TUNISIAN CROCHET 90

Drawings show you how to work with the afghan hook, an unusual cross between a knitting and a crochet needle, and how to do cross-stitch embroidery over the woven little boxlike afghan stitches. You are told how to make a single rose, a small nosegay or a large floral bouquet blossom into almost lifelike beauty even as you cross one small stitch over another onto the crocheted background. Limitless design possibilities are suggested, and many new afghan stitches are also shown, with directions for making them.

8. CHARTED DESIGNS 99

A folio of design charts, showing floral, stylized, and geometric patterns for use with the afghan stitch described in Chapter 7, and for filet crochet work described in Chapter 9. Suggestions are given for adapting these designs to the particular work being done, and for combining some and changing others so that suddenly completely new designs are created. Two different alphabet charts are also included for those wanting to use their name or monogram as part of their crochet design.

9. FILET CROCHET 109

A chapter about the particular type of open mesh work known as filet crochet, traditionally and still used for tablecloths, coverlets, placemats and other fine household linen, and beyond that, today, for contemporary high-fashion clothing, such as beach coats and long and short dinner skirts. There are directions and patterns for this type of crocheting which is generally done in a series of open spaces and blocks, the spaces forming the background of the work and the filled-in blocks the design which becomes an integral part of it.

10. MOTIFS 113

A picture dictionary of round, square, hexagonal, octagonal, and diamond-shaped motifs, the small pieces that are finished unto themselves and usually meant to be assembled into a larger piece of "patchwork." Directions are given for each and suggestions made for creating completely original motifs of your own by adding or leaving off rounds from those we have shown, or by making our solid-color ones in two, three, or four colors, changing them on the different rounds as it pleases you. A few fascinating methods of joining are also shown.

11. FRINGES, EDGINGS, AND INSERTIONS 139

A composite of plain and fancy trimmings, with directions for making them. There are many ideas on how to use them as embellishment and as a beautiful and interesting final touch wherever they are placed. Your imagination will be sparked by the thought of fashioning a skirt with strips of black material joined one to the other with crocheted inserts alternated colorwise in bands of brilliant red, strong yellow, and emerald green, or of lengthening your elegant but too-short damask draperies with an inch or two of a metallic gold crocheted trim worked across the bottom of them.

12. DESIGNER'S GUIDE   159

Here are secrets from a designer's notebook, telling you practically everything you might want to know about balance, proportion, and shaping in order to be able to create your own crocheted designs. Suggested basic measurements are given for twenty-six different sizes ranging from the six-month-infant size to size 46 for men, and guide rules are given for, among other things, the shaping of armholes, sleeves, shoulders, and necklines on sweaters, dresses, coats, and ponchos.

TRANSLATIONS OF CROCHET TERMS (Spanish, French, German, Italian)   169

Translations are given for many of the more popular crochet terms for those who choose to use the patterns here but are more familiar with the terminology in their native language, and for those who would like to adapt their own crocheting to designs and directions appearing in foreign periodicals.

INDEX: *A Complete Cross-Reference of All Material in This Book*   173

CROCHET and CREATIVE DESIGN

1. HISTORY AND LEGEND OF THE CROCHETING ART

The art of crocheting has grown only quite recently from one practiced by relatively very few to perhaps the most popular of the needlecraft skills today. The technique is rather a simple one to master, worked basically with a ball of yarn, a small needle hooked at one end, and a simple interlocking stitch, and those who enjoy a knowledge of it and the new methods of working with it are making many lovely things for their own personal and home use.

It is not quite understood why this interesting and very beautiful craft has taken so long to come into its own, or why so little is known about its early history. Unlike other needle-art work, about which there is much history and legend, crocheting has a vague background, with ancient scattered findings showing up in the Middle East and again in China, and more recent findings from the time of the Renaissance in Middle Europe, and then suddenly, and completely unrelated, a very crude form of crochet work has appeared among the relics of the primitive Pima Indians in Arizona.

Actually, the first real information of any consequence or logical sequence about crocheting refers to it as a lace-making art which was started during the Renaissance and as such gained some prominence at that time in Belgium, England and France,

and in Italy, where a particularly fine type of crochet work, known as Orvieto lace, was being made. It seems too that it was about this time that the art was finally given a name, and the word "crochet" began to appear, this being the diminutive of the French *croc,* meaning hook, and presumably referring to the type of needle used in crocheting.

The popular appeal of the new crocheted lace that appeared at that time soon waned, however. The people, who were fairly unimaginative and unfamiliar with the art and its potential for the many beautiful new patterns that could be developed, tired of it and preferred the very fine delicate lace that was being made in other ways. Once again crochet fell into a state of near oblivion, and it is certainly a tribute to the intrinsic fine qualities of the art that it survived at all. Some small work was being carried on here and there, but even though the early settlers in America—who were intrigued by the art, but had little spare time to devote to the working of fine lace—carried on the craft, not much else was being done anywhere with it until the mid-nineteenth century when an odd thing happened in the strange history of crochet.

Mid-nineteenth-century English ladies of the upper classes who had long regarded all needlecrafts

1

as "cottage work," done by the poor for the adornment of the rich, suddenly discovered that crocheting was a very satisfying, creative hobby. It was fun and offered a pleasant relief to their boredom; and it was their interest that caused once more a strong upsurge in the popularity of the craft. The ladies spent many hours at their new hobby and became quite excited by what they were doing. They could hardly wait to finish one project before starting another, and soon they began to vie and compete with each other for new stitches and patterns and in their individual skill in working out their own particular designs. Quite coincidentally, and just about at this time, a clever and talented Frenchwoman, Mlle Riego de la Blanchardière, who had also been working with the craft, succeeded in imitating with her crochet hook some lovely old Venetian needlepoint lace patterns. She gained much admiration for her work and gathered about her a wide following of people, among whom were English ladies who loved the things she was making. They begged her for lessons to show them how to reproduce some of her beautiful things for themselves.

Again, in the unusual chain of events that contributed toward the growth of the craft, just about the time that the ladies were busying themselves with their beautiful lace-making, in 1846 there occurred the dread potato famine in Ireland, causing a state of extreme poverty and great concern among the people. With the loss of the crops upon which much of their livelihood and sustenance depended, the Irish people were distraught and in serious trouble. The English ladies were aware of this problem, and wanting to be charitable and offer whatever help they could, they decided to introduce Mlle de la Blanchardière's lace-making patterns to the Irish to be carried on as "cottage work," and as such a means by which they could earn some money and thus alleviate their suffering to some degree.

The Irish were grateful for the knowledge that was being passed on to them, eager to do what they could, and quick to learn. They worked prolifically with their fine linen thread and the little hooked needle, were fascinated by the art, and did indeed help themselves through their plight with the great success of their new industry. Before long they were adding new patterns of their own to those which had been passed on to them, and the vivid imagination of the workers in creating new designs was indeed nothing less than inspired. Three-leafed shamrocks and roses bloomed on lacy backgrounds, and intricate knotting patterns blossomed into lovely effects. Nothing showed the creative possibilities of crochet better than this history of "Irish crochet" or "Irish lace," started during the time of the famine and still world famous today, the earlier more delicate work being equaled only by the later work, which became less fine in detail as the demand grew, but was a great deal more imaginative in design.

The art of crocheted lace-making was now a widely accepted one, and as instruction books began to appear, more and more people started to practice it. Working always with a very small, sliver-thin needle and very fine thread, people were making edgings on linens, lace collars, and camisole tops, doilies and antimacassars, and occasionally a larger piece such as a treasured bedspread or tablecloth to be completed in a lifetime, or if not, to be worked on by one's heirs. The work, however, though beautiful, was very painstaking because of its delicate nature, and as time went on and life seemed to become more complicated and demanding, the craft gradually was relegated to the elderly, the retired, and those who had a great deal of patience and a lot of time to spare.

And so it was with this very delicate craft until many years later when someone somewhere experimented a bit with a little wool and the thickest of the small crochet hooks, and discovered and opened then a whole new vista for the art of crochet. The use of soft wool and the comparative ease of working it with the heaviest of the small needles made it suddenly possible to adapt crochet to the making of many other types of things besides just the very dainty ornamental and decorative ones which had been made until this time. Though the lacy effect and the stitches remained the same, the supple, more pliable nature of wool worked well for such things as infant layette sets, and shawls and scarfs and afghans, and even sweaters and dresses. Cotton would not have done as well for the making of these garments, yet wool was just right. Strange that no one had thought of this earlier!

Contemporary crochet, then, was just starting on its way with this recent discovery of the many new and different types of things that could be made. It is almost incredible how, during the very short period of only the past few decades, it has developed from a fine lace-making art to a new means of making gossamer-sheer infant layette sets and lovely shawls and stoles and now, suddenly, to its current and very prominent position in the areas of high fashion and modern home decor. The knowledge that other materials besides cotton and very fine linen thread could be used in crocheting apparently stimulated much further thought. Crochet hooks could certainly be made larger, and since it is basically the size of the hook that determines the type of material that can be used, by making them in bigger sizes one could surely accommodate the working of the craft to many other types of yarn and, consequently, to many other types of things to be made.

Designers and manufacturers busied themselves toward this end, and soon aluminum and bone hooks began to appear in sizes numbered B, C, D, E, F, G, H, I, J and K, the B and C still quite small, but the No. E hook being just about the equivalent in size to the No. 00 steel hook, the largest in existence up to this time, and each next letter a fraction of a size larger. Needles formerly were made of either steel or bone only, and ranged in size from No. 00, the largest, to No. 0, and then from No. 1 through No. 14, the smallest. On the No. 14 hook, still in existence today but not in very common usage, one can use only the finest of threads, and the number of stitches one can get to the inch varies between 10 and 14. On a No. 5

hook one usually gets somewhere between 6 and 10 stitches to the inch (the number of stitches varying always in accordance with the type of thread being used, and the degree of tension in the hand of the one who is working with it), and on the No. 00, somewhere between 4 and 8 stitches. The new No. E hook works best, again, as the No. 00, with between 4 and 8 stitches to the inch, but as the aluminum hooks graduate in size, so the type of yarn that can be used becomes heavier, and on our large No. K hook we can get between 2 and 4 stitches to the inch.

Most people today, a little short of both time and patience, would certainly be more interested in making, to use an example, a 17″ placemat on somewhere between 34 and 68 stitches with a No. K hook and between 2 and 4 stitches to the inch, than that same placemat, in a different material on somewhere between 170 and 238 stitches with between 10 and 14 stitches to the inch on the sliver-thin No. 14 hook. That very same placemat worked in the same pattern stitch, with either the No. 14 or the No. K hook could be of equal texture interest, and, again, the only difference in working it would be the size of the needle and the type of material used. One would have to work with only the finest thread with the No. 14 hook, whereas one might conceivably use, for example, an interesting straw yarn or heavier-weight textured synthetic with the No. K hook. Aside from the difference in the time element involved in working the 17″ placemat on 68 or 238 stitches, actually the feel and look of the one made in one-third or one-quarter of the time might be more exciting than the other and much more in keeping with today's style of contemporary decor.

The comparable beauty between the two types of placemats we have just described, and the vast difference in the working ease and the amount of time involved in the making of each, occurs in the crocheting of all the other things, too, that people are making these days. As we have become aware of this, and have begun to take note of the beautiful new things that can be made in practically no time at all, one and then another of us has started to crochet and to make some of those beautiful things. Today once more the art has reached a peak of prominence. Hooks have grown already to the very large No. 15 wood or plastic ones, on which one can get as few as 2 stitches to the inch, and still beyond that to the "Jumbo Jet" needle with a not uncommon gauge of 1 stitch to 1". We are strong into contemporary crochet now, and vast numbers of women, both young and old, are either crocheting or would like to learn how.

2. CONTEMPORARY CROCHET

Contemporary crochet, now set on its way by the big new crochet hooks and the eye-opening revelation of all the different things that could be made with them, came finally and fully into its own in rather a strong and startling manner, and started an explosive rash of artistic endeavor such as was never heard of before. The skilled and the unskilled, the young and the old, practically everyone got hold of a crochet hook and a ball of some kind of yarn, and, with the two in hand, started to make something. So explosive actually was this latest revival of the centuries-old art of crochet that very recently there occurred because of it a business bonanza of almost unheard-of proportion among yarn and needle manufacturers. Current stocks of material to work with ran out, and older stockpiles of not-so-current materials ran out too. Supply could not keep up with demand, and try as they did to fill the needs of all the crocheters, the suppliers simply could not manage to cope or keep up with them. Stores were rationed as to the number of hooks and the amount of yarn they could buy; this was done in order to make the very limited supply of goods go around. Crocheters borrowed hooks and traded whatever they had for a No. F hook from one, and a No. K hook from another, and many of them went so far as to rip out older gar- ments in order to be able to get enough yarn to start something new. One reasons quite sensibly now that surely it could not have been just the produc- tion of a larger crochet hook that had brought about the tremendous new interest in the craft, one of the most unusual business happenings in twentieth- century peacetime America.

And it is a fact that something else did happen in the sixties, something actually of most important social significance. A mounting restlessness among our young people came to an unexpected and cli- mactic head at just about the time we are talking of. Incensed and rebellious against "the establish- ment," the futile wars that touched deeply into their own lives, and the economic inflation that seemed hopeless, hard to beat, and even hard to keep up with, many of our young adult generation sought and created for themselves a whole new way and style of living. Many of the youngsters retired into a world of their own, choosing to "do their thing," and let the rest of the world keep rushing along in its futile, frenzied way. Wanting peace and freedom for themselves above every- thing else, and a recognition of their way of living, they severed old ties and went about doing things in their own special manner. Among other ways in which they chose to identify their individuality and newly established freedom was their manner of dress. A whole new concept developed, depicting a casualness and thorough escape from absolutely everything that was at all reminiscent of the type of existence from which they were trying to run away.

Young women removed their dainty little white gloves and their neatly fitted coats and chose to wear, instead, blue jeans, a poncho, and a pair of woolen mittens. Young men took off their felt hats and neckties, opened their collars, tossed on some kind of casual sweater and cap, and began to feel suddenly liberated. These young people chose for themselves a new range of colors, shifting at will between blatantly loud combinations such as hot pink, orange, yellow, brilliant green, and royal blue, and somber dismal tones of brown, beige, copper, and black, any color or combination of colors removing them far away from the middle-class neutrals which might identify them with the establishment. Hair-styles changed too in the big battle against the old world, as did everything else that might in any way manifest proof of a new individual identity, and a return to a more real and basic way of living. Those involved in the movement not only chose to do their own thing, but also to make everything they possibly could by themselves, and with their own two hands. They sawed and hammered and built whatever furniture they needed rather than buy new, and they grew their own little gardens and invented wonderful new casserole recipes in which they could blend and cook what they had grown. They sewed their own clothes from hand-woven goods and began to knit and crochet as well.

It was, then, the happy marriage between so many people needing and wanting to make their own things and the complete change in the style of dress occurring quite coincidentally just at about the time of the appearance of the fascinating new easy-to-work big crochet hooks that brought about the enormous rise in the number of crocheters. All of the "new" people, many of whom had never even heard of the existence of a crochet hook before, started to work with one. A cap and scarf was a comparatively simple thing to make, and since it fitted in well with the new casual mode of dress, everyone began to make caps and scarfs for themselves. They mixed and matched their own colors, devised their own stitches and styles, and within a very short time after they had started, they proudly appeared among their friends wearing the new accessories they had made.

Usually it is the designers and the fashion experts who create and encourage new styles and the consumer who is ultimately guided by their dictates. In this instance, however, the unique chain of events that led to the popular cap-and-scarf fad turned the normal sequence of things exactly into reverse. So earnest was the enthusiasm of the young people toward creating their individual things, and so intense their endeavor toward this end, that even their first attempt toward a new style started a fashion trend, and indeed a very popular fad. Almost every young person was busy crocheting his own version of the new style, and soon their young brothers and sisters, watching them, began to copy what they were doing. Then older and more conservative people, observing what was going on, began to feel that truly a hand-made crocheted cap and scarf was a pretty practical idea for themselves, and those who had young children felt that such an outfit on hand was an easy way to keep the little ones warm and comfortable. They started making their own, too, generally more conservative in both style and color, but still hand-crocheted and attractive to wear. Practically everyone was crocheting now, young or old, established or searching, and the fad had caught on so quickly that quite a period of time passed before professional designers and manufacturers were able to pick up the strong cap-and-scarf fashion lead and accommodate their own production to it. Some of the styles they came up with were a bit different, but most of them, in any case, tried very hard to copy the popular hand-crocheted look.

By now people began to realize what a great deal of fun and relaxation there was in the very simple art of crocheting. Many were beginning to feel, perhaps for the first time in their lives, the joy of creativity, and of being able not only to choose their own color and size and pattern, but also to have the satisfaction of making something that took perhaps only a few days at most to make. Soon after they could put it on and wear it. It had cost them little money to make, and the experience had been such a very pleasant one that not long after they finished their first project they were ready and anxious to go on to another.

The cap-and-scarf fad had started early one fall, and people were busy with it all through the winter months. By the time spring came many, anxious to keep on crocheting and carried away to some degree by the things they were making and the success of the new style they had fostered, looked for something else to work on. They began making light-weight cotton caps and scarfs, not at all for function or warmth, but purely for fashion and fun; and when summer was over, they began again to make new woolen ones to replace those that they had thoroughly worn out during the previous winter. Today crocheted caps and scarfs are still a very important clothing accessory, and probably they will always remain in style.

Needing certainly now to go on, and still rather overwhelmed with their big success in starting a real new style trend with the very first thing they had chosen and wanted to make, the young people looked for something new. Their next innovation, not very long thereafter, was the crocheted poncho, again in either very brilliant or very earthy colors, and again a style fitting in comfortably with their new casual mode of dress. Before long everyone was making some kind of a poncho, again the young people first, then younger siblings, then more conservative groups for themselves and their little children, and finally the ready-to-wear manufacturers. Ponchos, long or short, round or pointed, and with V- or turtle-necks, became and are still a popular type of clothing, and most of them are either hand-crocheted or designed and manufactured with a hand-crocheted look in mind.

With excitement toward these new style creations running way out of bound now, more and more different things began to appear. The little filet mesh crocheted vests came next, and once more

caused a near riot in the worlds of both fashion and needlework. Most crocheters made two or three of them for themselves, and several more for gifts. Some of the styles were long, and some were short, and some were slipovers, some cardigans, and many just the simple open jacket types. The hooks used for these vests were big and bigger ones, ranging anywhere from the No. K aluminum to the very big Jumbo Jet, and while the stitches varied a little in detail, mostly they were some type of open mesh, very light and airy, and involving so little work that they could be made in just a very few hours with only a ball or two of yarn. And so one fad followed another during these recent years, another of the great successes being the crocheted "top-over" or potholder vest, easy and quick to make, designed to be worn over a blouse, and appearing in innumerable variations of color and style.

Certainly at this point much more is yet expected to come in the world of crocheted high fashion, and it will indeed be of interest to see if it appears in the form of brand-new innovations, or perhaps as some type of modern restyling of older, more classic designs.

We have discussed here at length the incredible number of new crocheters, and how this great increase in numbers came about. However with all these new modern craftsmen being so busy with the hobby they have discovered for themselves, others who have been crocheting for years are turning their hand more and more to the new type of crocheting too, copying some of the novelty styles, but very often making newer versions of more staple things of their own. Also intrigued by the wonderful things that can be made with the large crochet hooks and the new yarns, many who have always worked with a fine gauge on a small hook have laid aside their delicate work and transferred their skill and knowledge to the more modern way of doing things. Besides the smart and good-looking coats, jackets and suits to which the heavier yarn adapts itself so well, they are also making lovely lace dresses, hostess gowns, and sweaters and blouses for themselves. They find too that the very delicate lace edgings and inserts that were used before only for handkerchiefs, pillowcases, and other fine linens, worked on the big hooks and with heavier yarn, serve especially well now as edgings and inserts on dirndl skirts, capes, woolen sweaters, and many other types of clothing. By the same token, old granny squares designed solely for the making of granny-square afghans—worked to a big gauge with soft mohair, textured straw, or some other interesting novelty yarn—could now suddenly be joined together and blossom forth into a lovely stole or evening skirt or belt, or beyond that, to an unusual trim such as an oversized pocket on a simple dress, or the focal point of interest on the front of a shoulder-strap bag. Lacy, delicately patterned crocheted motifs formerly most effective and useful for heirloom tablecloths and bedspreads, today are still being used, in the very same patterns, for tablecloths and placemats, and bedspreads and coverlets, but worked again on the heavy needle, and probably with some miraculous machine-washable, machine-dryable synthetic yarn in a fraction of the time, and with equally beautiful and even more startling results.

Everything indeed has changed a great deal during recent years in the development of our quiet little craft. We've not yet mentioned how some of us are also making rugs, carpeting by the yard, throw pillows, exciting wall hangings, and a whole new variety of beautiful things for our homes, accessories and decorative touches that are original, good-looking, and indeed sometimes almost inspired in design. As you read on, we hope you too will become more impressed and more aware of the wonderful things that you can make easily, quickly, and with your own two hands, a crochet hook, and some yarn. We could go on now without end telling you about them, but perhaps a more simple way of describing so many of them is to make a categorical list for you, hoping that by looking at the list, and at all the beautiful stitches and patterns that appear in subsequent chapters in this book, your imagination will be inspired, and you will be motivated to the point of wanting to start making something and to make it as soon as you possibly can.

Things to Crochet for Infants and Babies

Afghans	Diaper bags	Ponchos
Bassinet Skirts	Diaper sets	Pram robes
Bibs	Dresses	Sacques
Blankets	Hammocks	Scarfs
Booties	High-chair pads	Shawls
Bottle warmers	Layette Sets	Snowsuits
Buntings	Mittens	Suits
Caps	Mobiles	Sweaters
Carriage covers	Nursery wall	Toys
Crib bumpers	hangings	
Crib Coverlets	Playpen pads	

Things to Crochet for Small Children

Afghans	Hats	Skirts
Bathing suits	Jackets	Slippers
Bathrobes	Laundry bags	Smocks
Capes	Mittens	Snowsuits
Coats	Pajama bags	Suits
Coverlets	Pinafores	Sunsuits
Dolls' clothes	Ponchos	Sweaters
Dresses	Scarfs	Toys
Gloves	Skating outfits	Vests

Things to Crochet for Men and Boys

Bathing suits	Polo shirts	Slippers
Belts	Ponchos	Sweaters
Caps	Robes	Tank shirts
Gloves	Scarfs	Ties
Jackets	Shaving coats	Vests
Mittens	Ski bands	Wraparongs

Things to Crochet for Women and Girls

Aprons	Coats	Purse accessories
Bags	Dresses	Robes
Bathing suits	Gloves	Scarfs
Beach coats	Halters	Skirts
Bedjackets	Hats	Slacks
Belts	Hostess coats	Stoles
Blazers	Jackets	Suits
Blouses	Mittens	Sweaters
Capes	Ponchos	Vests

Things to Crochet for Your Home

Afghans	Coverlets	Placemats
Bathroom accessories	Curtains	Potholders
Bedspreads	Doilies	Rugs
Bridge table covers	Doormats	Screen inserts
Carpeting by the yard	Kitchen accessories	Slip seat covers
Closet accessories	Lampshade covers	Tablecloths
Coasters	Pillows	Wall hangings

Things to Crochet for Small Gifts

Beach bags	Curler bags	Kerchiefs
Belts	Curler caps	Nursery rugs
Book covers	Dog blankets	Pillow covers
Bookmarks	Doilies	Purse accessories
Bottle covers	Glass jackets	Shoe bags
Bun warmers	Golf club covers	Shopping bags
Christmas decorations	Growing yardsticks	Tennis racquet covers
Covered hangers	Jewelry	Tote bags

And add to all the things mentioned above the infinite variety of beautiful crocheted motifs and insertions, to be used in self or contrast texture or color, and in light or heavy gauge as trim and embellishment, or as a possible focal point of interest on draperies and davenports and towels and tote bags—and shellacked or vinyl-sprayed, even on book covers and windowshades and lamps and furniture. Then too there are all the different kinds of tailored and fancy edgings to be used as finishing on practically anything to which you might want to add your own personal touch.

3. YOU CAN DESIGN YOUR OWN CROCHETS

Those of you who are experienced crocheters know already how to work with your needle, and those of you who have never held a crochet hook in your hand before can learn how to manipulate this simple tool by following the very basic "how to" instructions which appear in the Crocheter's Guide in Chapter 4 of this book. Once having read carefully through those pages, and practiced just a little bit with the things you have read about, you can assume that you are crocheters too. For all of you there lie ahead unending hours of pleasure and the relaxing yet stimulating joy of being able to make lovely things, and to make them with your own hands and your acquired knowledge of an interesting skill. And for any of you who want to add yet more to this delightful experience, there could be the further gratification of having designed for yourself whatever beautiful thing it might be that you are creating, whether it is an interesting large afghan made up of dozens of colorful little granny squares, a smart car-coat worked in a richly textured pattern stitch, or just inserts of beautiful crocheted lace to be added in tiers to the new velvet dinner skirt you are sewing for yourself.

Styles, original models, and directions for crochet work can be easily found today in numerous leaflets, pattern books, and current periodicals. Many of these are good and offer excellent ideas and very workable instructions for carrying out fresh ideas. However, there may be some of you who do have preconceived thoughts of your own as to exactly what it is that you want to make, and you may just not be able to find directions for those very things, despite the abundance of available material around. Perhaps you have found a style that you like, but the size given for making it will not in any way fit you, or on another style perhaps the directions are written in your size, but you would prefer to make it with a different type of pattern stitch, and possibly a round neck instead of the V-shaped one which is shown.

Indeed there are many reasons why you might want to know how to custom-make and design your very own crocheted things. For one, on the question of size, your body measurements may not conform at all to any of the standard measurements that are generally used in the designing of most clothing. Even though your hips may be a little broader, or your shoulders a little narrower, you should still be able to achieve the perfect fit that warrants the time and effort that you are putting into what you are making, and to be able to calculate your design so that this becomes entirely possible. Aside from being able to get a well-proportioned fit, you might also at some time or other want to copy in crochet one of your very favorite blouses, or something you've admired in a store window, or perhaps a dress or coat that you've taken a fancy to in one of the sewing pattern books, and for which there are no needlework directions given. As a matter of fact, it might even be that you've thought up a completely original idea of your own, and have been thinking about it for a long time now, and would like very much to be able to know how to go about making it.

Whatever the reason, it is certainly fun and a challenge to be able to design original things of your own, and a feeling actually that can be equaled only by the pleasure you will experience in executing the designs you have created. There is no special talent necessary to be able to gain this delightful sense of fulfillment, and really no special training or skill either beyond that which is offered to you in this book. Reading through the ''How to Design'' pages which follow in Chapter 5 and the ''Designer's Guide'' (Chapter 12), you can easily learn to make whatever it is you want and make it with the full confidence that it will come out right.

With the crocheting and designing knowledge you gain as you read on, and with the aid of many photographs of beautiful pattern stitches, motifs, edgings and inserts—all appearing in subsequent chapters, each with complete instructions on how to work them out—and with the ready availability of wonderful new yarns in the stores, you can be ready at any time you choose to start out on one of the most exciting and rewarding projects of your life.

For those of you, however, who might yet hesitate to design for yourselves, or have some possible inner doubt that your designs will be good, let us reassure you that, to quote an old adage, ''Beauty lies only in the eyes of the beholder,'' and if whatever it is you want to make looks good to you, then believe that it is good. There are no longer any very rigid standard rules of design, and those that do still exist today are only the ones of good balance and proportion. Actually, the best evidence of this very fact has been proven in Chapter 2, ''Contemporary Crochet.'' Novices, with certainly no experience in design or the art of crochet, thought of, fumbled through, perfected, and finally executed many new designs of their own which caused sensational style trends and sent professional designers scurrying to keep up with those trends, and possibly to foresee new design thoughts which might occur to and please the new group of novitiate designers. If you yourself still feel a little insecure, though, in spite of this reassurance, and would prefer a tighter rein in designing what may be your very first project, then perhaps a better way for you to start out on your new fun undertaking would be to begin with an already existing style and add to it just a little something of your own—perhaps a change of color, or measurements for the exact size you want, or possibly just a different pattern stitch that is more appealing to you. In this way, once you have seen that you are quite able to create new thoughts and to carry them out to perfection, you will be encouraged to go on next time with a completely new design of your own.

On the other hand, if you are more adventuresome and know exactly what it is you want to make, and are willing to try it all the way, press on, whether it be on that original design you've had in mind for a long time now, or perhaps some brand new thought from our lists of things to make in Chapter 2, using your own style, your own stitch and your own pattern. Read carefully Chapter 5, ''How to Design,'' almost as a lesson, and when you are done, choose your pattern stitch, select your yarn, refer as often as you like to the ''Crocheter's Guide'' (Chapter 4) and the ''Designer's Guide'' (Chapter 12), and then get started. You will be the first to enjoy what you are doing, and the first, too, to know that you have designed an original creation of your very own, and, having made it, to sense and experience what a wonderful feeling of creation this is.

4. CROCHETER'S GUIDE

In this chapter we attempt to answer all questions that might be asked about the various techniques involved in the art of crocheting. If you are just getting started as a crocheter you will want to know how to begin to learn, how to make your very first stitches, and then how to make more and more stitches until you feel that you do know how to crochet. We explain these things to you in the clearest and simplest way we know, starting with illustrations on how to make a foundation chain, which is the base and starting point for all crocheting, and then going on to describe for you all the basic stitches that you may need or want to learn, and beyond that to discuss all the many rules and guides that you and other more experienced crocheters might want to know about.

For those of you who are beginners, we suggest that you practice with a ball of yarn and a crochet hook on just a small piece for a little while, experimenting perhaps with the simple single crochet stitch which is one of the easiest to manipulate. In order to work this little piece you will need only to know how to make the foundation chain and how to make the single crochet stitch. Study our illustrations carefully and have a little patience with your first attempt. Crocheting is not a difficult craft to learn. A knowledge of the skill is so easy to acquire that once you have mastered this one simple stitch you are already a crocheter. With just this little knowledge you are practically ready to make something for yourself, such as a large straight piece of any size—perhaps a cozy rug for your bathroom, a colorful scarf, or a simple placemat.

Whether you decide to make any of these things, or maybe are more interested in a small baby blanket or a set of potholders, and even though you know that you are going to make whatever it is in single crochet, the stitch you've already mastered on your trial-practice piece, you will suddenly find that you have to know how many stitches you will need on your foundation chain in order to make the piece the size you want it to be. In the paragraphs on "gauge" which follow here we will tell you exactly how to measure and calculate in order to know the right number of stitches for whatever it is that you are going to make. Read this portion carefully, for a clear knowledge of the meaning of gauge is an invaluable asset toward the perfection of your work.

One thing leads to another, and when you have finished your piece you may want to put a fringe around the edges. Chapter 11 shows some very lovely ones, and shown there also are several other types of edgings, one of which you might prefer to use. In this case you will need to study further into this chapter, where you will find illustrations and clear explanations as to how to make every kind of stitch that might be involved in the making of your edging—or, as a matter of fact, in the making of anything else that you might want to crochet. And beyond this stitch information you will find a store of valuable hints and "how to" guides for everything involved in the art of crochet. Read it now and refer to it often as you progress in your work. With a little patience and a little practice you will soon know all there is to know about crocheting, and will be able to make anything you want, and to make it well.

Gauge

Gauge, in crocheting, means the number of stitches you are getting to an inch with your yarn, your crochet hook, and the pattern stitch you are working with. It is an important word to know, perhaps one of the most important in crocheting, because without a knowledge of gauge you cannot possibly know the number of stitches you need to work with in order to achieve the exact size or fit that you want. The number of stitches or patterns you get to each inch of your work, multiplied by the number of inches you want your work to measure, determines the number of stitches you will need to have on your foundation chain, and without this information you cannot even begin. The yarn you are using, the hook, the pattern stitch, and the tension in your own hand are what determine the gauge you are getting. Many yarn labels have printed on them a suggested good knitting gauge for that particular yarn, and tell you the size of the needles that are most apt to give you that gauge. Though the tension of your own hands may very well make it necessary for you to use different needles in order to achieve that gauge, even that type of suggested information is not available to crocheters. You yourself need to test the yarn you plan to use with various-sized hooks, and the one that is easiest to work with and gives you the "feel" that

you want in your finished work is the one that you will want to work with, and the one with which you will determine your own gauge.

There is a definite procedure to follow in establishing gauge, and that is to work a small piece about 3" square in the pattern stitch you are going to use and with the yarn you have selected and a crochet hook that you think might be the right size. You will know immediately how many stitches you are getting to the inch, and if the feel of the work is one that pleases you. If you are working from a pattern and it calls, for example, for 5 stitches to an inch and you are getting 7, you must change to a larger hook, experimenting with a few sizes until you get the one that gives you the 5; and if you are getting 3 stitches instead of 5, then you must switch to a smaller hook until you find the right one. In designs of your own, you experiment in exactly the same way until you reach your own desired stitch gauge.

In crocheting there is also a row gauge as well as the stitch gauge we have described above, and as you measure the number of stitches or patterns to an inch to get your stitch gauge, so you also measure the number of rows of your stitch or pattern to an inch to determine your row gauge. For many designs the row gauge does not matter at all, as long as you have established your stitch gauge and complete your work for the necessary number of inches. In others, however, it is very important to know your row gauge so that you can effect, for example, a necessary number of increases or decreases within the number of inches available for a total shaping of whatever you are working on.

If you plan to make a scarf and would like it to be 10 inches wide, and if, for example, you are getting a gauge of 3 stitches to 1" on your swatch, you would multiply 10 × 3 and chain 30 on your foundation; on a 5-stitch-to-1" gauge you would chain 50; and on a 7-stitch-to-1" gauge you would chain 70.

In making this particular scarf, the number of rows you get to an inch does not matter, and you would just work for a certain number of inches until you have reached the desired length. What does matter, however, is that you accommodate the 30 or 50 or 70 stitches that will work your scarf to its proper size to the multiple of the pattern you are using. The meaning and importance of a multiple in crocheting is very clearly defined in Chapter 6 on pattern stitches, and having referred to that chapter you will know that if your 30-stitch scarf were to be worked in a pattern with a stitch multiple of 3 + 1, you would need to chain 31, instead of 30; and if the multiple is 5 + 3, you would chain 28.

While the only mathematics you need to be involved with in the designing of your scarf are the stitch gauge and the multiple of the pattern you have chosen to work with, there are other instances, as we have mentioned earlier, when it is also necessary to include in your calculations the number of rows you are getting to an inch. For example, if you were shaping a raglan sleeve, you would definitely need to observe your row gauge and calculate the number of rows you are getting to, let us say, a presumed 8" armhole. Multiply the 8" by the number of rows to an inch and then divide the total number of rows by the number of stitches you must "lose," or decrease, for your shaping in that number of rows, and in as gradual a way as possible. If on a presumed gauge of 3 rows to 1" that armhole you want would involve rows, and if you were working on 72 stitches, and you were decreasing 1 stitch at each end of your row, you would need to figure the disposition of 72 stitches in the 24 rows. You would probably work your raglan by decreasing 2 stitches at each end of the first 12 rows, and 1 stitch at each end of the last 12 rows, thus decreasing your 72 stitches in 24 rows and having worked out a well-shaped raglan armhole.

Whether your crochet work of the moment involves both your stitch and row gauge or your stitch gauge only, remember that it is of utmost importance that you test first with your yarn and hook before attempting any project, swatching and sampling it out for a few inches to make sure that you have established a gauge that you like and that maintains itself at an even level and is comfortable to work with. Having done this much, you can be

sure that whatever you are making will be the proper size and that it will be right.

The Foundation Chain

Knot a loop onto hook. Holding hook in your right hand,† the end of yarn extending from the loop in your left hand and the main length of yarn over the index finger of your left hand, * place main length over hook, then draw the yarn and hook through the loop (1st stitch), repeat from * for the desired number of stitches on your foundation chain. Any pattern stitch may be worked on this foundation chain. Turning chains are worked in the same way, and where chain stitches are indicated in a pattern stitch, they are also done in the same way, using the last loop worked as the first one through which your yarn and hook are drawn.

The Stitch

All stitches are composed of two parts, the top and the base. The top remains the same in all stitches, and the base varies in height according to the stitch being used. All stitches should be worked

†If you are left-handed, see pp. 15–16.

through both loops of the top unless otherwise specified.

The Slip Stitch

Insert hook in stitch, yarn over hook and draw through stitch and through loop on hook.

The Single Crochet

Insert hook in stitch, yarn over hook and draw through stitch, yarn over and draw through remaining 2 loops on hook.

The Half Double Crochet

Yarn over hook, insert hook in stitch, yarn over and draw through the stitch, yarn over and draw through remaining 3 loops on hook.

The Double Crochet

Yarn over hook, insert hook in stitch, yarn over and draw through stitch, yarn over and draw through 2 loops on hook, yarn over and draw through remaining 2 loops on hook.

The Treble Crochet

Yarn over hook twice, insert hook in stitch, yarn over and draw through stitch, (yarn over and draw through 2 loops on hook) 3 times.

A *Double Treble Crochet* is worked as the treble crochet except that yarn is wrapped 3 times over the hook instead of twice, and 2 loops are taken off 4 times instead of 3 times.

A *Triple Treble Crochet* is worked as the treble crochet except that yarn is wrapped 4 times over the hook instead of twice, and 2 loops are taken off 5 times instead of 3 times.

Crocheting for Left-Handed People

Many left-handed people can make their own adjustments to anything that involves the use of their own two hands, which work just a little differently from those of right-handed people. With the needlecraft arts however some left-handed people do have a bit of a problem in being able to make that necessary adjustment and to manipulate their hands so that their work comes out right. We would like to offer a few suggestions here to those of you who crochet or would like to learn how to and find yourselves trying to substitute your right hand for your more dextrous left one, or not quite knowing how to transpose right-handed directions to ones that need to accommodate to the way you work.

Perhaps the simplest way to learn to adapt your own technique so that your finished work corresponds to that of others is to sit opposite a right-handed crocheter, watch what is being done, and then, observing everything you see as a mirrorlike image, work in exactly the opposite way. For example, working this opposite way, those of you who are left-handed would hold your work and your working strand of yarn in your right hand, your hook in your left hand, and you would work your rows from left to right instead of from right to left. If no one is available for you to observe, then you might just make use of the reverse reflection of the mirror itself to show you the way you need to work. Looking at stitch illustrations and reading right for left and left for right is another rather simple way of your being able to make the necessary changes so that you can work comfortably in your own way.

Chaining to Turn for the Next Row

The number of chain necessary to turn a row is given in each set of pattern stitches appearing in this book. If, however, you choose to work with a stitch that does not appear here, it is important to know that in most of our patterns we chain 1 to turn if the first stitch on the next row is a single crochet, 2 if it is a half double or a double crochet, 3 if a treble, and as many as are necessary for other stitches so that the height of the turning chain is the same as that of the first stitch on the next row that you are going to work, thus raising the position of your hook to a comfortable working level. The alternative way

of chaining to turn your work is to add 1 additional stitch to the number of chain we have indicated above, using, for example, 2 to chain if your first stitch on the next row is a single, 3 if it is a half double or double, and 4 if it is a treble. In this case the additional beginning chain counts as the top of the first stitch on the new row and the original number of chain counts for the necessary number to raise the height of your hook to working level.

Joining Yarn

Joining a new ball of yarn should be done at the beginning or end of a row whenever possible, in spite of the fact that the old ball of yarn may run out in the middle or toward the end of the row and a small length of the yarn may be wasted. When this is not possible for some reason, such as a shortage of yarn, work to within 3″ or 4″ of the end of the yarn, allow the same length end on the new ball, splice each end in half, twist them around each other to form one strand the equivalent thickness of the original yarn, then work the next 3 or 4 stitches with both strands, drop the old and continue with the new only. When your work is completed, weave about 1 inch of each of the remaining strands into the wrong side of work.

Changing Colors

When introducing a new color into your work, the last stitch of the original color is worked with that color to the point where 2 loops of that last stitch remain on the hook, and then those 2 loops are removed with the new color. When a change of color occurs at the start of a new row, the last 2 loops of the last stitch on the row just finished are the ones that are removed with the new color.

Ribbing

Ribbing is generally used to give shape, a snug fit, and a firm finish to parts of a garment that require it, such as around the bottom, neck and sleeve edges of a sweater, the armholes if your finished work is to be sleeveless, and for front bands if you are making a cardigan, vest, or other open-type garment. While there are a number of crocheted stitches that have a ribbed effect, to get the firm though elastic kind of ribbing to be used for the purposes mentioned just above, it is best to work in single crochet through the back loops of the stitches only. This type of ribbing is always made separately, and becomes part of the whole garment only after it has been finished to the desired size. For the waistband on the back of a sweater, for instance, you would work on 2", 3", or 4" (the desired height) for the necessary length (which is the width of the waistband), and then fasten off. You would then work 1 row of single crochet along one long side of this strip. This single crochet row becomes now the starting point for working the remainder of the back of your sweater. Ribbed cuffs at sleeve edges are worked in the same way. For other ribbings such as those for a neck, armholes, or front cardigan bands, the work is done in the same way, and then sewn in place onto the finished garment, the size of which would have been worked out initially to accommodate the addition of these extra pieces.

Increasing

Increasing basically involves the working of 2 stitches in the same stitch, thus forming an extra stitch. In most crochet stitches this is done by making the extra stitch in the same pattern as the original one in which the increase is being made, and this can be worked at any point of the row, as well as at the beginning and end. There are, however, many instances when increasing is done just a little differently and when it is best done at the beginning and the end of the row only, so that the sequence of the pattern stitch being used is maintained. When working with an afghan stitch, for instance, where all increases are made on the first half of the two-part afghan row, and where it would be feasible to add stitches only at each end of the row, to increase

at the beginning you would skip the first vertical bar of your work, draw up a loop in the next vertical bar and create your extra stitch at that end by drawing up another loop under the chain between the next 2 vertical bars; you would increase at the end of the row by picking up an extra loop between the last 2 vertical bars. When you are doing filet mesh, to add a space at the beginning of a row you would chain 7 at the end of the previous row for the added space, then work 1 double crochet into the top of the 1st vertical bar on the new row, and work the remainder of the row in pattern; and to add a space at the end of a filet row, you would chain 2, wrap yarn 3 times over your hook, insert your hook into the top of the last double crochet just worked, draw yarn through and draw yarn through 2 loops at a time until 1 loop remains on the hook, then continue with your next row in pattern. When you are working with other patterns which are composed of a combination of stitches such as possibly a single, double, and/or treble crochet which might be involved in a shell or cluster, for a gradual increase you would add parts of a pattern on every or every other row as necessary and finally add a whole or half a pattern when enough stitches have been added to fit in with the pattern being worked.

When several stitches are to be increased at the beginning and end of a row, you would make the necessary increases at the beginning of the row by making a chain at the end of your last row, using the number of extra stitches to be added plus the number necessary to turn your row. When they are to be added at the end of a row the necessary-size chain is made at the end of the row before the previous one, and when starting that previous row you slip stitch across that chain, then at the end of the following row you work across those slip stitches in whatever pattern you are using.

Decreasing

Decreasing when working with basic stitches involves the working off of 2 stitches as 1, thus decreasing, or "losing," one stitch whenever this is done. Again, as in increasing, this can be worked with many stitches on any part of the row, as well as at the beginning and end. For a few simple examples of how to decrease when using basic stitches on single crochet rows, you would draw up a loop in the next single crochet, draw up a loop in the following single crochet, then wrap yarn over hook and draw through all 3 loops at once. For double crochet you would work your 1st double crochet to the point where 2 loops remain on the hook, then yarn over and insert hook in next stitch, yarn over and draw through stitch, yarn over and draw through 2 loops, yarn over and draw through remaining 3 loops. This type of decreasing would apply in the working of many stitches, though there are, here again, many other stitches when decreasing is best done only at the beginning and end of the row. For example, working with the afghan stitch, which can be done only in this way, you would work as follows: On the first half of your two-part afghan row, skip the 1st vertical bar, insert hook under the next 2 vertical bars and draw up 1 loop only, then having worked your row through in basic or patterned afghan stitch, at the end of the row work a decrease in the same manner in the second and third vertical bars from the end.

When working with filet mesh, though a space can be decreased at each end of the row, the actual process of "losing" the spaces is always done at the end of a row. In decreasing a space at the beginning and end of a row you would work to within the last space of the row just before the one where you want your beginning decrease to occur. Do not work the last space but chain and turn, work in pattern to within the last space on the next row where you want your end decrease to occur. Do not work the last space but again chain and turn, and work your next row in established pattern with 2 spaces less on the row. For fancy patterned stitches you would either lose patterns or parts of patterns at the end of the row only, much as you did in decreasing spaces for the beginning and end of the row in working filet mesh, or for a more gradual decrease, lose parts of a pattern at the beginning

and end of every or every other row until the necessary number of whole patterns has been lost. When several stitches are to be decreased at the beginning and end of a row you would work this in the same manner as though you were binding off at the beginning and end of a row. We describe this technique in the following paragraph.

Binding Off

Binding off at the beginning of a row is done by working a slip stitch across the number of stitches to be bound off. A slip stitch is an invisible stitch which adds no height to your work and gives a firm finish to your bound-off edge. Binding off can be done only at the beginning of a row. Where it is important to have a certain number of stitches bound off at the beginning and end of a row, such as for the start of the shaping of armholes on a sweater, you would slip stitch across the necessary number of stitches at the beginning of the row, work to within that same number of stitches at the end of the row, chain and turn and work your next row on the stitches remaining, eliminating those which had been slip stitched across on the previous row.

Making a Circle

There are many times when one wants to crochet something circular such as a cap or hat, a centerpiece, a rug, or perhaps even a poncho. A circle is a perfect geometric form which will always come out right if it is calculated with more or less the same simple type of mathematics as that involved in working out any other shape or form. A piece of work of this kind is started with a small number of chain stitches joined into a ring with a slip stitch, and then graduated to the desired diameter by a number of evenly spaced increases on each round, the total number of increases depending primarily on the size of the round to be made, the gauge and the size of the hook being used, and the height of the stitches being worked. In Chapter 10 there is a motif, M24, which offers a very clear example of how a circular project is started. There is always the starting ring, followed by the first round of working a number of stitches into the ring, this number being a variable and needing to be a base multiple of the number of stitches to be increased on each round. For example, there will be 6 stitches worked into the center of the ring if there are to be 6 stitches increased on each round, 8 if there are to be 8 increases, and 10 if there are to be 10 increases. Usually the height of the stitches being used determines the number of stitches to be increased on each round. The taller the stitch, the more frequently the increases will need to occur. You yourself will be best able to determine the number of increases you need on each round once you have worked out just the first few rounds, since if the work does not lie flat you will know that more increases need to be made on each round, and if the work ruffles, you know that less will have to be made. Having established now the number of stitches you need on your first round, the second round would consist of working 2 stitches in each stitch around, the next round of increasing 1 stitch in every other stitch around, the next in every third stitch. You would continue in this manner, making the same number of increases evenly spaced on each round and having 1 stitch more between each point of increase until the desired diameter is reached.

It is best to use a fairly simple stitch when making a circle in order to avoid any confusion in the pattern of a more complicated one. If, however, for your own special project in the round it is most important that you do use a pattern stitch, then it is good to either alternate every other round of your pattern with a round of single crochet and make your increases on that single crochet round or in any case, whether you use the alternate single crochet rounds or not, be certain that the number of stitches you use for your periodic increases is a base multiple of the pattern you've chosen to work with.

Squares and Rectangles

Squares and rectangles are, like circles, perfect geometric forms which will always come out right if properly calculated. A square with its four equal sides and four right angles can be crocheted in a piece that is as long as it is wide, or started as a circle and then squared out when the desired size is reached. If you are starting with a square-shaped piece, you will probably finish that piece by working a row of single or double crochet around the four sides of it, working the same number of stitches along each of the four sides, that number being any amount so that the work lies flat, and you would work 3 stitches in each corner stitch to establish firmly the shaping of the square. If you are squaring a circle, your last row around the edge of the circle would need to be a number divisible by 4. Having established that, you would square your piece by marking off four corners, then working 1 single or double crochet in each stitch around each of the four sides (being certain that it is the same number of stitches on each side), and then working 3 stitches in each corner stitch as you pass. For example, if there are 20 stitches around the edge of your circle, you would work 4 along each side, and 3 in each corner stitch; and if there are 32, you would work 7 along each side and 3 in each corner. A simple way of being able to calculate immediately the number of stitches you have to work with for each of the four equal sides is to divide the total number of stitches by 4, then use 1 stitch less than your quotient for each of the sides, and allow the extra stitch for each of the four corners. Referring to our example above, 20 divided by 4 = 5, thus allowing you 4 for each side and 1 for each of the four corners; and 32 divided by 4 = 8, allowing you 7 for each side, and the remaining 1 for each of the four corners. A rectangle is similar to a square in that it is a four-sided piece with four corners, the difference in shape being that only opposite sides are equal to each other. Unlike a square, a rectangle must be crocheted to its original shape, and when the single or double crocheted edging is added to it, the number of stitches worked between the four 3-stitch corners is the same only on each of the two sets of parallel sides, the number across the two widths needing to be the same, and the number across the two lengths needing to be a different number, but both equal unto themselves.

Buttonholes and Buttonloops

To form a buttonhole, work to within the number of stitches at which point your buttonhole will occur, chain as many stitches as are necessary to accommodate the size of the button to be used, skip as many stitches of the previous row as the number you have chained, then complete the row. On the next row work as many stitches into the buttonhole chain as those that were skipped on the row below. Buttonloops, which differ from buttonholes in that they usually occur along the finished edge of a piece of work, are made on the last row of the work by chaining as many stitches as are necessary to accommodate the size of the button, skipping as many stitches of the previous row as the number that were chained, and then completing the final row.

Forming Hemlines

It is not too often that a hem is required for crochet work, since one of the characteristics of crocheting is that each row is finished unto itself, and the beginning or end of a piece needs no further finishing, except perhaps for trim. There are, however, a few instances when a hem is desired such as, for example, on the brim of a hat, where the double thickness added by the hem gives body to the brim. Hems are made by working for the desired number of rows, generally on a few stitches less than those to be on the work just above the hem, and one forms a firm, ridged hemline by

working the last turning row of the hem with a row of single crochet worked through the back loops of the stitches only. The number of increases to be made on the hemmed portion to make it equal in size to that portion of the work just above the hem are worked on the last row before the turning ridge. The rows immediately preceding and following the turning ridge must be wrong side rows of whatever pattern stitch is being used.

Waistband Casings

Waistband casings for the drawing through of elastic are generally done in one of two ways: the first a simple turn-under hem and the other a crocheted casing worked along the wrong side of a waistband. Of the two methods, the latter is the more desirable, since with it the garment is flatter at a place where it needs to be so. Crocheted casings are made as follows: Working on wrong side, attach yarn at one top end of waistband, work a slip stitch, * chain the equivalent of 1", slip stitch at bottom of waistband approximately ¾" beyond the last slip stitch, chain the equivalent of 1", slip stitch at top of waistband approximately ¾" beyond last slip stitch, repeat from * across waistband and fasten off.

Seaming

There are three popular methods of seaming and putting pieces together: a woven seam, a sewn seam, and a crocheted seam. In all three, the pieces to be joined must be matched carefully, and the seaming is done with the same yarn as that with which the pieces were worked. In the last two instances, a ¼" allowance on each side of each part of the garment needs to be made because this is approximately the amount that will be taken up in the seaming process. Woven seams are worked with a blunt-edged tapestry needle. Starting at an upper edge, sew top stitch of each side together, then insert needle through first stitch on one side, draw under 2 strands along the edge, then work in the same manner under 2 strands on opposite side edge and continue in this manner, sewing from side to side until the seam is completely woven. A sewn seam is usually worked with a running backstitch approximately ¼" long on the wrong side of the work. The crocheted seam is done with a fine crochet hook, also on the wrong side of the work, and is worked by inserting the hook through both loops of the stitches along each of the two side edges to be seamed.

Blocking

Blocking, the final finish to your crocheted garment, may be done before or after the pieces are assembled. Lay the work flat, cover it with a damp cloth and press lightly with a warm iron, allowing steam to form. Avoid pressing hard or holding the iron too long in any one place. When done, measure the piece to be sure it is the proper size. If it should need a little stretch in any direction at this time, do it while the garment is still damp, and then repeat the pressing process.

5. HOW TO DESIGN

The art of designing beautiful crocheted things is quite a simple one, as is also the actual technique of working with the craft itself. However, unlike any of the other needlework skills, crocheting is a many-faceted art which offers an incredible number of different possibilities of working with it. There are, for instance, the straight or "simple" crochet stitches, both plain and fancy, for which there exist innumerable patterns ranging a gamut from the basic stitches to the richly textured ones, the puffs and shells and clusters, the gossamer-sheer lacy ones, and those that are worked in combinations of two and three colors. Beyond this type of simple crochet, however, there is the "block" or motif piece-by-piece kind of work where each piece is a relatively small one, finished unto itself in squares, rounds, hexagonals, octagonals, and other varied shapes. Any and all of these are thought-inspiring for countless new designs, the designs depending on how many of the little pieces are used and how they are joined together. Just a single motif serves beautifully as an interesting type of trim on almost anything at all, whereas a group of anywhere from two to two hundred motifs can be handsomely connected together to create a complete whole of whatever it is you want to make, whether it be a lady's purse made of just two of them, an unusual tunic blouse of somewhere between twenty-five and fifty of them, depending on the size of the motifs and the tunic, or a beautiful afghan or tablecloth made up of somewhere between one hundred and two hundred pieces, the number depending again on the size of what you are making and the size of each of the individual motifs. There are various other types of crochet too, among them the afghan stitch, sometimes referred to as Tunisian crochet, (Chapter 7), worked in a little different manner with an elongated hook, and the filet mesh stitch, both of these particularly adaptable for working in one's own charted designs; also, the horizontal and vertical edgings and insertions, and many types of fringes, all basically used for trim and final finish on anything that has been straight-crocheted, or even sewn.

Although these variations of different types of crochet do exist, all are similar in being worked on the same single-hooked needle and with the same basic type of stitches, and the simple principles of design involving any of them are also quite the same. For a better way, however, of passing on a knowledge of this art to you, it would perhaps be easier and clearer if we were to use examples now for our straight simple stitches only, and then go on in other chapters to explain further the design possibilities of the various other types of crochet.

To be able to design any kind of crochet work you need only to remember your most elementary grade-school arithmetic lessons, and to be able to add a little, subtract a little, multiply and divide. The skill is not at all a difficult one to acquire, and it does indeed seem odd that the only requirement necessary to be able to design a stunning piece of handwork is, in addition to your own sense of good taste, a knowledge of only a few very simple mathematical manipulations. Just as you must know that 1 and 1 equals 2, so you should now know that to create your original crocheted clothing, you need only to multiply your body measurements by the gauge (number of stitches per inch) you are getting with your yarn and needle, and accommodate your final sum to the multiple of stitches necessary to work out the particular pattern you are using. And if, on the other hand, you are making a straight piece such as a rug or an afghan, you would work in the same manner, using the size of that piece as the basis for your original calculations.

Your very first step, once you've decided to venture forth into this rather stimulating design endeavor of your own, would be to decide what it is you want to make. Let us assume that it happens that you've been thinking for quite a while about doing something new and interesting for your home, maybe a rug or an afghan or perhaps just a nice small throw pillow for the divan. You have a little knowledge of crocheting, and you are aware by now that if there is anything further you need to know, you can refer easily and quickly to the Crocheter's Guide in Chapter 4 and find there whatever additional information you are looking for. For the time being, however, you think you'd be more secure working with a fairly simple stitch, although you feel also that you do want your design to have some interesting detail in it, maybe some kind of variegated stripe, a type of pattern to which you have always been partial anyhow. Since you're quite eager, but still just a little hesitant about starting out on this "first" project of your own, you've just about made up your mind, after thinking about it for a little while, that you do want to start out with

the smallest piece, the throw pillow, and that if that comes out well you might possibly want to go on to make a matching or coordinating large piece to go with it. You'd like the pillow to be fairly tailored, and in two colors, with perhaps skipper blue as the main color, and the striped pattern in emerald green. You've measured various pillow sizes and shapes, and you feel that a 16" square would be just about right for you, and you'd like to have some kind of trim around the edges to match the contrast color stripes, maybe an emerald loop fringe edging around each of the four sides, and a tassel in each of the corners. The pillow you have in mind probably looks very much like the one shown directly below, and now you'd like to get started on it.

At this point you need a crochet hook and some yarn, and a decision once again as to what kind of pattern stitch you want to use. Look carefully through all the straight stitches appearing in the following chapter and pick the one that you like the best, bearing in mind that you want to make a fairly tailored-looking pillow, and that you want some kind of a stitch that is quite easy to work with. You will find many of this type in the group of interesting textures appearing in that chapter, and you should have no problem at all in selecting one that you really like. Once having made this decision, you should now select your yarn, and a trip to your local yarn shop will be most helpful toward this end, and will show you what is available, what the price and advantage of each type is, and what the color range is in the one you finally decide to use. You do not know how much yarn you will be needing, but since most yarns do have a dye-lot number, and since a slight variation between dye lots cannot be avoided, you must be certain that you buy a sufficient amount of the particular dye lot you are using in order to be able to complete your project. Most shopkeepers can roughly estimate what your requirements will be, and are quite willing to give you their assurance, even though your undertaking this time may be a small one such as the making of a pillow, that if you have bought too much they will accept for return whatever is left over, and that if you buy only a starting amount they will lay away enough of the same dye lot so that you can pick up the remainder as you need it. In either case, your one obligation is to let the shopkeeper know as soon as you possibly can how much yarn you are actually going to need, and this you will be able to determine after you have completed approximately one-quarter of your work. Multiplying the amount used for that much work by 4, you can have a reasonably accurate calculation as to how much you will need. If you add to this amount an extra ball or two for "spare," in addition to whatever you may need for final finishing, you are in a position to complete your yarn order with the knowledge that you will finish your work with the same dye lot with which you started.

You now have your design roughly in mind, and your yarn on hand. It is time to determine what size crochet hook you want to use with the yarn you have selected, and this choice is, within limitations, largely up to you and the type of "feel" that you want to achieve in your work. If a needle is too small for your yarn, you will find it difficult to work with and your crocheting will have the stiff look of cardboard, and if it is too large, you will also find it difficult to use, and your work will appear sleazy. In either case you yourself will know if the choice

is not a good one simply by the effect that you are getting. There is, however, a very wide range of different-sized needles that you could use for a good effect with whatever yarn you have selected, and by experimenting just a little you will be able to decide which needle you really think is best for the "feel" you are looking for.

Make a small swatch about 3" square with your yarn, your pattern stitch, and a needle that you feel might be the right one. If you find the texture of your square too loose, try a smaller hook, and if you find it too tight, try a larger one. Continue to experiment in this way until you find exactly the tension you want in your work, and then you are ready to go on. Very carefully measure the 3" square of your choice to determine how many stitches you have to an inch, and how many rows. This will tell you the gauge you are going to work with. Now you go on to the final step in the designing of your pillow.

The gauge on the 3" square that pleased you most is 5 stitches and 7 rows to 1". The pattern stitch you've selected has a multiple of 3 (see Chapter 6 for a definition of "multiple"), but while you were looking through the stitches, you decided that you would like to work your pillow with the main color in the pattern stitch and the stripes in just plain single crochet. This you felt would add more texture design to your pillow, and there would be no problem with the multiple because single crochet can be worked on a multiple of any number of stitches. You were quite right in your decision, your pillow will have more interest, and you will have no problem with the multiple.

You still want the pillow to be 16" square, and you would like it to be reversible, the same on both sides, and the design to be a variegated stripe very similar, let us say, to the one shown above. At this point you return to your grade-school mathematics. The pillow will be made in two pieces, and each piece will be a 16" square. Looking at the illustration, you realize that with the vertical-striped design of the pillow, it would be best to work the design with your starting row at one side edge, and your finishing row at the opposite side edge in order to avoid the need to have to change colors after every few stitches, which would be necessary if your piece were worked from the bottom to the top edge.

Your 16" pillow with a gauge of 5 stitches to 1" would need to start out with 16 × 5 = 80 stitches, which needs to become 81 in order to accommodate and be divisible by the multiple of 3 in the pattern stitch. According to the illustration, you want to have 10 narrow contrast-color vertical stripes, and you need to calculate them now so that they will be properly spaced to form the variegated pattern you want. You are working with a total of 16". Let us assume that each contrast color stripe and each narrow main color stripe between the contrast colored ones will be worked with 2 rows of single crochet (or the necessary even number of rows on the gauge you are getting) to measure a little more than ¼". Since there are 10 contrast-color stripes, and 6 main-color stripes between the contrast stripes, also to be worked in single crochet, you would multiply 10 + 6 = 16 × ¼ = 4, and you would know that the 16 stripes would measure a total of approximately 4¼". You remain now with 11¾ more inches to work with, and in this amount of space you need to place your 5 main-color broad-textured stripes, of which the center one appears to be much wider than the other 4. If you were to calculate each of the narrower ones to be 2", you would have utilized 8" out of the remaining 11¾", which would leave approximately 3¾" free for the center broad main color stripe. This seems to be the right proportion, and you would probably work your pillow now in the following manner:

Make 2 Pieces: With MC (main color), chain 81. (*Note:* It is important for both new and experienced crocheters to refer now to the starting paragraphs of Chapter 6 for our explanation of the foundation, or starting chain, based on gauge and multiple, and telling how to turn for the first row.)

* Work even in pattern stitch for approximately 2", ending with a wrong side row. Attach CC (contrast color), and working in single crochet, work 2 rows with CC, 2 with MC, and 2 more with CC, then repeat from * once more and end with 1 additional MC and CC stripe. Fasten off CC, and work in MC pattern stitch until piece measures 8" in all. Place a marker on your work now to denote that this is the center of the pillow, and then work the second half to correspond to the first half, reversing the placing of the stripes. Fasten off yarn when the striped pattern has been completed and the piece measures approximately 16".

You now need to finish your pillow. Generally any straight piece of crochet needs a row or two of single crochet around the four sides in order to give it a firm solid edge, and in working this row or two one needs to work 3 single crochet in each of the 4 corner stitches in order to sharply define the corners. Also, when more than one color is used on a piece of work, the first row of single crochet is usually done in color over color in order to get a neat finish on the piece. With this information in mind, you would probably finish your pillow in this way:

Using color over color, work 1 row of single crochet around the entire outer edge of each piece, working 3 single crochet in each corner stitch as you turn. Fasten off MC now, and with CC only work 1 more row of single crochet in same manner. Fasten off CC. Block each piece carefully with a warm iron over a damp cloth according to directions in the Crocheter's Guide. Holding the 2 pieces together back to back now, join them on 3 sides with a row of CC single crochet, working your stitches through both pieces at one time, then stuff the pillow firmly with foam, cotton batting, or whatever filling material you choose and complete the joining of the fourth side. Your original thought was to use a loop fringe edging and 4 tassels as final finish on your piece. You will find very complete directions for these as well as many other types of edgings and trim in Chapter 11. Following directions for whichever finish you prefer, complete your pillow, place it on the divan, and be the first to enjoy and admire your own original crochet design!

The simple mathematical procedure involved in the designing of the pillow you've just completed remains much the same for anything else you might want to design. For just a little further illustration, your same pillow, if it were a 14" square, worked on a gauge of 6 stitches to 1", with a stitch multiple of 4, your mathematics would be: $14 \times 6 = 84$. 84 is divisible by 4, so that is the number of stitches you would be working on. Your 16 contrast and main-color single crochet stripes should each still be, for good proportion, approximately ¼" wide. $16 \times ¼ = 4$. That is the number of inches that would be used for your striping pattern. $14 - 4 = 10$, and that is the number of inches that would be left for your 5 main-color textured portions, of which the center one is wider than the other 4. In this case, each of your 4 textured stripes would be 1¾" wide (7" in all), and your center one would be approximately 3".

You are making progress in learning how to design now, and even as we are working out our simple mathematics together here, you have been looking at your own first design creation, and, remembering what fun it was to make it, you've just about decided that you want to go on and make something else—as a matter of fact, a few more things, like two more pillows in the emerald single crochet, one a 12" round, the other a small 8" × 10" rectangle, and maybe the coordinated striped rug and afghan shown on page 23, too. The fire has been sparked, and for just a little more support before you go out completely on your own, you'd be happy if we worked this ensemble out together. Let's do it!

To make your round pillow is again a simple thing to do, and follows basically the general rules applying to the making of any round piece of work, as described in the Crocheter's Guide. To make a circle or round you start with a very small circle and increase at even intervals on each round until the desired diameter is reached. You would probably work your round pillow in this manner:

Make 2 Pieces: Starting at center, chain 4 and join with a slip stitch to form a ring. Work 6 single crochet in center of ring. **Next Round:** Work 2 single crochet in each single crochet around—12 single crochet. **Next Round:** * Single crochet in next stitch, 2 single crochet in next stitch, repeat from * around—18 single crochet. **Next Round:** * Single crochet in each of the next 2 stitches, 2 single crochet in next stitch, repeat from * around —24 single crochet. Continue now in this manner to increase 6 stitches evenly spaced on each round, having 1 more stitch between each point of increase until piece measures 12" in diameter. Join and fasten off. Block each piece.

A round pillow of the size you've just made usually is best done with about a 1½" gusset joining the front and back portions. Assuming that you want to make your pillow this way, and that you are working with the gauge of 5 stitches to 1" as on your first pillow, you would now finish in this way: **Gusset:** Chain 8 and work in single crochet until piece measures around the circumference of the pillow. Join the last row to the first row with a row of slip stitch and fasten off. Work 1 row of single crochet around each side of the gusset. Holding wrong sides together, join one side now to the front or back round with a row of single crochet on the right side of the work. Join the other side of the gusset to the rest of the pillow three-quarters of the way around, then stuff pillow firmly and complete joining of the gusset to the remaining open portion of the pillow. Your round pillow is completed now, unless you would like to add a self-color loop fringe edging around it to give it a closer coordination to your first pillow. If you do choose to do this, it would be good design to work this border along the joining single crochet rows along each side of the gusset.

Now we have only to work out your 8" × 10" rectangular pillow before going on to your rug and afghan. Since your square pillow was worked from side edge to side edge, and the little rectangle you want to make now is part of the grouping you plan, it would be good to work this one in the same manner. The size you would like is 8" wide and 10" long. Calculating it on your same original gauge of 5 stitches to 1", $8 \times 5 = 40$. You should make your pillow this way:

Make 2 Pieces: Chain 40. Work even in single crochet until piece measures 10", then work 1 row single crochet around the entire outer edge of each piece, working 3 single crochet in each corner stitch as you turn. Fasten off. Block each piece. Holding the two pieces with wrong sides together now, join them on three sides with a row of single crochet, working your stitches through both pieces at one time, then stuff the pillow firmly and complete the joining of the fourth side. Whatever final finish you use now is purely a question of your own choice. A suggestion would be that since this new piece is part of a three-piece pillow setting, and since your square pillow is finished with loop fringe and tassels, and your round pillow with loop fringe only, it might be a good idea to finish this one with small tassels all around it, little miniatures of the four that were used on your square pillow.

Having completed your three pillows, you are now ready to go on to the afghan and rug. We feel quite certain that by this time a good working knowledge of the general mathematical design formula has been transmitted to you, and that, as for pillows, you could go on to make as many originals as you like, for yourself, for gifts, and for the fun of making them. Let's do your rug next.

In starting this new piece, or any other, the initial procedure remains exactly the same as when you started the first of your pillows. In this case, since you are going to work on just another part of a group of things that you have already started, you know what your design will be like, and you also know the pattern stitch that you are going to use. The texture of a rug, however, is quite different from that of the throw pillows you have made, and consequently even though your general stitch and pattern design are already determined, your yarn, your needle and your gauge need to be quite different. Your first decision now should be to choose what size rug you want to make and, with that and your colors in mind, the next thing you must do is to visit your local yarn shop again and look at what is available in heavy weight yarns and in colors that will match closely to the yarn you have already used on your pillows.

There is a great selection of bulky yarns in the stores, and many of them are very suitable and very attractive for rug-making. Some are wool, some are cotton, and many are made of some type of machine-washable, machine-dryable, synthetic composition. Inquire about the advantages of each type as to workability and wearability, and see for yourself which has colors closest to those you need, then make your purchase, again with careful regard as to the availability of a sufficient amount of the same dye lot, and with the shopkeeper's assurance that if you have bought too much he will accept for return what is left over, and if you are buying only a starting amount, he will lay away enough for you to be able to pick up when you are certain of exactly how much you will need.

With yarn in hand now, your next step once more is to determine the gauge or "feel" that you want to work with. Again you have the choice of a few different-sized needles to use with the yarn you have bought, although with a bulky yarn the size range of your hooks needs to be fairly large to start with. A good gauge for a rug made of heavy yarn could be 5 stitches to 2", 3 stitches to 1", 7 stitches to 2", or, at the tightest, 4 stitches to 1". Experiment with your yarn and different hooks as you have done before on little 3" swatches and when you find the gauge that pleases you most, you're ready to design your rug.

Let us assume that the size of the rug you want to make is 30" wide by 42" long, and the gauge that you like best is 3 stitches to 1". Since your pillows were worked vertically, you should work your rug in that way too. 30 × 3 = 90, and since 90 is divisible by your multiple of 3, that becomes the number of stitches you will be working on for your 42". On your striped pillow there were 10 contrast-color single crochet stripes, and each one was calculated in the design to measure ½". On your coordinated rug as shown in the illustration above, there are 20 contrast-color single crochet stripes in the design, and since the rug is a much larger piece, we should assume that each of these stripes is ¾" wide, and that each of the 14 main-color single-crochet stripes (between the contrast-color ones) are also ¾" wide. 20 + 14 = 34 × ¾ = 25½. This tells us that 25½" of our 42" rug will be used for the single crochet striped pattern. $42 - 25\frac{1}{2} = 16\frac{1}{2}$. You remain now with 16½" more within which to work your 7 main-color broad-textured stripes, of which the center one appears to be a little broader than any of the other 6. If you were to calculate each of the narrower ones to be about 2¼" wide, you would have utilized approximately 13½" out of the remaining 16½" which would leave 3" free for the center main-color stripe. This seems to be the right proportion, and so you would probably work your rug in the following manner:

With MC (main color), chain 90. * Work even in pattern stitch for approximately 2¼", ending with a wrong side row. Attach CC (contrast color), and working in single crochet, work ¾" with CC, ¾" with MC, ¾" more with CC, then repeat from * once and end with 1 additional MC and CC stripe (5 stripes), then repeat from * once again and end with 9 single crochet stripes. Fasten off CC, and work in MC pattern stitch until piece measures 21" in all. Place a marker on your work now to denote that this is the center of your rug, and then work the second half to correspond to the first half, reversing the placing of the stripes. Fasten off yarn when the striped pattern has been completed, and the piece measures 42". To finish your rug you would work, as on the first of your pillows, a row of color over color single crochet around the four sides, working 3 single crochet in each corner stitch as you turn, and then probably work 1 more row of single crochet in MC only. In planning our own illustration, we felt that adding a thick MC fringe between 4" and 6" long along each short end of the rug would be a good way of final finishing it. If this pleases you too, there are directions for making this type of fringe in Chapter 11, and if you would prefer another style of final finishing, you will also find many other suggestions in that chapter.

And so, as your rug is finished, let it lie in cozy comfort and beauty on the floor at the foot of the divan, part of a handsome composition, and a silent acclamation of one of your very own handcraft creations. We're glad you've decided to make the afghan too; it will complete the beautiful setting and be a lovely thing to own, and functional besides. Shall we go on? Afghans have no standard size, they can be as large or as small as you want them to be. More often than not they are rectangular in shape, and also more often than not the length will be a minimum of 12" more than the width, and a maximum of 20" more. Popular sizes are 48" × 60", 54" × 66", 60" × 74", and 70" × 84". Since even the smallest of afghans is basically a large piece, however, they are usually worked in strips or squares, and then the pieces are either sewn or crocheted together with a plain or fancy stitch. Presume now that you have decided to make your afghan 60" wide by 72" long. An afghan should be worked on a somewhat looser gauge than your pillows were (so that it does not become too heavy a piece), and also, generally, with a yarn that is not quite as bulky as that used on your rug. The popular preferred afghan gauge usually varies between 4 stitches to 1", 9 stitches to 2", and, at the tightest, 5 stitches to 1", and the popular preferred yarn is of knitting worsted weight, though it need not be knitting worsted yarn at all, since there are many other yarns which are of the same weight. Since you have the design of your afghan quite clearly in mind, and you know the size you want it to be, go once again to the yarn shop. The shopkeeper will be happy to see that you have been enjoying the work you've been doing, as you must be and as we are too, and he will be glad to help you with your selection of yarn, and to guarantee you enough of the dye lot you will be needing. Once again then, with yarn in hand, make your little 3" swatches, decide which tension you prefer, and calculate your afghan and set it up ready to put into work.

Let us assume that of the swatches you have worked you prefer the one that gives you a gauge of 4 stitches to 1". You have decided that your afghan will be a fairly large one, 60" wide by 72" long, and you know that to correspond to your other pieces it should be worked in the same manner, from one side edge to the other. Our illustration above depicting the three-piece ensemble (to which you have added two more pillows) seems to indicate a finishing with a striped border around the entire outer edge of the afghan. There appear to be a total of 7 contrast and main-color stripes in this border, and judging from the other parts of the group that you have made, each of these narrow stripes should measure approximately ½″ in width. 7 × ½ = 3½″. 3½″ would be the width of the border on each of the four sides of the afghan, and since borders or edgings of any type are added as final finish after an entire piece of work has been completed, you need to subtract 7″ (double the 3½″, since the border is to be worked along all four sides) from both the width and the length of the afghan you are about to calculate. Your 60″ × 72″ afghan needs now to be calculated at 53″ × 65″. With a presumed gauge of 4 stitches to 1″, 65 × 4 = 260. The figure 260 is not divisible by your pattern stitch multiple of 3, so you must accommodate to that multiple by adding 1 more stitch. You will be working now on 261 stitches for 53″. Obviously, this is too large and unwieldy a piece to be able to work all in one, so you need now to figure out, in addition to the placement of your striping pattern, the manner in which you will divide your work for ease of handling. According to the design you are going to have, as on your rug, 34 single crocheted stripes, each one measuring approximately ½″ in width: 34 × ½″ = 17″; and the balance of your 53″, which is 53″ − 17″ = 36″, will be used for your 7 main-color broad-textured stripes, of which the center one is wider than the other 6. Your proportion would be right if, in this instance, each of your 6 stripes were to measure approximately 4¾″, and your center one 7½″. Your calculations would add up to 6 × 4¾″ = 28½″ + 7½″ = 36″, and that is the width you need. A good way to divide a piece of this size and design would probably be to make it in 3 strips, each one on your 261 stitches. Working it this way and starting on the left side of the afghan, you would do the first strip through 2½″ of the third broad main-color stripe, the second one beginning with 2½″ of the same broad main-color stripe (allowing ¼″ extra on this stripe for seaming) and working through 2½″ of

the third broad main-color stripe from the right side, and the last one beginning with 2½″ of the same broad main-color stripe (allowing ¼″ extra on this stripe for seaming) and working to completion of the afghan.

The choice of finishing on afghans is a wide one, as discussed at length in the Designer's Guide. However, since you already know how you want to finish this one, you would work now in this manner: Block each piece, then seam them together carefully on the wrong side of work, matching the stripes and making the seam as inconspicuous as possible. Work 1 row of color over color single crochet around the entire outer edge, working 3 single crochet in each corner stitch as you turn, then work your 7-stripe single crochet final border. Your afghan is finished now. Block the entire piece, toss it casually over a corner of the divan (as though you were not mighty proud of your achievement)—and enjoy it!

It is our feeling that by now a good knowledge of the art of designing has been imparted to you through the pages you've just read, and that with that knowledge and all the information available to you in the Crocheter's Guide and the Designer's Guide you will be able to go on to create many new original things of your own. However, with the exception of your round pillow which involved the standard shaping that applies to all round pieces of crochet work, all the other pieces you've made have been straight ones worked with the same few mathematical exercises, but little else in the way of shaping such as one might need to be concerned with in, for instance, a piece of clothing which has, among other things, sleeves and shoulders and a neckline and armholes, all of which require a little calculation of their own. Perhaps it would be wise now to further your knowledge in the art of design by working out together another piece or two which would involve this additional skill of shaping, although let us reassure you again that incredible as it may seem, once you have shaped one or two pieces of clothing, you will be able to design many more, since here again basic and quite firm rules do exist, and as you have become more familiar with the Crocheter's and Designer's Guides, you will also become very aware of this fact.

The little girl's dress shown below here is a pretty one, and one that you might want to make for your own child or a member of the family or, in a larger size, even for yourself. It would be a lovely thing worked in a fluffy soft mauve or eggshell mohair yarn, with a simple textured stitch for the body and a very lacy one for all the ruffled trim. Finish it with a very narrow black velvet ribbon border between the main portions and the ruffled trim, a small bow at the neck and a few tiny black buttons, and here is a festive party dress for any size and any age! In the Designer's Guide there are suggested standard-size measurement charts with basic measurements for twenty-six different sizes, one of which will surely approximate the size you want to make. Since, however, the model pictured here is a child's dress, it might be good to work it out that way, although actually you would employ the same calculating route for whatever size you choose to make it. For purpose of example now, however, let us presume that you want to make it in a child's size 8. Given here now for your working purpose, just below the dress illustration, is a chart with the standard measurements for a child's size 8. How do you start?

Standard Measurements for a Child's Size 8

Chest	26″	Armhole depth	5½″
Shoulder back	10¾″	Waist to underarm	7½″
Shoulder	3¼″	Underarm sleeve length	12½″
Back of neck	4¼″	Sleeve width at underarm	10″

Choose your yarn first, again with the reassurance as already discussed that you will have enough of the dye lot you are using to be able to complete your garment. Select the pattern stitch that you want for the main portion of the dress, and the very lacy one that you will want to use for the ruffled trim. Swatch out the textured body stitch (the gauge and number of stitches you will use for the lacy trim, which is added last, can be determined later on) to decide what size hook you want to use, measure your gauge, note the multiple of the textured stitch, then consult the standard size 8 chart. Measure the body proportions of the child for whom you are making the dress to be certain that her actual body measurements do conform to those on the standard-size chart. Wherever there is a variation, if there is one, in those parts you must substitute the child's measurements for those on the chart. You need now only to determine what length you want to make the dress in order to be able to start your design. Dress length is always a complete variable, depending on the style and the height of the person for whom it is being made, and for this reason it never appears on standard-size measurement charts. Let us assume now for purpose of example that in this instance you want the total length of the dress from the very bottom to the underarm to be 28″, of which the last 4″ will be ruffled flounce to be added last, thus making your bottom to underarm working measurement 24″.

If we do plan now that you have selected a pattern stitch for the main portion of your dress with a gauge of 2 patterns to 3", and a multiple of 7 + 4, we are ready to start your calculations much as you did in the designing of your lovely afghan, rug and pillow ensemble, needing, however, to take into consideration the additional mathematics involved in the various shapings of your garment, and the increasing and decreasing necessary to accomplish these. The Designer's Guide offers this information in great detail, and includes all the facts as to where to place and how to shape every portion of a garment, such as sleeves and armholes and various kinds of necklines, and the Crocheter's Guide contains helpful information as to how to work out the particular pattern stitch you have chosen and how to increase and decrease with it. Refer to these sections of the book as often as you need in order to be able to work out your various shapings, but meanwhile right now let us review here just a few design rules which you must know before we can even begin to work out our lesson together.

For most garments one works the back first, the front or fronts (if the garment is a cardigan type) next, and the sleeves last before the final finishing of sewing seams and adding details such as neckbands, collars, pockets, and whatever other trim may be used. For slipover sweaters or dresses, the number of stitches is the same on both back and front, and that number of stitches is half the number involved in the total calculation of the bust or chest measurement, plus a small allowance for seaming, and additional allowance for any particular shaping that occurs below the waist. To determine the number of stitches on the foundation chain for the back and front of the dress you are about to make now, divide your chest measurement in half. 26" divided by 2 = 13". This would be the number of inches you would need to start the back of a standard size 8 dress, except that there is an A-line shaping at the bottom of the dress you are going to design now, and since a 2" A-line seems to be a good proportion for this size (see the Designer's Guide on A-line shaping), you would be starting with 13" + 2" = 15". Taking into consideration now your gauge of 2 patterns to 3", divide the number of inches

needed by the 3" figure in that gauge. 15 divided by 3 = 5. 5 × 2 (the number of patterns to each 3") tells you that you need 10 patterns to achieve your 15" with the particular stitch you have chosen. The multiple of that stitch is 7 + 4. Multiply now the number of patterns you need by the number of stitches in each pattern (the base multiple). 10 × 7 = 70. 70 + 4 (the number necessary to complete the multiple) = 74. This becomes the number of stitches in your starting foundation chain, and in this particular instance you do not need to add anything for seam allowance, since the 4 stitches you added to complete your pattern multiple will accommodate this allowance.

You need to know now just a few more design rules before going on. On a 24" dress with a 2" A-line shaping, that shaping should, for good proportion, occur during the first 8" of your work. Also, your 12½" sleeve, minus the 3" for the ruffled cuff, will start with a 3" above-the-wrist measurement, and you will need to increase it gradually in the 9½" remaining to the full 10" width at the underarm, although in this particular instance since the sleeve appears to be a fairly full one, your increases should take place somewhere along the first 6½" of that remaining portion, rather than in the total 9½"; and a round-neck shaping on the front of a garment usually occurs 2" below the start of the shoulder shaping in the front and, in a style such as this, particularly a garment where there is a ruffled neck trim in addition to the high round neck, it is wise to have some kind of an opening at the top of the back. Bearing all the above information in mind now, and continuing to refer as necessary to the Crocheter's Guide and the Designer's Guide, you would probably work your dress in the following manner:

Back: Chain 74. Work even in pattern stitch for approximately 2", ending with a wrong side row (most shaping begins on a right side row). Work your first A-line decrease at the beginning and end of the next row, and, being careful to maintain your pattern stitch throughout, continue to decrease gradually and at even intervals until your piece measures 13" in width, and 8" in length have been worked. (*Note:* Since the method of increasing and decreasing varies with the type of stitch being used, refer now to the Crocheter's Guide for information on how to decrease with the particular stitch you are working with.) Work even now until the piece measures approximately 24" to the underarm (again ending with a wrong side row), then **Shape Armholes:** Slip stitch across 1 pattern, or as many patterns or stitches necessary to reduce your garment by a little less than ½ the number of inches necessary to be bound off to come to the difference between your chest and shoulder-back measurement (refer here to the Designer's Guide for armhole shaping), work to within last pattern (or an equal number of stitches or patterns as at the beginning of the row), chain and turn. Next Row: Work even. Decrease now, if necessary, in keeping with your pattern stitch as you did in the shaping of your A-line skirt on every other row until 10¾" remain for your shoulder back. Work 1 row even, then **Divide for Neck Opening:** Next Row: Work to center of back, chain and turn. Work even in pattern on these stitches only until piece measures 5½" above start of armhole shaping, ending with a wrong side row. **Shape Shoulders:** Slip stitch across 2 patterns (or as many patterns or stitches as necessary to equal the number of inches to be bound off for one shoulder), complete row. Next Row: Slip stitch across remaining stitches for half of back of neck. Fasten off. Return now to row where stitches were first divided for neck opening, join yarn and complete other half of shoulder back to correspond, reversing all shaping. **Front:** Work as for Back until piece measures same as Back to start of armhole shaping. Shape armholes as on Back, then work even on remaining stitches until piece measures 3½" above start of armhole shaping, ending with a wrong side row. **Shape Neck:** Work across the number of patterns or stitches to measure approximately 1" more than that measurement used for the shoulder bind-off, chain and turn. Decrease at beginning of next row and repeat the decrease at same edge every other row until that number used for the shoulder bind-off remains. Work even on these stitches until piece measures

same as Back to shoulder and shape shoulder as on Back. Return now to row where neck shaping began, skip center stitches, join yarn and complete other half of shoulder front to correspond, reversing all shaping. **Sleeves:** Chain 32—the size of this foundation chain to measure 6" and accommodate your stitch multiple of 7 + 4. Work even in pattern stitch for approximately 1", then, being careful to maintain pattern as established, increase at each end of work and at even intervals until piece measures 10½" in width, and approximately 6" of work has been done. Work even now until piece measures 9½", ending with a wrong side row, then **Shape Cap:** Slip stitch across 1 pattern (or the same number of patterns or stitches as at the beginning of the armhole shaping), work to within the same number of patterns or stitches, chain and turn. Work 1 row even, then decrease at beginning and end of every other row until piece measures approximately 2½" above start of cap shaping. Fasten off. (*Note:* See shaping of Sleeve Caps in the Designer's Guide.) **Finishing:** Sew side, sleeve and shoulder seams, working a thin seam with an overhand back stitch. (*Note:* The choice of other methods of seaming appears in the Crocheter's Guide.) Work 1 row single crochet around all outer edges of dress, including back neck opening. **Bottom Flounce:** Bearing in mind the stitch multiple for the lacy pattern you are going to use for trim, make a chain to measure twice the circumference of the bottom of the dress (see the Designer's Guide for Ruffles), and work even in that lacy pattern for 4". Fasten off. Gathering the extra fullness evenly, sew the flounce to the bottom of the dress, sewing the foundation chain of the flounce to the final single crochet row around the bottom of the dress. Work the sleeve ruffle in the same manner, making that one 3" instead of 4" as on the bottom. Make another ruffle 1" wide and to measure double the circumference of the neck, and sew that one around the neck, rounding the shape of the neckline as you sew. Measure the length of the distance of the top of the front of the dress from the top of the shoulders to 2" below the start of the armhole shaping, double this amount, measure the width of the front neck opening, and the total of double these figures will give you the amount you need to chain for the lacy ruffled front trim of the dress. Make a chain to measure this length and work in the pattern stitch for 1". Fasten off. Place this last piece around the top of the front of the dress as shown and sew into place, squaring out the bottom corners. Sew a length of ribbon along each point of joining of ruffle to dress, and a small ribbon bow at the neck as shown. Trim with 3 small buttons and complete the dress by sewing a zipper along the back neck opening. The dress is finished now, and we hope that you are delighted with it, and will remember too that it can be made in any size at all and that, having been through this lesson together, you are probably quite able to design and make it yourself to any specification you choose. Perhaps now however we should work out just one more lesson together before you take to wings on your own, and feel absolutely free to go ahead and design whatever you want to make. Let's assume that this time it is a long sleeveless surplice type slipover for yourself, the kind that does so well over a blouse with slacks or a skirt.

You are a size 12, and you'd like your sweater to be in a small all-over textured stitch, and in a light-weight yarn with a very loose gauge. The garment you're thinking about probably resembles the one pictured below here. Under the picture you will find the chart for standard measurements for a woman's size 12.

Standard Measurements for a Woman's Size 12

Bust	34"	Armhole depth	7¼"
Waist	25"	Waist to underarm	8"
Shoulder back	13"	Underarm sleeve length	18"
Shoulder	4¼"	Sleeve width at underarm	12"
Back of neck	4½"		

Starting again in the same manner as with your other designs, select your yarn (we might suggest here a sport weight worked on a No. K hook for the type of "feel" you seem to want), choose your pattern stitch, make your swatch, then compare your own body measurements to the standard ones appearing on the chart. In this case you know that, although you are a size 12, your bust measures 36" instead of the 34" on the standard size chart, so you will need to take that into consideration in working out your final calculations. Aside from referring to the Crocheter's Guide and the Designer's Guide for whatever help or information you may

need, there are just two more rules that you should know now, in addition to those you have learned in working out our last garment together. Hip measurement is usually the same as bust measurement; and any type of garment such as a cardigan, jacket, coat or vest meant to be worn over something else usually needs an allowance of approximately an extra inch in overall measurement for "ease" of fit. Bearing these two rules in mind, plus all else you have learned, and presuming that you have chosen to use a gauge of 3 stitches to 1" with your thin yarn, and a stitch multiple of 5, you are ready now to begin your calculations.

Your bust measurement is 36", half of which is 18". 18 × 3 (your gauge) = 54. 54 + 3 (for "ease" allowance) = 57. 57 + 2 (for seam allowance) = 59. Since 59 is not divisible by your multiple of 5, you would add 1 more stitch, and start your foundation chain with 60 stitches and then work in this manner:

Back: Chain 60. Work even in pattern stitch for 18", ending with a wrong side row, then **Shape Armholes:** Slip stitch across the number of stitches to equal approximately 1", work to within the same number of stitches at the end of the row, chain and turn. Next Row: Work even. Decrease now at each end of work on every other row (See Crocheter's Guide for decreasing) until 13" remain for your shoulder back. Work even now on 13" until piece measures 7¾" (an extra ½" is added here to armhole depth for "ease") above start of armhole shaping, ending with a wrong side row. **Shape Shoulders:** Slip stitch across the number of stitches to equal approximately 2¼", or ½ the shoulder measurement, work to within the same number of stitches at the end of the row, chain and turn. Next Row: Work even. Next Row: Slip stitch across the remaining number of stitches to equal your complete shoulder bind-off of 4¼", work to within the same number of stitches at the end of the row, chain and turn. Next Row: Slip stitch across remaining stitches for back of neck. Fasten off. **Front:** Start as for Back and work even for 6". Place a marker on left side edge to denote point at which surplice effect will begin. Continue to work even now until piece measures 12", then **Shape Neck:** Work across 10", chain and turn. Being careful to maintain pattern, decrease gradually and at even intervals the necessary number of stitches (being sure to allow for stitches needed at armhole shaping) so that you remain with 4¼" when your piece measures the same as the Back to the shoulder, and *at same time* when piece measures 18", ending at side edge, shape your armhole as on Back. When 4¼" remain and your piece measures 7¾" above the start of the armhole shaping, ending at side edge, shape your shoulder as on Back. Return now to row where neck shaping began, attach yarn and work other side of front to correspond, reversing all shaping. **Finishing:** Sew side and shoulder seams. Work 1 row single crochet around all outer edges. **Trim:** Chain 5 and work in single crochet through back loops of stitches only (for ribbed effect) until piece measures from left side edge marker 6" above the bottom, around neck and ending at center point of V-neck shaping. Fasten off. Sew this ribbed trim onto sweater as shown.

You've worked out quite a few things now, and you've come a far way. We hope that you are happy about having learned this new creative skill of designing, and are stimulated to go on to enjoy many pleasant leisure hours with it. Making always the same starting choice of a style and a pattern stitch, and yarn and a hook and a gauge, and working the same rudimentary mathematical calculations, with the help of whatever additional information you might need from the Crocheter's Guide and the Designer's Guide, you will certainly be able to achieve whatever it is that you want in the way of a new design. We believe that with this new knowledge you will have found an interesting avenue of release for personal expression, and perhaps even discovered some latent talent that, unknown to yourself, has bottled up within you for years. In subsequent chapters we will tell you of many other exciting facets of crochet design beyond those of the simple crochet you have learned now, and involving, as we had mentioned at the start of this chapter, "block" or motif crocheting, filet mesh, the afghan or Tunisian type of work, and the many uses of all kinds of interesting trim, including beautiful edgings and insertions and plain and fancy fringes.

6. PATTERN STITCHES

Photographed here now are many beautiful pattern stitches, any one of which you might want to select for use in your own crochet designs, or to substitute for other patterns in designs you have seen elsewhere. Some of the stitches are quite easy to work, others more intricate. Among those shown are simple patterns and rich textures, shells, clusters, puffs and popcorns, delicate lacy designs and patterns of two and three colors. Directions are given for making all of the stitches shown, and practically any one can be used in the place of another for whatever piece of work you are planning. The choice of which you use is completely your own, and you need only to be mindful that the one you do decide to work with, and the gauge and size of the hook you use with it, will be strong contributing factors to the design you finally achieve. A basic sweater made with a simple textured stitch can metamorphose into a sheer creation with the use of one of the delicate lacy patterns. And by the same token, if you were making a belted hip-length coat with a knitting-worsted-weight yarn and a No. G hook on a gauge of 5 stitches to 1", you would probably be working toward a very useful, attractive garment to wear for everyday getting-about, whereas that same garment, worked with the same stitch, and maybe even the same yarn, with a No. 15 hook and a presumable gauge of 5 stitches to 2" would undoubtedly take on a softer, much more supple look, thus rendering it more of an evening going-out-for-dinner coat. Your imagination has complete free rein at this point, and though certain stitches may be more suitable for certain types of garments (one would not use a lacy stitch for a man's crocheted jacket!), still the choice of the one you do use is entirely your own, and up to the dictates of your own good taste.

Given directly below here is an explanation of the various abbreviations used in our pattern stitches, and beyond that a few detailed descriptive interpretations of certain terms accompanying the pattern stitches. Any additional information that you might need on how to work the basic stitches involved in the patterns will be found, many of them illustrated, in the Crocheter's Guide in Chapter 4; any other information on how to work out or complete your own particular piece of work will be found in the Designer's Guide in Chapter 12.

beg	beginning
bl	block
ch	chain
CC	contrast color
dbl	double
dc	double crochet
dec	decrease
F.O.	fasten off
hdc	half double crochet
hk	hook
inc	increase
j	join
lp(s)	loop(s)
MC	main color
pat	pattern
rnd	round
sc	single crochet
sk	skip
sl st	slip stitch
sp(s)	space(s)
st(s)	stitch(es)
tog	together
tr	treble
yo	yarn over

The word *Multiple* which appears at the beginning of each set of directions given below tells the number of stitches to be used on the foundation or starting chain in order to complete one pattern. The number of stitches you use in your work needs to be divisible by the number of the original multiple. For example, in working a pattern with a multiple of 4, you must start out with any number of stitches divisible by 4, such as 8, 12, 16, or any other multiple of the original 4. The variation where a multiple has an additional figure at the end, such as, let us say, 4 + 1, means that the number of stitches needs again to be divisible by the original multiple with 1 stitch added just at the end. In this case, the number of stitches on the foundation chain might be 9, 13, 17, or any other multiple of 4 + 1.

The foundation chain as worked in our directions indicates the actual number of stitches for you to start with considering the multiple, gauge, and size of the piece of work you are doing, and does not include the number of chains needed to turn at the end of the row. The last loop on your hook does not count as a chain, and for best results your chain should be made very loosely, since there is not much "give" in this part of your work.

All stitches are worked through both loops at the top of the stitch unless otherwise specified. Refer to the illustration in the Crocheter's Guide where we clearly define the top and the base, the two component parts of any stitch.

An asterisk (*), which appears in all of our directions, indicates that the instructions immediately following it are to be repeated the additional number of times necessary to accommodate the number of stitches involved on the piece of work you are doing.

When a portion of any set of directions is set within parentheses, those instructions within the parentheses must be repeated in the exact order they are given for the number of times indicated by the numeral immediately following the close of the parentheses. This has to be done before going on to the remaining instructions for the completion of the pattern row in which they appear and must be worked in the same way as often as you need to repeat it in order to accommodate the number of stitches you are working with.

When a set of brackets [ ] occurs, directions and a set of parentheses are generally included between the opening and closing of the brackets. When this appears, all instructions within the brackets must be repeated in the exact order they are given for the number of times indicated by the numeral immediately following the closing bracket. This is to be done before the completion of all directions following the brackets.

Note: In the making of our two-color patterns, we used a light color for the main color and a deeper one for the contrast color. In our three-color patterns we used a light color for A, a dark color for B, and a medium color for C. If other color gradations are used, your work may be equally attractive, but will show some variation in the appearance of the pattern.

(1)

Multiple of any number of ch: **Row 1:** Ch 1, 1 sc in 2nd ch from hk, * 1 sc in next ch, repeat from * across, ch 1, turn. **Row 2:** Work 1 sc in each st across, ch 1, turn. Repeat row 2 for pattern.

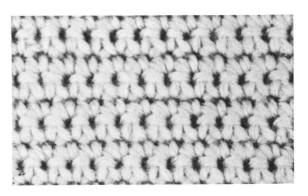

(2)

Multiple of any number of ch: **Row 1:** Ch 2, 1 dc in 3rd ch from hk, * 1 dc in next ch, repeat from * across, ch 2, turn. **Row 2:** Work 1 dc in each st across, ch 2, turn. Repeat row 2 for pattern.

(3)

Multiple of any number of ch: **Row 1:** Ch 2, 1 hdc in 3rd ch from hk, * 1 hdc in next ch, repeat from * across, ch 2, turn. **Row 2:** Work 1 hdc in each st across, ch 2, turn. Repeat row 2 for pattern.

(4)

Multiple of any number of ch: **Row 1:** Ch 3, 1 tr in 4th ch from hk, * 1 tr in next ch, repeat from * across, ch 3, turn. **Row 2:** Work 1 tr in each st across, ch 3, turn. Repeat row 2 for pattern.

(5)

Multiple of 2 ch: **Row 1:** Ch 1, 1 sc in 2nd ch from hk, * 1 dc in next ch, 1 sc in next ch, repeat from * across and end 1 dc in last ch, ch 1, turn. **Row 2:** * 1 sc in next dc, 1 dc in next sc, repeat from * across, ch 1, turn. Repeat row 2 for pattern.

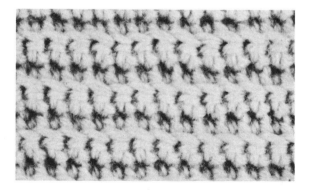

(6)

Multiple of any number of ch: **Row 1:** Ch 1, 1 sc in 2nd ch from hk, * 1 sc in next ch, repeat from * across, ch 1, turn. **Row 2:** Work 1 sc through back lp only of each st across, ch 1, turn. Repeat row 2 for pattern.

(7)

Multiple of 2 ch: **Row 1:** Ch 2 (counts as 1 st), yo, insert hk in 3rd ch from hk, yo and draw through, yo, insert hk in next ch, yo and draw through, yo and draw through 5 lps on hk, * ch 1, yo, insert hk in next ch, yo and draw through, yo, insert hk in next ch, yo and draw through, yo and draw through 5 lps on hk, repeat from * across, ch 3, turn. **Row 2:** Yo, insert hk in 3rd ch from hk, yo and draw through, yo, insert hk in next ch-1 sp, yo and draw through, yo and draw through 5 lps on hk, * ch 1, yo, insert hk in same ch-1 sp, yo and draw through, yo, insert hk in next ch-1 sp, yo and draw through, yo and draw through 5 lps on hk, repeat from * across and end ch 1, yo, insert hk in same ch-1 sp, yo and draw through, yo, insert hk in turning ch of previous row, yo and draw through, yo and draw through 5 lps on hk, ch 3, turn. Repeat row 2 for pattern.

(8)

Multiple of 2 ch: **Row 1:** Ch 2 (counts as 1 st), insert hk in 3rd ch from hk, yo and draw through, insert hk in next ch, yo and draw through, yo and draw through 2 lps on hk, yo and draw through last 2 lps on hk, * ch 1, (insert hk in next ch, yo and draw through) twice, yo and draw through 2 lps on hk, yo and draw through last 2 lps on hk, repeat from * across, ch 3, turn. **Row 2:** Insert hk in 3rd ch from hk, yo and draw through, insert hk in next ch-1 sp, yo and draw through, yo and draw through 2 lps on hk, yo and draw through last 2 lps on hk, * ch 1, insert hk in same ch-1 sp, yo and draw through, insert hk in next ch-1 sp, yo and draw through, yo and draw through 2 lps on hk, yo and draw through last 2 lps on hk, repeat from * across and end ch 1, insert hk in same ch-1 sp, yo and draw through, insert hk in turning ch of previous row, yo and draw through, yo and draw through 2 lps on hk, yo and draw through last 2 lps on hk, ch 3, turn. Repeat row 2 for pattern.

(9)

Multiple of 2 ch: **Row 1:** Ch 2, 1 dc in 3rd ch from hk, * 1 dc in next ch, repeat from * across, ch 2, turn. **Row 2:** Yo, insert hk in 1st dc, yo and draw through, yo, insert hk in next dc, yo and draw through, yo and draw through 5 lps on hk, * ch 1, yo, insert hk in same dc, yo and draw through, yo, insert hk in next dc, yo and draw through, yo and draw through 5 lps on hk, repeat from * across, ch 3, turn. **Row 3:** 1 dc in 3rd ch from hk, * 1 dc in next ch-1 sp, repeat from * across and end 1 dc in turning ch of previous row, ch 2, turn. Repeat rows 2 and 3 for pattern.

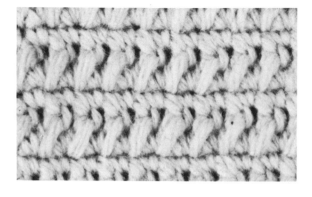

(10)

Multiple of 2 ch: **Row 1:** Ch 1, 1 sc in 2nd ch from hk, * 1 sc in next ch, repeat from * across, ch 2, turn. **Row 2:** Yo, insert hk in 1st sc, yo and draw through, yo, insert hk in next sc, yo and draw through, yo and draw through 5 lps on hk, * ch 1, yo, insert hk in same sc, yo and draw through, yo, insert hk in next sc, yo and draw through, yo and draw through 5 lps on hk, repeat from * across, ch 2, turn. **Row 3:** 1 sc in 2nd ch from hk, * 1 sc in next ch-1 sp, repeat from * across and end 1 sc in turning ch of previous row, ch 2, turn. Repeat rows 2 and 3 for pattern.

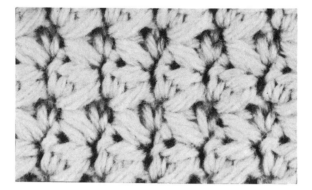

(11)

Multiple of 3 ch plus 1: **Row 1:** Ch 1, 1 sc in 2nd ch from hk, * (yo, insert hk in same ch, yo and draw through) twice, yo and draw through 5 lps on hk (puff st made), sk 2 ch, 1 sc in next ch, repeat from * across, ch 1, turn. **Row 2:** * (1 sc, 1 puff st) in next sc, repeat from * across and end 1 sc in last sc, ch 1, turn. Repeat row 2 for pattern.

(12)

Multiple of 4 ch: **Row 1:** Ch 1, 1 sc in 2nd ch
from hk, * 1 sc in next ch, repeat from * across,
ch 1, turn. **Rows 2 and 4:** * 1 sc through back lp
only of next sc, repeat from * across, ch 1, turn.
Row 3: * 1 sc through back lp only in each of
next 3 sc, insert hk in top of st 1 row below next
sc, yo and draw up a long lp, yo and draw
through 2 lps on hk, sk 1 sc, repeat from * across,
ch 1, turn. **Row 5:** * 1 sc through back lp only of
next sc, insert hk in top of st 1 row below next sc,
yo and draw up a long lp, yo and draw through
2 lps on hk, sk 1 sc, 1 sc through back lp only in
each of next 2 sc, repeat from * across, ch 1,
turn. Repeat rows 2 through 5 for pattern.

(13)

Multiple of 2 ch plus 1: **Row 1:** Ch 3, 1 sc in
4th ch from hk, * ch 1, sk 1 ch, 1 sc in next ch,
repeat from * across, ch 2, turn. **Row 2:** * 1 sc in
next ch-1 sp, ch 1, repeat from * across and end
1 sc in turning ch of previous row, ch 2, turn.
Repeat row 2 for pattern.

(14)

Multiple of 2 ch plus 1: **Row 1:** Ch 1, 2 sc in
2nd ch from hk, * sk 1 ch, 2 sc in next ch, repeat
from * across, ch 1, turn. **Row 2:** * Sk 1 sc, 2 sc
in next sc, repeat from * across, ch 1, turn.
Repeat row 2 for pattern.

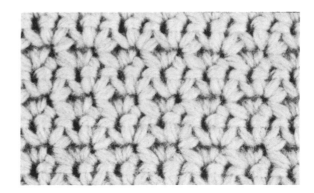

(15)
Multiple of 2 ch plus 1: **Row 1:** Ch 3, 1 sc in 4th ch from hk, * ch 1, sk 1 ch, 1 sc in next ch, repeat from * across, ch 2, turn. **Row 2:** * 1 sc in next ch-1 sp, ch 1, repeat from * across and end 1 sc in turning ch of previous row, ch 2, turn. **Row 3:** * Sk 1 sc, insert hk in top of sc 1 row below next ch-1, yo and draw up a long lp, yo and draw through 2 lps on hk, ch 1, repeat from * across, ch 2, turn. Repeat row 3 for pattern.

(16)
Multiple of 2 ch plus 1: **Row 1:** Ch 1, (1 sc, 1 dc) in 2nd ch from hk, * sk 1 ch, (1 sc, 1 dc) in next ch, repeat from * across and end 1 sc in last ch, ch 1, turn. **Row 2:** * (1 sc, 1 dc) in next sc, sk 1 dc, repeat from * across and end 1 sc in last sc, ch 1, turn. Repeat row 2 for pattern.

(17)
Multiple of 2 ch: **Row 1:** Ch 2, 1 dc in 3rd ch from hk, * 1 dc in next ch, repeat from * across, ch 1, turn. **Rows 2 and 4:** * 1 sc in next dc, repeat from * across, ch 2, turn. **Row 3:** * Sk 1 sc, yo, insert hk horizontally from right to left under dc 1 row below skipped sc, yo and draw up a long lp, yo and draw through 3 lps on hk, 1 dc in next sc, repeat from * across, ch 1, turn. **Row 5:** * 1 dc in next sc, repeat from * across, ch 1, turn. Repeat rows 2 through 5 for pattern.

(18)

Multiple of 6 ch: **Row 1:** Ch 2, 1 dc in 3rd ch from hk, * 1 dc in next ch, repeat from * across, ch 1, turn. **Rows 2 and 4:** * 1 sc in next st, repeat from * across, ch 2, turn. **Row 3:** * 1 dc in each of next 3 sc, (yo, insert hk horizontally from right to left under dc 1 row below next st, yo and draw up a long lp, yo and draw through 2 lps on hk, yo and draw through last 2 lps on hk) 3 times, sk 3 sc behind 3 sts just made, repeat from * across, ch 1, turn. **Row 5:** * (Yo, insert hk horizontally from right to left under dc 1 row below next st, yo and draw up a long lp, yo and draw through 2 lps on hk, yo and draw through last 2 lps on hk) 3 times, sk 3 sc behind 3 sts just made, 1 dc in each of next 3 sc, repeat from * across, ch 1, turn. Repeat rows 2 through 5 for pattern.

(19)

Multiple of 10 ch: **Row 1:** Ch 1, 1 sc in 2nd ch from hk, * 1 sc in each of next 4 ch, 1 dc in each of next 5 ch, 1 sc in next ch, repeat from * across and end 1 dc in each of last 5 ch, ch 1, turn.
Row 2: * 1 sc in each of next 5 dc, 1 dc in each of next 5 sc, repeat from * across, ch 1, turn. Repeat row 2 for pattern.

(20)

Multiple of 3 ch plus 1: **Row 1:** Ch 2, (1 sc, 2 dc) in 3rd ch from hk, * sk 2 ch, (1 sc, 2 dc) in next ch, repeat from * across and end 1 sc in last ch, ch 1, turn. **Row 2:** * (1 sc, 2 dc) in next sc, sk 2 dc, repeat from * across and end 1 sc in last sc, ch 1, turn. Repeat row 2 for pattern.

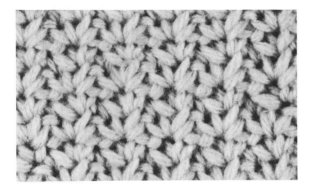

(21)
Multiple of 2 ch plus 1: **Row 1:** Ch 2, 1 sc in 3rd ch from hk, * (1 sc, ch 1, 1 sc) in next ch, sk 1 ch, repeat from * across and end 1 sc in last ch, ch 2, turn. **Row 2:** * (1 sc, ch 1, 1 sc) in next ch-1 sp, repeat from * across and end 1 sc in turning ch of previous row, ch 2, turn. Repeat row 2 for pattern.

(22)
Multiple of 2 ch plus 1: **Row 1:** Ch 1, 1 sc in 2nd ch from hk, * ch 1, sk 1 ch, 1 sc in next ch, repeat from * across, ch 1, turn. **Row 2:** 1 sc in 1st sc, * 1 long sc in ch below next ch-1 sp, 1 sc in next sc, repeat from * across, ch 1, turn.
Row 3: 1 sc in 1st sc, * ch 1, sk 1 long sc, 1 sc in next sc, repeat from * across, ch 1, turn. **Row 4:** 1 sc in 1st sc, * 1 long sc in skipped long sc below next ch-1 sp, 1 sc in next sc, repeat from * across, ch 1, turn. Repeat rows 3 and 4 for pattern.

(23)
Multiple of 2 ch: **Row 1:** Ch 1, keeping all lps on hk, insert hk in 2nd ch from hk, yo and draw through, (insert hk in next ch, yo and draw through) 3 times, yo and draw through 5 lps on hk, * ch 1, keeping all lps on hk, insert hk in ch-1 sp just made, yo and draw through, insert hk in last ch worked, yo and draw through, (insert hk in next ch, yo and draw through) twice, yo and draw through 5 lps on hk, repeat from * across, ch 4, turn. **Row 2:** Keeping all lps on hk, insert hk in 2nd ch from hk, yo and draw through, (insert hk in next ch, yo and draw through) twice, insert hk in top of next st, yo and draw through, yo and draw through 5 lps on hk, * ch 1, keeping all lps on hk, insert hk in ch-1 sp just made, yo and draw through, insert hk in top of last st of

previous row, yo and draw through, insert hk in next ch-1 sp, yo and draw through, insert hk in top of next st, yo and draw through, yo and draw through 5 lps on hk, repeat from * across, ch 4, turn. Repeat row 2 for pattern.

(24)
Multiple of 2 ch: **Row 1:** Ch 1, 1 sc in 2nd ch from hk, * 1 dc in next ch, 1 sc in next ch, repeat from * across and end 1 dc in last ch, ch 1, turn. **Row 2:** * 1 sc through back lp only of next dc, 1 dc through front lp only of next sc, repeat from * across, ch 1, turn. Repeat row 2 for pattern.

(25)
Multiple of 3 ch plus 2: **Row 1:** Ch 1, 1 sc in 2nd ch from hk, * 1 sc in next ch, repeat from * across, ch 1, turn. **Row 2:** 1 sc through back lp only in each of next 2 sc, * 1 sc in top of st 1 row below next sc, 1 sc through back lp only in each of next 2 sc, repeat from * across, ch 1, turn. **Row 3:** * 1 sc in next st, repeat from * across, ch 1, turn. Repeat rows 2 and 3 for pattern.

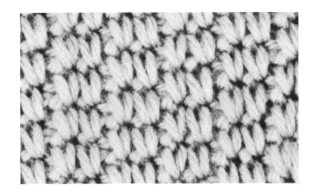

(26)
Multiple of 4 ch: **Row 1:** Ch 1, 1 sc in 2nd ch from hk, * 1 sc in next ch, repeat from * across. F.O., working in the loose thread on next row. Return to beg of row. **Row 2:** Attach yarn to back lp of 1st sc, 1 sc through back lp only of next sc, * (1 sc in top of st 1 row below next sc) twice, 1 sc through back lp only in each of next 2 sc, repeat from * across and end (1 sc in top of st 1 row below next sc) twice. F.O. Return to beg of row. **Row 3:** Attach yarn to back lp of 1st sc,

1 sc in top of st 1 row below same sc, 1 sc in top of st 1 row below next sc, * 1 sc through back lp only in each of next 2 sc, (1 sc in top of st 1 row below next sc) twice, repeat from * across and end 1 sc through back lp only in each of last 2 sc. F.O. Return to beg of row. Repeat rows 2 and 3 for pattern.

(27)
Multiple of 2 ch plus 1: **Row 1:** Ch 1, 1 sc in 2nd ch from hk, * 1 tr in next ch, 1 sc in next ch, repeat from * across, ch 1, turn. **Row 2:** * 1 sc in next st, repeat from * across, ch 1, turn. **Row 3:** * 1 sc in next sc, sk 1 sc, yo twice, insert hk horizontally from right to left under tr 1 row below skipped sc, yo and draw through, (yo and draw through 2 lps on hk) 3 times, repeat from * across and end 1 sc in last sc, ch 1, turn. Repeat rows 2 and 3 for pattern.

(28)
Multiple of 2 ch: **Row 1:** Ch 1, 1 sc in 2nd ch from hk, * 1 sc in next ch, repeat from * across, ch 4, turn. **Row 2:** Sk 1st sc, * 1 tr through back lp only of next sc, repeat from * across, ch 1, turn. **Row 3:** * Insert hk through back lp only of next tr, insert hk in free lp of sc 1 row below same tr, yo and draw through, yo and draw through 2 lps on hk, repeat from * across and end 1 sc in turning ch of previous row, ch 1, turn. **Row 4:** * 1 sc in next st, repeat from * across, ch 1, turn. **Row 5:** * 1 sc in next sc, repeat from * across, ch 4, turn. Repeat rows 2 through 5 for pattern.

(29)

Multiple of 2 ch: **Row 1:** Ch 1, 1 sc in 2nd ch from hk, * 1 sc in next ch, repeat from * across, ch 3, turn. **Row 2:** Keeping all lps on hk, yo, insert hk in 1st sc, * yo and draw through, yo, insert hk in same sc, yo and draw through, sk 1 sc (unworked), yo, insert hk in next sc, yo and draw through, yo, insert hk in same sc, yo and draw through, yo and draw through 9 lps on hk, ch 1, yo, insert hk in skipped sc, repeat from * across and end yo and draw through, yo, insert hk in same sc, yo and draw through, (yo, insert hk in last st, yo and draw through) twice, yo and draw through 9 lps on hk, ch 1, turn. **Row 3:** * 1 sc in next ch-1, 1 sc in next st, repeat from * across, ch 3, turn. Repeat rows 2 and 3 for pattern.

(30)

Multiple of 2 ch: **Row 1:** Ch 1, 1 sc in 2nd ch from hk, * 1 sc in next ch, repeat from * across, ch 1, turn. **Row 2:** * 1 sc in next sc, 1 tr in next sc, repeat from * across, ch 1, turn. **Rows 3 and 5:** * 1 sc in next st, repeat from * across, ch 1, turn. **Row 4:** 1 sc in each of 1st 2 sc, * 1 tr in next sc, 1 sc in next sc, repeat from * across, ch 1, turn. Repeat rows 2 through 5 for pattern.

(31)

Multiple of 2 ch: **Row 1:** Ch 2, 1 hdc in 3rd ch from hk, * 1 hdc in next ch, repeat from * across, ch 2, turn. **Row 2:** 1 sc in sp between 2nd and 3rd hdc of previous row, * ch 2, sk 2 hdc, 1 hdc in sp before next hdc, repeat from * across and end 1 sc in turning ch of previous row, ch 2, turn. **Row 3:** * 2 hdc in next ch-2 sp, repeat from * across and end 2 hdc in turning ch of previous row, ch 2, turn. Repeat rows 2 and 3 for pattern.

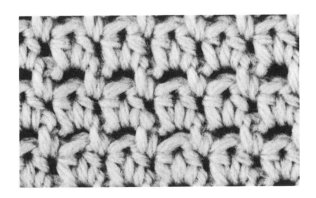

(32)

Multiple of 4 ch plus 2: **Row 1:** Ch 2, 1 dc in 3rd ch from hk, 1 dc in next ch, * 1 sc in each of next 2 ch, 1 dc in each of next 2 ch, repeat from * across, ch 1, turn. **Row 2:** * 1 sc in each of next 2 dc, 1 dc in each of next 2 sc, repeat from * across and end 1 sc in each of last 2 dc, ch 2, turn. **Row 3:** * 1 dc in each of next 2 sc, 1 sc in each of next 2 dc, repeat from * across and end 1 dc in each of last 2 sc, ch 1, turn. Repeat rows 2 and 3 for pattern.

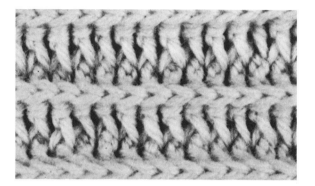

(33)

Multiple of 2 ch: **Row 1:** Ch 2, 1 dc in 3rd ch from hk, * 1 dc in next ch, repeat from * across, ch 2, turn. **Row 2:** * Yo, insert hk horizontally from right to left under next dc, yo and draw through, yo and draw through 2 lps on hk, yo and draw through last 2 lps on hk, repeat from * across, ch 2, turn. Repeat row 2 for pattern.

(34)

Multiple of 10 ch plus 5: **Row 1:** Ch 2, 1 dc in 3rd ch from hk, * 1 dc in next ch, repeat from * across, ch 1, turn. **Row 2:** * (Insert hk horizontally from right to left under next dc, yo and draw up a long lp, yo and draw through 2 lps on hk) 5 times, (1 dc in next dc, 1 sc in next dc) twice, 1 dc in next dc, repeat from * across and end (insert hk horizontally from right to left under next dc, yo and draw up a long lp, yo and draw through 2 lps on hk) 5 times, ch 2, turn. **Rows 3 and 5:** * 1 dc in next st, repeat from * across, ch 2, turn. **Row 4:** * (1 dc in next dc, 1 sc in next dc) twice, 1 dc in next dc, (insert hk horizontally from right to left under next dc, yo and draw up a long lp, yo and draw through 2 lps on hk) 5 times, repeat from * across and end (1 dc in next dc, 1 sc in next dc) twice, 1 dc in last dc, ch 2, turn. Repeat rows 2 through 5 for pattern.

(35)
Multiple of 4 ch: **Row 1:** Ch 2, 1 dc in 3rd ch from hk, * 1 dc in next ch, repeat from * across, ch 2, turn. **Row 2:** * (Yo, insert hk horizontally from right to left under next dc, yo and draw through, yo and draw through 2 lps on hk, yo and draw through last 2 lps on hk) twice, (yo, insert hk from back to front, over and around next dc, yo and draw through, yo and draw through 2 lps on hk, yo and draw through last 2 lps on hk) twice, repeat from * across, ch 2, turn. Repeat row 2 for pattern.

(36)
Multiple of 2 ch plus 1: **Row 1:** Ch 1, 1 sc in 2nd ch from hk, * 1 sc in next ch, repeat from * across, ch 1, turn. **Row 2:** 1 sc in 1st sc, * ch 1, sk 1 sc, 1 sc in next sc, repeat from * across, ch 1, turn. **Row 3:** * 1 sc in next sc, 1 sc in next ch-1 sp, repeat from * across and end 1 sc in last sc, ch 1, turn. Repeat rows 2 and 3 for pattern.

(37)
Multiple of 3 ch plus 1: **Row 1:** Ch 1, 1 sc in 2nd ch from hk, 2 dc in same ch, * sk 2 ch, (1 sc, 2 dc) in next ch (shell made), repeat from * across and end 1 sc in last ch, ch 1, turn. **Row 2:** * 1 shell in next sc, sk 2 dc, repeat from * across and end 1 sc in last sc, ch 1, turn. Repeat row 2 for pattern.

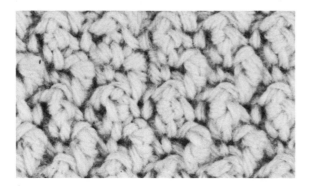

(38)
Multiple of 2 ch: **Row 1:** Ch 1, 1 sc in 2nd ch from hk, * 1 tr in next ch, 1 sc in next ch, repeat from * across and end 1 tr in last ch, ch 1, turn. **Row 2:** * 1 sc in next tr, 1 tr in next sc, repeat from * across, ch 1, turn. Push tr's to right side of work. Repeat row 2 for pattern.

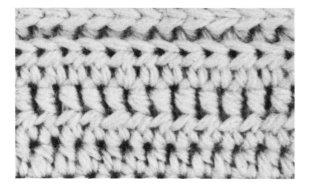

(39)
Multiple of any number of ch: **Row 1:** Ch 2, 1 hdc in 3rd ch from hk, * 1 hdc in next ch, repeat from * across, ch 2, turn. **Row 2:** * 1 hdc through back lp only of next hdc, repeat from * across, ch 2, turn. **Row 3:** Yo, insert hk in next hdc, * insert hk from back to front through next hdc, yo and draw through, yo and draw through 3 lps on hk, yo, insert hk in same hdc, repeat from * across and end insert hk from back to front through last hdc, yo and draw through, yo and draw through 3 lps on hk, 1 hdc in same hdc, ch 2, turn. **Row 4:** * 1 hdc in next hdc, repeat from * across, ch 2, turn. Repeat rows 2 through 4 for pattern.

(40)
Multiple of 4 ch: **Row 1:** Ch 2, 1 dc in 3rd ch from hk, 1 dc in next ch, sk 1 ch, 1 dc in next ch, 1 dc in skipped ch, * 1 dc in each of next 2 ch, sk 1 ch, 1 dc in next ch, 1 dc in skipped ch, repeat from * across, ch 2, turn. **Row 2:** * 1 dc in each of next 2 dc, sk 1 dc, 1 dc in next dc, 1 dc in skipped dc, repeat from * across, ch 2, turn. Repeat row 2 for pattern.

(41)

Multiple of 3 ch plus 1: **Row 1:** Ch 3, 2 dc in 4th ch from hk, * sk 2 ch, (sl st, ch 3, 2 dc) in next ch, repeat from * across and end sl st in last ch, ch 3, turn. **Row 2:** 2 dc in 1st sl st, * sk 2 dc, (sl st, ch 3, 2 dc) in next ch-3 sp, repeat from * across and end sl st in turning ch of previous row, ch 3, turn. Repeat row 2 for pattern.

(42)

Multiple of 6 ch plus 1: **Row 1:** Ch 1, 1 sc in 2nd ch from hk, * sk 2 ch, 5 dc in next ch, sk 2 ch, 1 sc in next ch, repeat from * across, ch 3, turn. **Row 2:** 2 dc in 1st sc, * sk 2 dc, 1 sc in next dc, sk 2 dc, 5 dc in next sc, repeat from * across and end 3 dc in last sc, ch 1, turn. **Row 3:** 1 sc in 1st dc, * sk 2 dc, 5 dc in next sc, sk 2 dc, 1 sc in next dc, repeat from * across and end 1 sc in turning ch of previous row, ch 3, turn. Repeat rows 2 and 3 for pattern.

(43)

Multiple of 6 ch plus 1: **Row 1:** Ch 3, 2 dc in 4th ch from hk, * sk 2 ch, 1 sc in next ch, sk 2 ch, 5 dc in next ch, repeat from * across and end 3 dc in last ch, ch 1, turn. **Row 2:** 1 sc in 1st dc, * sk 1 dc, 2 dc in next dc, 4 dc in next sc, take lp off hk, insert hk in 1st dc of 4-dc group, pick up and draw lp of 4th dc through, ch 1 (popcorn made), 2 dc in next dc, sk 1 dc, 1 sc in next dc, repeat from * across and end 1 sc in turning ch of previous row, ch 3, turn. **Row 3:** 2 dc in 1st sc, * sk 2 dc, 1 sc in top of next popcorn, sk 2 dc, 5 dc in next sc, repeat from * across and end 3 dc in last sc, ch 1, turn. Repeat rows 2 and 3 for pattern.

(44)
Multiple of 2 ch plus 1. **Row 1:** Ch 2, yo, insert hk in 3rd ch from hk, yo and draw through, yo and draw through 2 lps on hk, * (yo, insert hk in same ch, yo and draw through, yo and draw through 2 lps on hk) twice, yo and draw through 4 lps on hk, ch 1, sk 1 ch, yo, insert hk in next ch, yo and draw through, yo and draw through 2 lps on hk, repeat from * across and end yo and draw through last 2 lps on hk, ch 2, turn. **Row 2:** * Yo, insert hk in next ch-1 sp, yo and draw through, yo and draw through 2 lps on hk, (yo, insert hk in same ch-1 sp, yo and draw through, yo and draw through 2 lps on hk) twice, yo and draw through 4 lps on hk, ch 1, repeat from * across and end 1 dc in turning ch of previous row, ch 2, turn. Repeat row 2 for pattern.

(45)
Multiple of 6 ch plus 1: **Row 1:** Ch 1, 1 sc in 2nd ch from hk, * ch 2, sk 2 ch, (1 dc, ch 2, 1 dc) in next ch, ch 2, sk 2 ch, 1 sc in next ch, repeat from * across, ch 3, turn. **Row 2:** 2 dc in 1st sc, * sk (ch-2 sp, 1 dc), 1 sc in next ch-2 sp, sk (1 dc, ch-2 sp), 5 dc in next sc, repeat from * across and end 3 dc in last sc, ch 3, turn. **Row 3:** 1 sc in 1st dc, * ch 2, sk 2 dc, (1 dc, ch 2, 1 dc) in next sc, ch 2, sk 2 dc, 1 sc in next dc, repeat from * across and end 1 sc in turning ch of previous row, ch 3, turn. Repeat rows 2 and 3 for pattern.

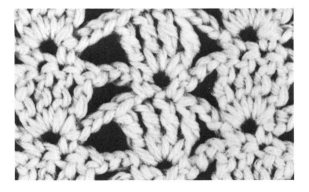

(46)
Multiple of 9 ch plus 1: **Row 1:** Ch 4, 1 tr in 5th ch from hk, * ch 3, sk 3 ch, 1 sc in next ch, ch 3, 1 sc in next ch, ch 3, sk 3 ch, 4 tr in next ch, repeat from * across and end 2 tr in last ch, ch 1, turn. **Row 2:** 1 sc in 1st tr, * ch 3, sk (1 tr, ch-3 sp, 1 sc), 4 tr in next ch-3 sp, ch 3, sk (1 sc, ch-3 sp, 1 tr), 1 sc in next tr, ch 3, 1 sc in next tr, repeat from * across and end 1 sc in turning ch of previous row, ch 4, turn. **Row 3:** 1 tr in 1st sc,

ch 3, sk (ch-3 sp, 1 tr), * 1 sc in next tr, ch 3, 1 sc in next tr, ch 3, sk (1 tr, ch-3 sp, 1 sc), 4 tr in next ch-3 sp, ch 3, sk (1 sc, ch-3 sp, 1 tr), repeat from * across and end 2 tr in last sc, ch 1, turn. Repeat rows 2 and 3 for pattern.

(47)

Multiple of 6 ch plus 4: **Row 1:** Ch 3, 2 dc in 4th ch from hk, * sk 2 ch, 1 sc in next ch, sk 2 ch, 5 dc in next ch, repeat from * across and end 1 sc in last ch. Drop yarn. Return to beg of row. **Row 2:** Attach another ball of yarn to turning ch, 1 sc in turning ch, (1 sc through back lp only of next dc) twice, * 1 sc in next sc, (1 sc through back lp only of next dc) 5 times, repeat from * across and end 1 sc in last sc, drop yarn, draw last lp of previous row through, ch 3, turn. **Row 3:** 2 dc in 1st sc, * sk 2 sc, 1 sc in next sc, sk 2 sc, 5 dc in next sc, repeat from * across and end 1 sc in last sc. Drop yarn. Return to beg of row. **Row 4:** Pick up attached yarn, 1 sc in turning ch, (1 sc through back lp only of next dc) twice, * 1 sc in next sc, (1 sc through back lp only of next dc) 5 times, repeat from * across and end 1 sc in last sc, drop yarn, draw last lp of previous row through, ch 3, turn. Repeat rows 3 and 4 for pattern.

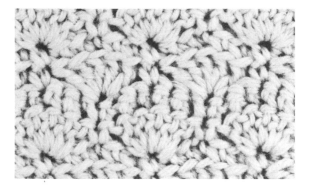

(48)

Multiple of 4 ch plus 3: **Row 1:** Ch 1, 1 sc in 2nd ch from hk, * keeping last lp of each tr on hk, 3 tr in next ch, yo and draw through 4 lps on hk (popcorn made), 1 sc in each of next 3 ch, repeat from * across and end 1 sc in last ch, ch 1, turn. **Rows 2 and 4:** * 1 sc in next st, repeat from * across, ch 1, turn. **Row 3:** * 1 sc in each of next 3 sc, 1 popcorn in next sc, repeat from * across and end 1 sc in each of last 3 sc, ch 1, turn. **Row 5:** 1 sc in 1st sc, * 1 popcorn in next sc, 1 sc in each of next 3 sc, repeat from * across and end 1 sc in last sc, ch 1, turn. Repeat rows 2 through 5 for pattern.

(49)

Multiple of 4 ch plus 1: **Row 1:** Ch 3, keeping last lp of each dc on hk, 2 dc in 4th ch from hk, yo and draw through 3 lps on hk, * ch 3, sk 3 ch, keeping last lp of each dc on hk, 5 dc in next ch, yo and draw through 6 lps on hk (cluster made), repeat from * across and end keeping last lp of each dc on hk, 3 dc in last ch, yo and draw through 4 lps on hk (half cluster made), ch 1, turn. **Row 2:** 1 dc in 1st st, * ch 3, 1 cluster in next ch-3 sp, repeat from * across and end ch 3, 1 dc in turning ch of previous row, ch 3, turn. **Row 3:** Keeping last lp of each dc on hk, 2 dc in next ch-3 sp, yo and draw through 3 lps on hk, * ch 3, 1 cluster in next ch-3 sp, repeat from * across and end ch 3, half cluster in last ch-3 sp, ch 2, turn. Repeat rows 2 and 3 for pattern.

(50)

Multiple of 2 ch plus 1: **Row 1:** Ch 2, yo, insert hk in 3rd ch from hk, yo and draw through, * (yo, insert hk in same ch, yo and draw through) 3 times, yo and draw through 8 lps on hk, yo and draw through last 2 lps on hk, ch 1 (cluster made), sk 1 ch, yo, insert hk in next ch, yo and draw through, repeat from * across and end 1 dc in last ch, ch 2, turn. **Row 2:** Sk 1st dc, * 1 cluster in next ch-1 sp, repeat from * across and end 1 dc in turning ch of previous row, ch 2, turn. Repeat row 2 for pattern.

(51)

Multiple of 6 ch plus 1: **Row 1:** Ch 2, 1 dc in 3rd ch from hk, * sk 2 ch, (2 dc, ch 1, 2 dc) in next ch (shell made), sk 2 ch, 1 dc in next ch, repeat from * across, ch 2, turn. **Row 2:** Sk 3 dc, * 1 shell in next ch-1 sp, sk 2 dc, yo, insert hk horizontally from right to left under next dc, yo and draw through, yo and draw through 2 lps on hk, yo and draw through last 2 lps on hk (dc around post made) sk 2 dc, repeat from * across, ch 3, turn. **Row 3:** Sk 3 dc, * 1 shell in next ch-1 sp, sk 2 dc, 1 dc around post of next dc, sk 2 dc, repeat from

* across and end 1 dc in turning ch of previous row, ch 3, turn. Repeat row 3 for pattern.

(52)
Multiple of 6 ch plus 1: **Row 1:** Ch 1, 1 sc in 2nd ch from hk, ch 5, 1 sc in same ch, * sk 2 ch, 5 dc in next ch (shell made), sk 2 ch, (1 sc, ch 5, 1 sc) in next ch (lp made), repeat from * across and end (1 sc, ch 2, 1 dc) in last ch, ch 1, turn. **Row 2:** 1 lp in 1st ch-2 sp, * 1 shell in center dc of next shell, 1 lp in next ch-5 sp, repeat from * across and end (1 sc, ch 2, 1 dc) in last lp, ch 1, turn. Repeat row 2 for pattern.

(53)
Multiple of 5 ch plus 1: **Row 1:** Ch 1, 1 sc in 2nd ch from hk, * ch 4, 4 tr in same ch, sk 4 ch, 1 sc in next ch, repeat from * across and end 1 sc in last ch, ch 1, turn. **Row 2:** * (1 sc, ch 4, 4 tr) in next sc, sk (4 tr, ch-4), repeat from * across and end 1 sc in last sc, ch 1, turn. Repeat row 2 for pattern, keeping all shells on right side of work.

(54)
Multiple of 5 ch plus 1: **Row 1:** Ch 1, 1 sc in 2nd ch from hk, * ch 4, 4 tr in same ch, sk 4 ch, 1 sc in next ch, repeat from * across and end 1 sc in last ch, ch 1, turn. **Row 2:** * (1 sc, ch 4, 4 tr) through back lp only of next sc, sk (4 tr, ch-4), keeping shells of row 2 behind shells of previous row, repeat from * across and end 1 sc through back lp only of last sc, ch 1, turn. **Row 3:** * (1 sc, ch 4, 4 tr) through front lp only of next sc, sk (4 tr, ch-4), keeping shells of row 3 behind shells of row 2, repeat from * across and end 1 sc through front lp only of last sc, ch 1, turn. Repeat rows 2 and 3 for pattern.

(55)

Multiple of 6 ch plus 1: **Row 1:** Ch 1, 1 sc in 2nd ch from hk, * sk 2 ch, 5 dc in next ch, sk 2 ch, 1 sc in next ch, repeat from * across, ch 3, turn. **Row 2:** 2 dc in 1st sc, * sk 2 dc, 1 sc through back lp only of next dc, sk 2 dc, 5 dc through back lp only of next sc, repeat from * across and end 3 dc in last sc, ch 1, turn. **Row 3:** 1 sc in 1st dc, * sk 2 dc, 5 dc through back lp only of next sc, sk 2 dc, 1 sc through back lp only of next dc, repeat from * across and end 1 sc in turning ch of previous row, ch 3, turn. Repeat rows 2 and 3 for pattern.

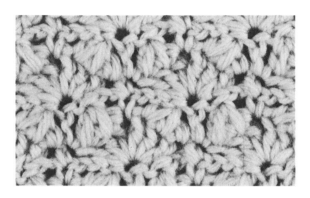

(56)

Multiple of 6 ch plus 1: **Row 1:** Ch 1, 1 sc in 2nd ch from hk, * sk 2 ch, (3 dc, ch 1, 3 dc) in next ch (shell made), sk 2 ch, 1 sc in next ch, repeat from * across, ch 3, turn. **Row 2:** * 1 dc in next sc, (yo, insert hk in next dc, yo and draw through) 3 times, yo and draw through 6 lps on hk, yo and draw through last 2 lps on hk (dc cluster made), ch 2, 1 sc in next ch-1 sp, ch 2, 1 dc cluster over next 3 dc, repeat from * across and end 1 dc in last sc, ch 3, turn. **Row 3:** 4 dc in 1st dc, * sk (1 dc cluster, ch-2), 1 sc in next sc, sk (ch-2, 1 dc cluster), 1 shell in next dc, repeat from * across and end 4 dc in last dc, ch 1, turn. **Row 4:** 1 sc in 1st dc, * ch 2, 1 dc cluster over next 3 dc, 1 dc in next sc, 1 dc cluster over next 3 dc, ch 2, 1 sc in next ch-1 sp, repeat from * across and end 1 sc in last dc, ch 1, turn. **Row 5:** * 1 sc in next sc, sk (ch-2, 1 dc cluster), 1 shell in next dc, sk (1 dc cluster, ch-2), repeat from * across and end 1 sc in last sc, ch 3, turn. Repeat rows 2 through 5 for pattern.

(57)

Multiple of 11 ch plus 9: **Row 1:** Ch 1, 1 sc in 2nd ch from hk, 1 sc in each of next 3 ch, 3 sc in next ch, 1 sc in each of next 4 ch, * sk 2 ch, 1 sc in each of next 4 ch, 3 sc in next ch, 1 sc in each of next 4 ch, repeat from * across, ch 1, turn. **Row 2:** Working through back lps of sts only, sk 1 sc, * 1 sc in each of next 4 sc, 3 sc in next sc, 1 sc in each of next 4 sc, sk 2 sc, repeat from * across and end 1 sc in each of next 4 sc, 3 sc in next sc, 1 sc in each of next 3 sc, sk 1 sc, 1 sc in last sc, ch 4, turn. **Row 3:** (1 dc, ch 1, 1 dc) in 1st sc, * sk 4 sc, 1 sc in next sc, sk 5 sc, (1 dc, ch 1) 4 times and 1 dc in skipped 2-sc sp of previous row (shell made), sk 1 sc, repeat from * across and end (1 dc, ch 1) twice and 1 dc in last sc, ch 1, turn. **Row 4:** 2 sc in 1st dc, (1 sc in next ch-1 sp, 1 sc in next dc) twice, * sk 1 sc, (1 sc in next dc, 1 sc in next ch-1 sp) twice, 3 sc in next dc, (1 sc in next ch-1 sp, 1 sc in next dc) twice, repeat from * across and end 1 sc in next dc, 1 sc in next ch-1 sp, 1 sc in last dc, 3 sc in turning ch of previous row, ch 1, turn. **Row 5:** Working through back lps of sts only, 2 sc in 1st sc, 1 sc in each of next 4 sc, * sk 2 sc, 1 sc in each of next 4 sc, 3 sc in next sc, 1 sc in each of next 4 sc, repeat from * across and end 2 sc in last sc, ch 1, turn. **Row 6:** 1 sc in 1st sc, * sk 5 sc, 1 shell in skipped 2-sc sp of previous row, sk 5 sc, 1 sc in next sc, repeat from * across and end 1 sc in last sc, ch 1, turn. **Row 7:** * Sk 1 sc, (1 sc in next dc, 1 sc in next ch-1 sp) twice, 3 sc in next dc, (1 sc in next ch-1 sp, 1 sc in next dc) twice, repeat from * across and end sk last dc, 1 sc in last sc, ch 1, turn. Repeat rows 2 through 7 for pattern.

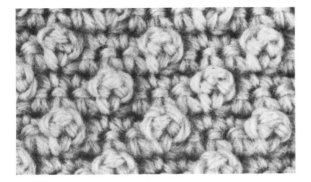

(58)

Multiple of 4 ch plus 3: **Row 1:** Ch 1, 1 sc in 2nd ch from hk, * 1 sc in next ch, repeat from * across, ch 1, turn. **Row 2:** 1 sc in 1st sc, (1 sl st, ch 4, 1 sl st) in next sc (picot made), * 1 sc in each of next 3 sc, 1 picot in next sc, repeat from * across and end 1 sc in last sc, ch 1, turn. **Row 3:** 1 sc in 1st sc, * ch 1, sk next picot (keep picot in front of ch-1), 1 sc in each of next 3 sc, repeat from * across and end ch 1, sk next picot, 1 sc in last sc, ch 1, turn. **Row 4:** 1 sc in 1st sc, * 1 sc in next ch-1 sp, 1 sc in next sc, 1 picot in next sc, 1 sc in next sc, repeat from * across and end 1 sc in next ch-1 sp, 1 sc in last sc, ch 1, turn.**Row 5:** * 1 sc in each of next 3 sc, ch 1, sk next picot, repeat from * across and end 1 sc in each of last 3 sc, ch 1, turn. **Row 6:** 1 sc in 1st sc, * 1 picot in next sc, 1 sc in next sc, 1 sc in next ch-1 sp, 1 sc in next sc, repeat from * across and end 1 picot in next sc, 1 sc in last sc, ch 1, turn. Repeat rows 3 through 6 for pattern.

(59)

Multiple of 7 ch plus 4: **Row 1:**Ch 1, 1 sc in 2nd ch from hk, sk 2 ch, 3 dc in next ch, * ch 3, sk 3 ch, 1 sc in next ch, sk 2 ch, 3 dc in next ch, repeat from * across, ch 1, turn. **Row 2:** 1 sc in 1st dc, sk 2 dc, 3 dc in next sc, * ch 3, 1 sc in next ch-3 sp, sk 3 dc, 3 dc in next sc, repeat from * across, ch 1, turn. Repeat row 2 for pattern.

(60)
Multiple of 4 ch: **Row 1:** Ch 3, (2 dc, ch 1, 1 dc) in 4th ch from hk, * sk 3 ch, (3 dc, ch 1, 1 dc) in next ch, repeat from * across and end sk 2 ch, 1 dc in last ch, ch 3, turn. **Row 2:** Sk 2 dc, (2 dc, ch 1, 1 dc) in ch-1 sp, * sk 4 dc, (3 dc, ch 1, 1 dc) in next ch-1 sp, repeat from * across and end sk 2 dc, 1 dc in turning ch of previous row, ch 3, turn. Repeat row 2 for pattern.

(61)
Multiple of 3 ch plus 1: **Row 1:** Ch 1, 1 sc in 2nd ch from hk, * 1 sc in next ch, repeat from * across, ch 1, turn. **Row 2:** 1 sc in 1st sc, * yo, insert hk in next st, yo and draw through, (yo and draw through 2 lps on hk, yo, insert hk in same st, yo and draw through) 4 times, yo and draw through 2 lps on hk, yo and draw through last 6 lps on hk (popcorn made), 1 sc in each of next 2 sc, repeat from * across, ch 1, turn. **Rows 3 and 5:** * 1 sc in next st, repeat from * across, ch 1, turn. **Row 4:** 1 sc in each of 1st 3 sc, * 1 popcorn in next sc, 1 sc in each of next 2 sc, repeat from * across and end 1 sc in last sc, ch 1, turn. Repeat rows 2 through 5 for pattern.

(62)
Multiple of 2 ch plus 1: **Row 1:** Ch 1, 1 sc in 2nd ch from hk, * 1 dc in next ch, 1 sc in next ch, repeat from * across, ch 2, turn. **Row 2:** 1 dc through back lp only of 1st sc, * 1 sc through front lp only of next dc, 1 dc through back lp only of next sc, repeat from * across, ch 1, turn. **Row 3:** 1 sc through front lp only of 1st dc, * 1 dc through back lp only of next sc, 1 sc through front lp only of next dc, repeat from * across, ch 2, turn. Repeat rows 2 and 3 for pattern.

(63)

Multiple of 3 ch plus 1: **Row 1:** Ch 1, 1 sc in 2nd ch from hk, * ch 2, sk 2 ch, 1 sc in next ch, repeat from * across, ch 3, turn. **Row 2:** 1 dc in 1st sc, * 3 dc in next sc, repeat from * across and end 2 dc in last sc, ch 1, turn. **Row 3:** * 1 sc in next dc, ch 2, sk 2 dc, repeat from * across and end 1 sc in turning ch of previous row, ch 3, turn. Repeat rows 2 and 3 for pattern.

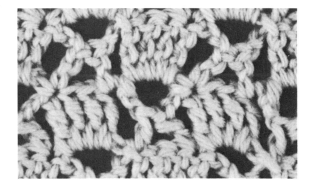

(64)

Multiple of 6 ch plus 7: **Row 1:** Ch 4, 1 tr in 5th ch from hk, ch 2, 1 dc in same ch, sk 2 ch, 1 dc in next ch, ch 2, turn, sk (2 dc, ch-2), 1 tr in next tr, turn, * 1 tr in each of next 4 ch, ch 2, 1 dc in last ch worked, sk 2 ch, 1 dc in next ch, ch 2, turn, sk (2 dc, ch-2), 1 tr in next tr, turn (cross st made), repeat from * across and end 1 tr in each of last 2 ch, ch 4, turn. **Row 2:** Sk 2 tr, * 4 tr in next sp above cross st of previous row, ch 2, 1 dc in next tr, sk 2 tr, 1 dc in next tr, ch 2, turn, sk (2 dc, ch-2), 1 tr in next tr, turn, repeat from * across and end 4 tr in next sp above cross st, sk last tr, 1 tr in turning ch of previous row, ch 4, turn. **Row 3:** Sk 1st tr, 1 tr in next tr, ch 2, 1 dc in same tr, sk 2 tr, 1 dc in next tr, ch 2, turn, sk (2 dc, ch-2), 1 tr in next tr, turn, * 4 tr in next sp above cross st, ch 2, 1 dc in next tr, sk 2 tr, 1 dc in next tr, ch 2, turn, sk (2 dc, ch-2), 1 tr in next tr, turn, repeat from * across and end 1 tr in last tr worked, 1 tr in turning ch of previous row, ch 4, turn. Repeat rows 2 and 3 for pattern.

(65)

Multiple of 6 ch plus 1: **Row 1 (wrong side):**
Ch 1, 1 sc in 2nd ch from hk, * sk 2 ch, 6 dc in
next ch, sk 2 ch, 1 sc in next ch, repeat from
* across, take lp off hk. Return to beg of row.
Row 2: Attach 2nd ball of yarn to 1st sc, 3 dc in
same sc, * sk 3 dc, 1 sc in sp before next dc,
sk 3 dc, 6 dc in next sc, repeat from * across and
end 3 dc in last sc, yo, insert hk in same sc, yo
and draw through, yo and draw through 2 lps on
hk, break off 2nd strand of yarn, pick up lp of
previous row, draw through last 2 lps on hk, ch 1,
turn. **Row 3:** 1 sc in 1st dc, * keeping all lps on
hk (insert hk horizontally from right to left over
base of next st into next sp, yo and draw through)
7 times, yo and draw through 8 lps on hk (cluster
made), ch 3, 1 sc in sp before next dc, repeat
from * across and end 1 sc in turning ch of
previous row, ch 1, turn. **Row 4:** 1 sc in 1st sc,
* 6 dc in eye of next cluster, 1 sc in next sc,
repeat from * across, take lp off hk. Return to beg
of row. Repeat rows 2 through 4 for pattern.

(66)

Multiple of 7 ch plus 8: **Row 1:** Ch 3, 2 dc in
4th ch from hk, ch 1, sk 3 ch, 1 dc in next ch,
ch 1, * sk 2 ch, (3 dc, ch 1, 3 dc) in next ch (shell
made), ch 1, sk 3 ch, 1 dc in next ch, ch 1, repeat
from * across and end 3 dc in last ch, ch 3, turn.
Row 2: 2 dc in 1st dc, ch 1, sk (2 dc, ch-1),
* 1 dc in next dc, ch 1, sk (ch-1, 3 dc) 1 shell in
next ch-1 sp, ch 1, sk (3 dc, ch-1) repeat from
* across and end 3 dc in turning ch of previous
row, ch 3, turn. Repeat row 2 for pattern.

(67)

Multiple of 8 ch plus 9: **Row 1:** Ch 3, 4 dc in 4th ch from hk, * sk 3 ch, 1 sc in next ch, sk 3 ch, 9 dc in next ch, repeat from * across and end 5 dc in last ch, ch 1, turn. **Row 2:** * 1 sc in next st, repeat from * across, ch 3, turn. **Row 3:** (Yo, insert hk in next st, yo and draw through, yo and draw through 2 lps on hk) 4 times, yo and draw through 5 lps on hk, ch 1 (eye made), * ch 3, 1 sc in next st, ch 3, (yo, insert hk in next st, yo and draw through, yo and draw through 2 lps on hk) 9 times, yo and draw through 10 lps on hk, ch 1, repeat from * across and end (yo, insert hk in next st, yo and draw through, yo and draw through 2 lps on hk) 5 times, yo and draw through 6 lps on hk, ch 2, turn. **Row 4:** * 1 sc in eye of next st, 3 sc in next ch-3 sp, 1 sc in next sc, 3 sc in next ch-3 sp, repeat from * across and end 1 sc in eye of last st, ch 3, turn. **Row 5:** 4 dc in 1st sc, * sk 3 sc, 1 sc in next sc, sk 3 sc, 9 dc in next sc, repeat from * across and end 5 dc in last sc, ch 1, turn. Repeat rows 2 through 5 for pattern.

(68)

Multiple of 8 ch plus 7: **Row 1:** Ch 2, 1 dc in 3rd ch from hk, * (yo, insert hk in next ch, yo and draw through, yo and draw through 2 lps on hk) 5 times, yo and draw through 6 lps on hk (cluster made), ch 5, 1 dc in each of next 3 ch, repeat from * across and end 1 dc in last ch, ch 2, turn. **Row 2:** 1 dc in 1st dc, * 1 cluster over next ch-5, ch 5, 1 dc in each of next 3 dc, repeat from * across and end 1 dc in last dc, ch 2, turn. Repeat row 2 for pattern.

(69)
Multiple of 4 ch plus 1: **Row 1:** Ch 2, (1 sl st, 1 sc, 1 hdc, 1 dc) in 3rd ch from hk (shell made), * sk 3 ch, 1 shell in next ch, repeat from * across and end 1 sl st in last ch, ch 2, turn. **Row 2:** * 1 shell in next sl st, sk (1 dc, 1 hdc, 1 sc) repeat from * across and end 1 sl st in turning ch of previous row, ch 2, turn. Repeat row 2 for pattern.

(70)
Multiple of 8 ch plus 1: **Row 1 (wrong side):** Ch 1, 1 sc in 2nd ch from hk, * 1 sc in next ch, repeat from * across, ch 2, turn. **Rows 2 and 6:** 1 dc in each of 1st 4 sc, * 5 dc in next sc, take lp off hk, insert hk through 1st dc of 5-dc group, draw lp of 5th dc through (popcorn made), 1 dc in each of next 3 sc, ch 1, sk 1 sc, 1 dc in each of next 3 sc, repeat from * across and end 1 dc in each of last 4 sc, ch 1, turn. **Rows 3, 5, 7, 9, 11, and 13:** * 1 sc in next st, repeat from * across, ch 2, turn. **Row 4:** 1 dc in each of 1st 2 sc, * (1 popcorn in next sc, 1 dc in next sc) twice, 1 popcorn in next sc, 1 dc in each of next 3 sc, repeat from * across and end 1 dc in each of last 2 sc, ch 1, turn. **Rows 8 and 12:** 1 dc in each of 1st 4 sc, * ch 1, sk 1 sc, 1 dc in each of next 3 sc, 1 popcorn in next sc, 1 dc in each of next 3 sc, repeat from * across and end 1 dc in each of last 4 sc, ch 1, turn. **Row 10:** 1 dc in each of 1st 6 sc, * (1 popcorn in next sc, 1 dc in next sc) twice, 1 popcorn in next sc, 1 dc in each of next 3 sc, repeat from * across and end 1 dc in each of last 6 sc, ch 1, turn. Repeat rows 2 through 13 for pattern.

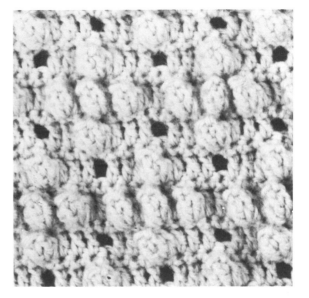

(71)

Multiple of 5 ch: **Row 1:** * Draw up lp on hk to ½", yo and draw through, insert hk between long lp and single strand, yo and draw through, yo and draw through 2 lps on hk (single knot st made), 1 single knot st (double knot st made), sk 4 ch, 1 sc in next ch, repeat from * across and end 1 sc in last ch, 1 double knot st, 1 single knot st, turn. **Row 2:** Sk 1st single knot st, * 1 sc between long lp and single strand of 1st half of next double knot st, 1 sc between long lp and single strand of 2nd half of same double knot st, 1 double knot st, repeat from * across and end 1 double knot st, 1 single knot st, turn. **Row 3:** Sk 1st single knot st, * 1 sc between long lp and single strand of 1st half of next double knot st, 1 sc between long lp and single strand of 2nd half of same double knot st, 1 double knot st, repeat from * across and end 1 sc in turning knot st of previous row, 1 double knot st, 1 single knot st, turn. Repeat row 3 for pattern.

(72)

Multiple of 6 ch plus 1: **Row 1:** Ch 3, yo, insert hk in 4th ch from hk, * yo and draw through, yo and draw through 2 lps on hk, yo, insert hk in same ch, yo and draw through, (yo and draw through 2 lps on hk) 3 times, ch 2, sl st in same ch, ch 3, (yo, insert hk in same ch, yo and draw through, yo and draw through 2 lps on hk) twice, (yo and draw through 2 lps on hk) twice (cluster made), ch 1, sk 5 ch, yo, insert hk in next ch, repeat from * across and end 1 cluster in last ch, ch 2, sl st in same ch, ch 4, turn. **Row 2:** * (1 cluster, ch 2, sl st, ch 3, 1 cluster) in next ch-1 sp, ch 1, repeat from * across and end (1 cluster, ch 2, sl st) in turning ch of previous row, ch 4, turn. Repeat row 2 for pattern.

(73)

Multiple of 9 ch: **Row 1:** Ch 2, 1 dc in 3rd ch from hk, 1 dc in next ch, * (yo, insert hk in next ch, yo and draw through, yo and draw through 2 lps on hk) 5 times, yo and draw through 6 lps on hk (cluster made), ch 5, 1 dc in each of next 4 ch, repeat from * across and end 1 cluster, ch 5, 1 dc in each of last 2 ch, ch 2, turn. **Row 2:** 1 dc in each of 1st 2 dc, * 1 cluster, ch 5, 1 dc in each of next 4 dc, repeat from * across and end 1 cluster, ch 5, 1 dc in each of last 2 dc, ch 2, turn. Repeat row 2 for pattern.

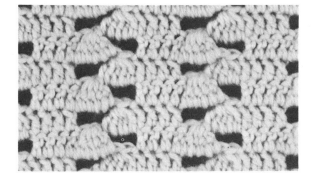

(74)

Multiple of 4 ch plus 1: **Row 1:** Ch 2, 2 dc in 3rd ch from hk, * sk 1 ch, 3 dc in next ch (shell made), repeat from * across, ch 3, turn. **Row 2:** * 1 shell in sp between shells, repeat from * across and end 1 dc in turning ch of previous row, ch 3, turn. **Row 3:** 2 dc in sp between 1st dc and 1st shell, * 1 shell in sp between shells, repeat from * across and end 2 dc in turning ch of previous row, ch 3, turn. Repeat rows 2 and 3 for pattern.

(75)

Multiple of 8 ch plus 4: **Row 1:** Ch 1, 1 sc in 2nd ch from hk, * 1 sc in next ch, repeat from * across, ch 6, turn. **Row 2:** Sk 3 sc, 1 sc in next sc, * ch 5, sk 3 sc, 1 sc in next sc, repeat from * across, ch 4, turn. **Row 3:** 1 sc in 1st ch-5 sp, * ch 3, 3 dc in next ch-5 sp, ch 3, 1 sc in next ch-5 sp, repeat from * across, ch 6, turn. **Row 4:** 1 sc in 1st ch-3 sp, * ch 5, 1 sc in next ch-3 sp, repeat from * across and end ch 5, 1 sc in turning ch of previous row, ch 4, turn. **Row 5:** 2 dc in 1st ch-5 sp, * ch 3, 1 sc in next ch-5 sp, ch 3, 3 dc in next ch-5 sp, repeat from * across, ch 6, turn. **Row 6:** 1 sc in 1st ch-3 sp, * ch 5, 1 sc in next ch-3 sp, repeat from * across and end 1 sc in turning ch of previous row, ch 4, turn. Repeat rows 3 through 6 for pattern.

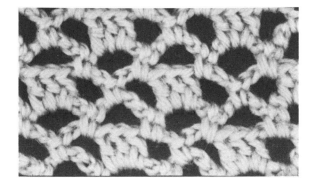

(76)

Multiple of 3 ch plus 1: **Row 1:** Ch 6, 1 dc in 7th ch from hk, * ch 2, sk 2 ch, 1 dc in next ch, repeat from * across, ch 3, turn. **Row 2:** 2 dc in 1st ch-2 sp, * ch 1, 2 dc in next ch-2 sp, repeat from * across and end 2 dc in turning ch of previous row, ch 5, turn. **Row 3:** * Sk 2 dc, 1 dc in next ch-1 sp, ch 2, repeat from * across and end 1 dc in turning ch of previous row, ch 3, turn. Repeat rows 2 and 3 for pattern.

(77)

Multiple of 4 ch plus 3: **Row 1:** Ch 3, 1 dc in 4th ch from hk, * ch 1, sk 1 ch, 1 dc in next ch, repeat from * across, ch 4, turn. **Row 2:** Sk (1 dc, ch-1), * yo, insert hk in next dc, yo and draw through, (yo, insert hk in same dc, yo and draw through) 3 times, yo and draw through 8 lps on hk, yo and draw through last 2 lps on hk (popcorn made), ch 1, sk ch-1, 1 dc in next dc, ch 1, sk ch-1, repeat from * across and end ch 1, 1 dc in turning ch of previous row, ch 4, turn. **Row 3:** Sk (1 dc, ch-1), * 1 dc in next st, ch 1, sk ch-1, repeat from * across and end 1 dc in 3rd ch of turning ch of previous row, ch 2, turn. **Row 4:** 1 popcorn in 1st dc, * ch 1, sk ch-1, 1 dc in next dc, ch 1, sk ch-1, 1 popcorn in next dc, repeat from * across and end 1 popcorn in 3rd ch of turning ch of previous row, ch 4, turn. **Row 5:** Sk (1 popcorn, ch-1), * 1 dc in next st, ch 1, sk ch-1, repeat from * across and end 1 dc in last popcorn, ch 4, turn. Repeat rows 2 through 5 for pattern.

(78)

Multiple of 3 ch plus 1: **Row 1:** Ch 2, 1 sc in 3rd ch from hk, ch 2, sk 2 ch, 1 sc in next ch, * ch 4, 1 sc in 3rd ch from hk (picot made), ch 2, sk 2 ch, 1 sc in next ch, repeat from * across, ch 5, turn. **Row 2:** 1 sc in 3rd ch from hk, ch 2, 1 sc in ch-2 sp after 1st picot, * ch 4, 1 sc in 3rd ch from hk, ch 2, 1 sc in ch-2 sp after next picot, repeat from * across, ch 5, turn. Repeat row 2 for pattern.

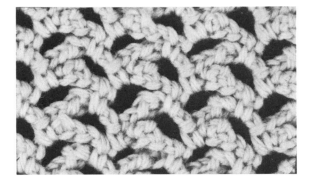

(79)

Multiple of 4 ch plus 1: **Row 1:** Ch 5, 1 sc in 6th ch from hk, * ch 3, sk 3 ch, 1 sc in next ch, repeat from * across, ch 5, turn. **Row 2:** 1 sc in 1st ch-3 sp, * ch 3, 4 dc in next ch-3 sp, take lp off hk, insert hk through 1st dc of 4-dc group, draw lp of 4th dc through (popcorn made), ch 3, 1 sc in next ch-3 sp, repeat from * across and end 1 sc in turning ch of previous row, ch 5, turn.
Rows 3 and 5: 1 sc in 1st ch-3 sp, * ch 3, 1 sc in next ch-3 sp, repeat from * across and end 1 sc in turning ch of previous row, ch 5, turn. **Row 4:** 1 popcorn in 1st ch-3 sp, * ch 3, 1 sc in next ch-3 sp, ch 3, 1 popcorn in next ch-3 sp, repeat from * across, ch 5, turn. Repeat rows 2 through 5 for pattern.

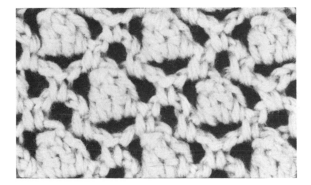

(80)

Multiple of 4 ch plus 1: **Row 1:** Ch 4, (1 dc, ch 2, 1 dc) in 5th ch from hk, * ch 1, sk 1 ch, 1 dc in next ch, ch 1, sk 1 ch, (1 dc, ch 2, ch 2, 1 dc) in next ch (shell made), repeat from * across, ch 4, turn. **Row 2:** Sk (1 dc, ch-2), (1 dc, ch 2, 1 dc) in next dc, * ch 1, sk (ch-2, 1 dc, ch-1) 1 dc in next dc, ch 1, sk (ch-1, 1 dc, ch-2), 1 shell in next dc, repeat from * across, ch 4, turn. Repeat row 2 for pattern.

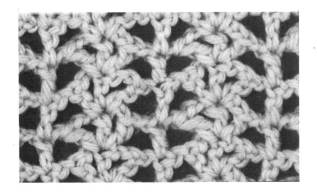

(81)

Multiple of 2 ch: **Row 1:** Ch 1, 1 sc in 2nd ch from hk, * 1 sc in next ch, repeat from * across, ch 3, turn. **Row 2:** Sk 1st sc, * 1 dc in next sc, ch 1, sk 1 sc, repeat from * across and end 1 dc in last sc, ch 1, turn. **Row 3:** * Sk 1 dc, 2 sc in next ch-1 sp, repeat from * across and end 2 sc in turning ch of previous row, ch 3, turn. Repeat rows 2 and 3 for pattern.

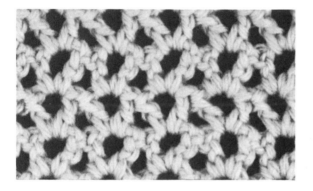

(82)

Multiple of 3 ch plus 1: **Row 1:** Ch 2, (1 dc, ch 3, 1 dc) in 3rd ch from hk, * sk 2 ch, (1 dc, ch 3, 1 dc) in next ch, repeat from * across, ch 2, turn. **Row 2:** * (1 dc, ch 3, 1 dc) in next ch-3 sp, repeat from * across, ch 2, turn. Repeat row 2 for pattern.

(83)

Multiple of 3 ch plus 1: **Row 1:** Ch 6, 1 dc in 7th ch from hk, * ch 3, sk 2 ch, 1 dc in next ch, repeat from * across, ch 4, turn. **Row 2:** Sk (1 dc, 1 ch), * 1 sc in next ch, ch 2, sk 1 ch, 1 dc in next dc, ch 2, sk 1 ch, repeat from * across and end 1 sc in 2nd ch of turning ch of previous row, ch 6, turn. **Row 3:** Sk (1 sc, ch-2), * 1 dc in next dc, ch 3, sk (ch-2, 1 sc, ch-2), repeat from * across and end 1 dc in turning ch of previous row, ch 4, turn. Repeat rows 2 and 3 for pattern.

(84)

Multiple of 3 ch plus 1: **Row 1:** Ch 2, insert hk in 3rd ch from hk, yo and draw through, (yo and draw through 1 lp on hk) twice, yo and draw through last 2 lps on hk (long st made), * ch 3, 1 long st in same ch, sk 2 ch, 1 long st in next ch, repeat from * across and end ch 3, 1 long st in same ch, ch 2, turn. **Row 2:** * (1 long st, ch 3, 1 long st) in next ch-3 sp, repeat from * across, ch 2, turn. Repeat row 2 for pattern.

(85)

Multiple of 7 ch plus 5: **Row 1:** Ch 2, 1 dc in 3rd ch from hk, 1 dc in next ch, * (1 dc, ch 2, 1 dc) in next ch, 1 dc in each of next 2 ch, (yo, insert hk in next ch, yo and draw through, yo and draw through 2 lps on hk) twice, yo and draw through 3 lps on hk, 1 dc in each of next 2 ch, repeat from * across and end (1 dc, ch 2, 1 dc) in next ch, 1 dc in each of last 2 ch, ch 2, turn. **Row 2:** 1 dc in each of next 2 dc, sk 1 dc, * (1 dc, ch 2, 1 dc) in next ch-2 sp, 1 dc in each of next 2 dc, (yo, insert hk in next st, yo and draw through, yo and draw through 2 lps on hk) 3 times, yo and draw through 4 lps on hk, 1 dc in each of next 2 dc, repeat from * across and end (1 dc, ch 2, 1 dc) in last ch-2 sp, sk 1 dc, 1 dc in last 2 dc, ch 2, turn. Repeat row 2 for pattern.

(86)

Multiple of 6 ch plus 2: **Row 1:** Ch 2, 1 dc in 3rd ch from hk, 1 dc in next ch, * ch 2, sk 1 ch, 1 sc in each of next 2 ch, ch 2, sk 1 ch, 1 dc in each of next 2 ch, repeat from * across, ch 1, turn. **Row 2:** 1 sc in each of 1st 2 dc, *ch 2, sk ch-2, 1 dc in each of next 2 sc, ch 2, sk ch-2, 1 sc in each of next 2 dc, repeat from * across, ch 2, turn. **Row 3:** 1 dc in each of 1st 2 sc, * ch 2, sk ch-2, 1 sc in each of next 2 dc, ch 2, sk ch-2, 1 dc in each of next 2 sc, repeat from * across, ch 1, turn. Repeat rows 2 and 3 for pattern.

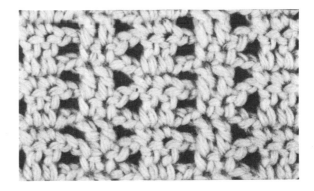

(87)

Multiple of 2 ch: **Row 1:** Ch 1, 1 sc in 2nd ch from hk, * 1 sc in next ch, repeat from * across, ch 1, turn. **Row 2:** * 1 sc in next sc, repeat from * across, ch 1, turn. **Row 3:** * 1 sc in next sc, repeat from * across, ch 4, turn. **Row 4:** Sk 1st sc, * 1 tr in next sc, ch 1, sk 1 sc, repeat from * across and end 1 tr in last sc, ch 1, turn. **Row 5:** * Sk 1 tr, 2 sc in next ch-1 sp, repeat from * across and end 2 sc in turning ch of previous row, ch 1, turn. Repeat rows 2 through 5 for pattern.

(88)

Multiple of 4 ch plus 1: **Row 1:** Ch 1, 1 sc in 2nd ch from hk, * ch 5, sk 3 ch, 1 sc in next ch, repeat from * across, ch 7, turn. **Row 2:** Sk (1 sc, 2 ch), * 1 sc in next ch, ch 5, sk (2 ch, 1 sc, 2 ch), repeat from * across and end 1 sc in next ch, ch 7, turn. Repeat row 2 for pattern.

(89)

Multiple of 6 ch plus 5: **Row 1:** Ch 2, 1 dc in 3rd ch from hk, * ch 3, sk 3 ch, 1 dc in each of next 3 ch, repeat from * across and end 1 dc in last ch, ch 3, turn. **Row 2:** Sk 1st dc, 2 dc in next ch-3 sp, * ch 3, sk 3 dc, 3 dc in next ch-3 sp, repeat from * across, ch 6, turn. **Row 3:** Sk 3 dc, * 3 dc in next ch-3 sp, ch 3, sk 3 dc, repeat from * across and end sk 2 dc, 1 dc in turning ch of previous row, ch 3, turn. Repeat rows 2 and 3 for pattern.

(90)

Multiple of 8 ch plus 3: **Row 1:** Ch 2, 1 dc in 3rd ch from hk, * 1 dc in next ch, repeat from * across, ch 3, turn. **Row 2:** Sk 1st dc, * 1 dc in each of next 2 dc, ch 2, holding last lp of next 3 sts on hk, 1 tr in same st as last dc, sk 2 dc, 1 dc in next dc, sk 2 dc, 1 tr in next dc, yo and draw through 4 lps on hk, ch 2, 1 dc in same st as last tr, repeat from * across and end 1 dc in each of last 2 dc, ch 3, turn. **Row 3:** Sk 1st dc, * 1 dc in next dc, holding last lp of next 2 sts on hk, 1 dc in next st, sk ch-2, 1 tr in next st, yo and draw through 3 lps on hk, ch 2, 1 dc in same st as last tr, ch 2, holding last lp of next 2 sts on hk, 1 tr in same st as last dc, sk ch-2, 1 dc in next st, yo and draw through 3 lps on hk, repeat from * across and end 1 dc in last st, 1 dc in turning ch of previous row, ch 3, turn. **Row 4:** 1 dc in each st and 2 dc in each ch-2 sp across and end 1 dc in turning ch of previous row, ch 3, turn. Repeat rows 2 through 4 for pattern.

(91)

Multiple of 4 ch plus 1: **Row 1:** Ch 3, (1 sc, ch 3, 1 sc) in 4th ch from hk (picot made), * ch 5, sk 3 ch, 1 picot in next ch, repeat from * across and end 1 sc in last ch, ch 5, turn. **Row 2:** Sk (1 sc, 2 ch), * 1 picot in next ch, ch 5, sk (2 ch, 1 picot, 2 ch), repeat from * across and end 1 sc in turning ch of previous row, ch 5, turn. Repeat row 2 for pattern.

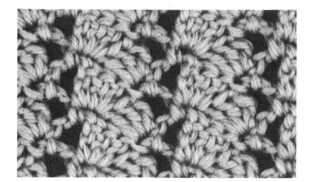

(92)

Multiple of 7 ch plus 4: **Row 1:** Ch 3, 3 dc in 4th ch from hk, sk 2 ch, 1 sc in next ch, * ch 3, sk 3 ch, 3 dc in next ch, sk 2 ch, 1 sc in next ch, repeat from * across, ch 3, turn. **Row 2:** * 3 dc in next sc, 1 sc in next ch-3 sp, ch 3, repeat from * across and end 3 dc in last sc, 1 sc in turning ch of previous row, ch 3, turn. Repeat row 2 for pattern.

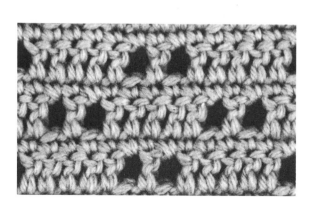

(93)

Multiple of 2 ch plus 1: **Row 1:** Ch 3, 1 hdc in 4th ch from hk, * ch 1, sk 1 ch, 1 hdc in next ch, repeat from * across, ch 3, turn. **Row 2:** * Sk 1 hdc, 1 hdc in next ch-1 sp, ch 1, repeat from * across and end 1 hdc in turning ch of previous row, ch 3, turn. Repeat row 2 for pattern.

(94)

Multiple of 8 ch plus 5: **Row 1:** Ch 1, 1 sc in 2nd ch from hk, * 1 sc in next ch, repeat from * across, ch 3, turn. **Row 2:** 1 dc in each of next 5 sc, * ch 1, sk 1 sc, 1 dc in next sc, ch 1, sk 1 sc, 1 dc in each of next 5 sc, repeat from * across, ch 1, turn. **Row 3:** 1 sc in each dc and each ch-1 sp across, ch 4, turn. **Row 4:** Sk 2 sc, 1 dc in next sc, * ch 1, sk 1 sc, 1 dc in each of next 5 sc, ch 1, sk 1 sc, 1 dc in next sc, repeat from * across and end ch 1, sk 1 sc, 1 dc in last sc, ch 1, turn. **Row 5:** 1 sc in each dc and each ch-1 sp across and end 2 sc in turning ch of previous row, ch 3, turn. Repeat rows 2 through 5 for pattern.

(95)

Multiple of 3 ch plus 1: **Row 1:** Ch 2, (1 sl st, ch 4, 4 dc) in 3rd ch from hk, * sk 2 ch, (1 sl st, ch 4, 4 dc) in next ch, repeat from * across and end sk 2 ch, 1 sc in last ch, ch 4, turn. **Row 2:** Sk 4 dc, * (1 sl st, ch 4, 4 dc) in next ch-4 sp, sk (1 sl st, 4 dc), repeat from * across and end (1 sl st, ch 4, 4 dc) in last ch-4 sp, ch 4, turn. Repeat row 2 for pattern.

(96)

Multiple of 3 ch plus 1: **Row 1:** Ch 2, 1 dc in 3rd ch from hk, * 1 dc in next ch, repeat from * across, ch 2, turn. **Row 2:** 1 sc in sp between 1st and 2nd dc, * sk 3 dc, 1 sc in sp between last skipped dc and next dc, repeat from * across and end 1 sc in turning ch of previous row, ch 3, turn. **Row 3:** * 2 dc in next sc, 1 dc in sp between last sc and next sc, repeat from * across and end 1 dc in last sc, ch 2, turn. Repeat rows 2 and 3 for pattern.

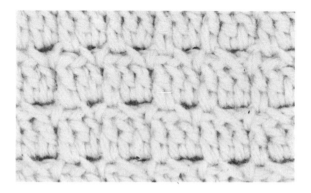

(97)

Multiple of 4 ch plus 3: **Row 1:** Ch 4, (1 dc, ch 3, 1 dc) in 5th ch from hk, * sk 3 ch, (1 dc, ch 3, 1 dc) in next ch, repeat from * across and end sk 1 ch, 1 dc in last ch, ch 1, turn. **Row 2:** 1 sc in 1st dc, * sk 1 dc, 3 sc in next ch-3 sp, sk 1 dc, yo, insert hk in next sp, yo and draw through, yo and draw through 2 lps on hk, (yo, insert hk in same sp, yo and draw through, yo and draw through 2 lps on hk) 4 times, yo and draw through 6 lps on hk, ch 1 (puff st made), repeat from * across and end 3 sc in last ch-3 sp, 1 sc in turning ch of previous row, ch 1, turn. **Row 3:** 1 sc in each sc and in top of each puff st across, ch 3, turn. **Row 4:** Sk 1st 2 sc, * (1 dc, ch 3, 1 dc) in next sc, sk 3 sc, repeat from * across and end sk 1 sc, 1 dc in last sc, ch 1, turn. **Row 5:** 1 sc in 1st dc, * sk 1 dc, 3 sc in next ch-3 sp, sk 1 dc, 1 sc in next sp,

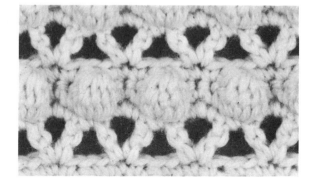

repeat from * across and end 1 sc in turning ch of previous row, ch 1, turn. **Row 6:** 1 sc in each of 1st 4 sc, * 1 puff st in next sc, 1 sc in each of next 3 sc, repeat from * across and end 1 sc in each of last 4 sc, ch 1, turn. Repeat rows 3 through 6 for pattern.

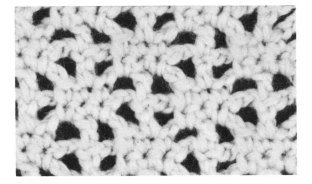

(98)

Multiple of 8 ch plus 6: **Row 1:** Ch 5, 1 sc in 6th ch from hk, 1 sc in each of next 2 ch, * ch 2, sk 2 ch, 1 dc in next ch, ch 2, sk 2 ch, 1 sc in each of next 3 ch, repeat from * across and end ch 2, sk 2 ch, 1 dc in last ch, ch 1, turn. **Row 2:** 1 sc in 1st dc, 1 sc in next ch-2 sp, * ch 2, sk 1 sc, 1 dc in next sc, ch 2, sk 1 sc, 1 sc in next ch-2 sp, 1 sc in next dc, 1 sc in next ch-2 sp, repeat from * across and end 2 sc in turning ch of previous row, ch 1, turn. **Row 3:** 1 sc in each of 1st 2 sc, * ch 2, sk ch-2, 1 dc in next dc, ch 2, sk ch-2, 1 sc in each of next 3 sc, repeat from * across and end 1 sc in each of last 2 sc, ch 3, turn. **Row 4:** Sk 1st 2 sc, * 1 sc in next ch-2 sp, 1 sc in next dc, 1 sc in next ch-2 sp, ch 2, sk 1 sc, 1 dc in next sc, ch 2, sk 1 sc, repeat from * across and end 1 sc in next ch-2 sp, 1 sc in next dc, 1 sc in next ch-2 sp, ch 2, sk 1 sc, 1 dc in last sc, ch 5, turn. **Row 5:** Sk (1st dc, ch-2), * 1 sc in each of next 3 sc, ch 2, sk ch-2, 1 dc in next dc, ch 2, sk ch-2, repeat from * across and end 1 sc in each of next 3 sc, ch 2, 1 dc in turning ch of previous row, ch 1, turn. Repeat rows 2 through 5 for pattern.

(99)

Multiple of 5 ch: **Row 1:** Ch 3, keeping last lp of each dc on hk, 1 dc in 4th ch from hk, 1 dc in next ch, yo and draw through 3 lps on hk, * ch 4, 1 dc in each of next 5 ch, yo and draw through 6 lps on hk (cluster made), repeat from * across and end ch 4, 3-dc cluster over last 3 ch, ch 3, turn. **Row 2:** 2 dc in top of 3-dc cluster, * sk ch-4, 5 dc in top of 5-dc cluster, repeat from * across and end 3 dc in top of last cluster, ch 3, turn. **Row 3:** Sk 1st dc, 2-dc cluster over next

2 dc, * ch 4, 5-dc cluster over next 5 dc, repeat
from * across and end 3-dc cluster over last 2 dc
and turning ch of previous row, ch 3, turn. Repeat
rows 2 and 3 for pattern.

(100)
Multiple of 2 ch plus 1: **Row 1:** Ch 3, 1 dc in
5th ch from hk, 1 dc in 4th ch from hk, * sk 1 ch,
1 dc in next ch, 1 dc in skipped ch, repeat from
* across and end 1 dc in last ch, ch 3, turn. **Row
2:** * Sk 1 dc, 1 dc in next dc, 1 dc in skipped dc,
repeat from * across and end 1 dc in last dc,
ch 3, turn. Repeat row 2 for pattern.

(101)
Multiple of 4 ch plus 1: **Row 1:** Ch 2, (2 dc, ch 1,
1 dc) in 3rd ch from hk, * sk 3 ch, (2 dc, ch 1,
1 dc) in next ch, repeat from * across and end
1 dc in last ch, ch 2, turn. **Row 2:** Sk 2 dc,
* (2 dc, ch 1, 1 dc) in next ch-1 sp, sk 3 dc,
repeat from * across and end sk 2 dc, 2 dc in
turning ch of previous row, ch 1, turn. **Row 3:**
* Sk 1 dc, 1 sc in next dc, sk 1 dc, 3 dc in next
ch-1 sp, repeat from * across and end 1 sc in last
dc, ch 2, turn. **Row 4:** 1 dc in 1st sc, * sk 1 dc,
1 sc in next dc, sk 1 dc, 3 dc in next sc, repeat
from * across and end 2 dc in last sc, ch 2, turn.
Row 5: Sk 1 dc, 1 dc in next dc, * (2 dc, ch 1,
1 dc) in next sc, sk 3 dc, repeat from * across and
end 1 dc in last dc, ch 2, turn. Repeat rows 2
through 5 for pattern.

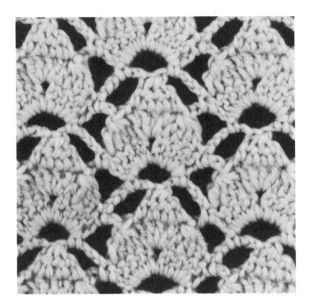

(102)

Multiple of 16 ch plus 5: **Row 1:** Ch 1, 1 sc in 2nd ch from hk, ch 5, sk 3 ch, * (1 sc in next ch, ch 5, sk 3 ch) 4 times, repeat from * across and end 1 sc in last ch, ch 2, turn. **Row 2:** * (4 dc, ch 1, 4 dc) in next ch-5 sp, (1 sc in next ch-5 sp, ch 5) twice, 1 sc in next ch-5 sp, repeat from * across and end (4 dc, ch 1, 4 dc) in last ch-5 sp, 1 sc in last sc, ch 5, turn. **Row 3:** Sk 1st sc, * keeping last lps on hk, work 1 dc in each of next 4 dc, yo and draw through 5 lps on hk (closed 4-dc group made), 4 dc in next ch-1 sp, 1 closed 4-dc group over next 4 dc, (ch 5, 1 sc in next ch-5 sp) twice, ch 5, repeat from * across and end 1 closed 4-dc group over next 4 dc, 4 dc in last ch-1 sp, 1 closed 4-dc group over last 4 dc, ch 5, 1 sc in turning ch of previous row, ch 5, turn. **Row 4:** * 1 sc in next ch-5 sp, ch 5, sk 1 closed 4-dc group, 1 closed 4-dc group over next 4 dc, ch 5, sk 1 closed 4-dc group, 1 sc in next ch-5 sp, (4 dc, ch 1, 4 dc) in next ch-5 sp, repeat from * across and end 1 sc in turning ch of previous row, ch 5, turn. **Row 5:** * (1 sc in next ch-5 sp, ch 5) twice, 1 closed 4-dc group over next 4 dc, 4 dc in next ch-1 sp, 1 closed 4-dc group over next 4 dc, ch 5, repeat from * across and end 1 sc in turning ch of previous row, ch 5, turn. **Row 6:** * 1 sc in next ch-5 sp, (4 dc, ch 1, 4 dc) in next ch-5 sp, 1 sc in next ch-5 sp, ch 5, sk 1 closed 4-dc group, 1 closed 4-dc group over next 4 dc, ch 5, sk 1 closed 4-dc group, repeat from * across and end 1 sc in turning ch of previous row, ch 5, turn. Repeat rows 3 through 6 for pattern.

(103)

Multiple of 6 ch plus 3: **Row 1:** Ch 5, 1 dc in 6th ch from hk, * ch 1, sk 1 ch, 1 dc in next ch, repeat from * across, ch 4, turn. **Row 2:** Sk (1 dc, ch 1), * 4 dc in next dc, take lp off hk, insert hk through 1st dc of 4-dc group, draw lp of 4th dc through (popcorn made), (ch 1, sk ch-1, 1 dc in next dc) twice, ch 1, sk ch-1, repeat from * across and end 1 popcorn in next dc, ch 1, sk 1 ch, 1 dc in next ch of turning ch of previous row, ch 4, turn. **Row 3:** Sk (1 dc, ch-1), * 1 dc in next popcorn, (ch 1, sk ch-1, 1 dc in next dc) twice, ch 1, sk ch-1, repeat from * across and end 1 dc in next popcorn, ch 1, sk 1 ch, 1 dc in next ch of turning ch of previous row, ch 4, turn. Repeat rows 2 and 3 for pattern.

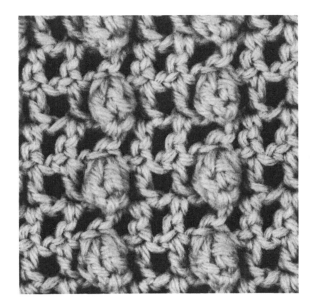

(104)

Multiple of 14 ch plus 11: **Row 1:** Ch 2, 1 dc in 3rd ch from hk, sk 2 ch, * (2 dc, ch 2, 2 dc) in next ch (4 dc group made), sk 3 ch, 1 4-dc group in next ch, ch 9, sk 9 ch, repeat from * across and end 1 4-dc group in next ch, sk 3 ch, 1 4-dc group in next ch, sk 2 ch, 1 dc in last ch, ch 2, turn. **Rows 2, 5 and 6:** 1 dc in 1st dc, * (sk 2 dc, 1 4-dc group in next ch-2 sp, sk 2 dc) twice, ch 9, sk ch-9, repeat from * across and end 1 dc in last dc, ch 2, turn. **Row 3:** 1 dc in 1st dc, * (sk 2 dc, 1 4-dc group in next ch-2 sp, sk 2 dc) twice, ch 5, 1 sl st in 5th ch of ch-9 3 rows below, ch 3, turn, 6 tr in ch-5 sp just made, ch 2, turn, 1 dc in each tr just made, sk 2nd half of ch-9, repeat from * across and end 1 dc in last dc, ch 2, turn.
Row 4: 1 dc in 1st dc, * (sk 2 dc, 1 4-dc group in next ch-2 sp, sk 2 dc) twice, ch 9, sk 6 dc, repeat from * across and end 1 dc in last dc, ch 2, turn. Repeat rows 3 through 6 for pattern.

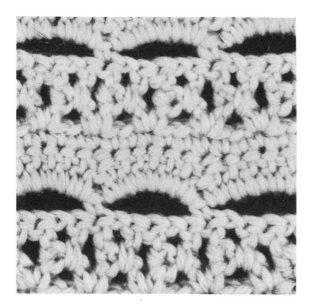

(105)

Multiple of 6 ch plus 7: **Row 1:** Ch 1, 1 sc in 2nd ch from hk, * 1 sc in next ch, repeat from * across, ch 4, turn. **Row 2:** Yo twice, insert hk in 1st sc, yo and draw through, * yo and draw through 2 lps on hk, sk 2 sc, yo, insert hk in next sc, yo and draw through, (yo and draw through 2 lps on hk) 4 times, ch 1, 1 dc in center of st just made (X st made), yo twice, insert hk in last sc worked, yo and draw through, repeat from * across and end 1 X st, 1 tr in last sc worked, ch 1, turn. **Row 3:** 1 sc in 1st tr, * ch 5, sk 5 sts, 1 sc in next st, repeat from * across, ch 3, turn. **Row 4:** 6 dc in 1st ch-5 sp, * yo, insert hk in same ch-5 sp, yo and draw through, yo and draw through 2 lps on hk, yo, insert hk in next ch-5 sp, yo and draw through, yo and draw through 2 lps on hk, yo and draw through last 3 lps on hk, 5 dc in same ch-5 sp, repeat from * across and end 1 dc in last sc, ch 1, turn. **Row 5:** * 1 sc in next st, repeat from * across, ch 4, turn. Repeat rows 2 through 5 for pattern.

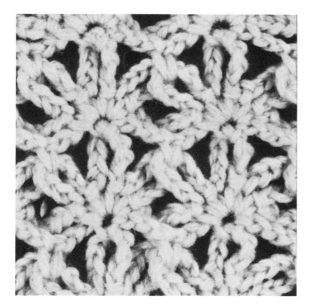

(106)

Multiple of 5 ch plus 1: **Row 1:** Ch 1, 1 sc in 2nd ch from hk, ch 9, 1 sc in same ch (petal made), 1 petal in same ch, ch 6, * sk 4 ch, (1 sc, 3 petals) in next ch, ch 6, repeat from * across and end (1 sc, 2 petals) in last ch, ch 6, turn. **Row 2:** 1 sc in 1st petal, * ch 3, insert hk in next 2 petals, yo and draw through, yo and draw through 2 lps on hk, ch 3, 1 sc in next petal, repeat from * across, ch 1, turn. **Row 3:** (1 sc, 2 petals) in 1st sc, * ch 6, sk (ch-3, 1 sc, ch-3), (1 sc, 3 petals) in next sc, repeat from * across and end (1 sc, 2 petals) in last sc, ch 6, turn. Repeat rows 2 and 3 for pattern.

(107)

Multiple of 9 ch plus 8: **Row 1:** Ch 4, 1 tr in 5th ch from hk, * ch 4, sk 1 ch, 1 dc in each of next 3 ch, ch 4, sk 1 ch, 1 tr in each of next 4 ch, repeat from * across and end 1 tr in each of last 2 ch, ch 1, turn. **Row 2:** 1 sc in each of 1st 2 tr, * ch 4, sk ch-4, 1 dc in each of next 3 dc, ch 4, sk ch-4, 1 sc in each of next 4 tr, repeat from * across and end 1 sc in last tr, 1 sc in turning ch of previous row, ch 1, turn. **Rows 3 and 4:** 1 sc in each of 1st 2 sc, * ch 4, sk ch-4, 1 dc in each of next 3 dc, ch 4, sk ch-4, 1 sc in each of next 4 sc, repeat from * across and end 1 sc in each of last 2 sc, ch 1, turn. **Row 5:** Ch 4, sk 1 sc, 1 tr in next sc, * ch 1, sk ch-4, 1 dc in each of next 3 dc, sk ch-4, (ch 1, 1 tr in next sc) 4 times, repeat from * across and end (ch 1, 1 tr in next sc) twice, ch 3, turn. **Row 6:** Sk 1 tr, 1 dc in next ch-1 sp, 1 dc in next tr, * 1 dc in next ch-1 sp, 1 dc in each of next 3 dc, (1 dc in next ch-1 sp, 1 dc in next tr) 4 times, repeat from * across and end 1 dc in last tr, 1 dc in turning ch of previous row, ch 4, turn. **Row 7:** Sk 1 dc, 1 tr in next dc, * ch 4, sk 1 dc, 1 dc in each of next 3 dc, ch 4, (sk 1 dc, 1 tr in next dc) 4 times, repeat from * across and end sk 1 dc, 1 tr in next dc, sk last dc, 1 tr in turning ch of previous row, ch 1, turn. Repeat rows 2 through 7 for pattern.

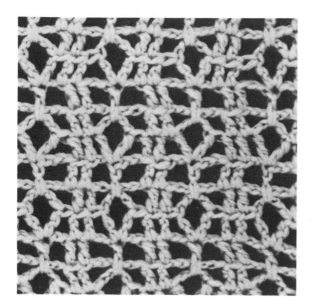

(108)
Multiple of 7 ch plus 1: **Row 1:** Ch 3, yo twice, insert hk in 4th ch from hk, yo and draw through, yo and draw through 2 lps on hk, yo and draw through last 3 lps on hk (half tr made), * sk 2 ch, (1 half tr, ch 4, 1 half tr) in next ch, sk 2 ch, 1 half tr in each of next 2 ch, repeat from * across, ch 3, turn. **Row 2:** Sk 1st half tr, 1 half tr in next half tr, * ch 5, sk (1 half tr, ch-4, 1 half tr), 1 half tr in each of next 2 half tr, repeat from * across and end 1 half tr in last half tr, 1 half tr in turning ch of previous row, ch 3, turn. **Row 3:** Sk 1st half tr, 1 half tr in next half tr, * ch 2, yo, insert hk under ch-4 below ch-5 of previous row, yo and draw through, (yo and draw through 2 lps on hk) twice, ch 2, 1 half tr in each of next 2 half tr, repeat from * across and end 1 half tr in last half tr, 1 half tr in turning ch of previous row, ch 3, turn. **Row 4:** Sk 1st half tr, 1 half tr in next half tr, * sk ch-2, (1 half tr, ch 4, 1 half tr) in next st, sk ch-2, 1 half tr in each of next 2 half tr, repeat from * across and end 1 half tr in last half tr, 1 half tr in turning ch of previous row, ch 3, turn. Repeat rows 2 through 4 for pattern.

(109)
Multiple of 9 ch: **Row 1:** Ch 1, 1 sc in 2nd ch from hk, 1 sc in each of next 2 ch, * ch 7, sk 2 ch, 1 sc in each of next 7 ch, repeat from * across and end 1 sc in each of last 4 ch, ch 1, turn. **Row 2:** Sk 1st sc, 1 sc in each of next 2 sc, * ch 3, sk (1 sc, 3 ch), 1 sc in next ch of ch-7, ch 3, sk (3 ch, 1 sc), 1 sc in each of next 5 sc, repeat from * across and end 1 sc in each of last 2 sc, ch 1, turn. **Row 3:** Sk 1st sc, 1 sc in next sc, * ch 3, sk 2 ch, 1 sc in next ch, 1 sc in next sc, 1 sc in next ch, ch 3, sk (2 ch, 1 sc), 1 sc in each of next 3 sc, repeat from * across and end 1 sc in last sc, ch 4, turn. **Row 4:** * Sk (1 sc, 2 ch), 1 sc in next ch, 1 sc in each of next 3 sc, 1 sc in next ch, ch 3, sk (2 ch, 1 sc), 1 sc in next sc, ch 3, repeat from * across and end 1 sc in last sc, ch 3, turn. **Row 5:** * Sk (1 sc, 2 ch), 1 sc in next ch,

1 sc in each of next 5 sc, 1 sc in next ch, ch 7, sk 2 ch, repeat from * across and end ch 3, 1 sc in 1st ch of turning ch of previous row, ch 4, turn. **Row 6:** Sk (1 sc, ch-3, 1 sc), * 1 sc in each of next 5 sc, ch 3, sk (1 sc, 3 ch), 1 sc in next ch of ch-7, ch 3, sk (3 ch, 1 sc), repeat from * across and end ch 3, 1 sc in last ch of turning ch of previous row, ch 1, turn. **Row 7:** 1 sc in 1st sc, 1 sc in next ch, * ch 3, sk (2 ch, 1 sc), 1 sc in each of next 3 sc, ch 3, sk (1 sc, 2 ch), 1 sc in next ch, 1 sc in next sc, 1 sc in next ch, repeat from * across and end ch 3, sk (1 sc, 2 ch), 1 sc in each of last 2 ch, ch 1, turn. **Row 8:** 1 sc in each of 1st 2 sc, * 1 sc in next ch, ch 3, sk (2 ch, 1 sc), 1 sc in next sc, ch 3, sk (1 sc, 2 ch), 1 sc in next ch, 1 sc in each of next 3 sc, repeat from * across and end 1 sc in each of last 2 sc, ch 1, turn. **Row 9:** 1 sc in each of 1st 3 sc, sk (ch-3, 1 sc, 2 ch), * ch 7, 1 sc in next ch, 1 sc in each of next 5 sc, 1 sc in next ch, sk (2 ch, 1 sc, 2 ch), repeat from * across and end ch 7, 1 sc in next ch, 1 sc in each of last 3 sc, ch 1, turn. Repeat rows 2 through 9 for pattern.

(110)

Multiple of 9 ch plus 2: **Row 1:** Ch 3, 1 dc in 4th ch from hk, 1 dc in each of next 2 ch, * ch 5, sk 4 ch, 1 dc in each of next 5 ch, repeat from * across and end 1 dc in each of last 4 ch, ch 3, turn. **Row 2:** 1 dc in each of next 2 dc, sk 2 dc, * ch 3, 1 dc in ch-5 sp, ch 3, sk 1 dc, 1 dc in each of next 3 dc, sk 1 dc, repeat from * across and end sk 1 dc, 1 dc in each of last 2 dc, 1 dc in turning ch of previous row, ch 3, turn. **Row 3:** 1 dc in 1st dc, sk 2 dc, * ch 3, 1 dc in ch-3 sp, 1 dc in next dc, 1 dc in next ch-3 sp, ch 3, sk 1 dc, 1 dc in next dc, sk 1 dc, repeat from * across and end sk 1 dc, 1 dc in last dc, 1 dc in turning ch of previous row, ch 5, turn. **Row 4:** Sk 1st 2 dc, 1 dc in ch-3 sp, * 1 dc in each of next 3 dc, 1 dc in next ch-3 sp, ch 5, 1 dc in next ch-3 sp, repeat from * across and end ch 3, 1 dc in turning ch of previous row, ch 3, turn. **Row 5:**

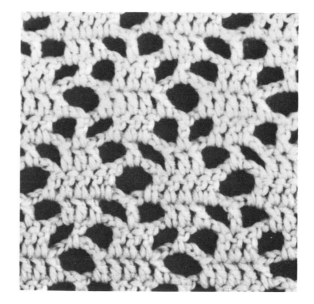

Sk 1st dc, 1 dc in ch-3 sp, * ch 3, sk 1 dc, 1 dc in each of next 3 dc, ch 3, sk 1 dc, 1 dc in next ch-5 sp, repeat from * across and end ch 3, 2 dc in turning ch of previous row, ch 3, turn. **Row 6:** 1 dc in 1st dc, 1 dc in ch-3 sp, * ch 3, sk 1 dc, 1 dc in next dc, sk 1 dc, ch 3, 1 dc in next ch-3 sp, 1 dc in next dc, 1 dc in next ch-3 sp, repeat from * across and end 1 dc in last dc, 1 dc in turning ch of previous row, ch 3, turn. **Row 7:** 1 dc in each of 1st 2 dc, 1 dc in ch-3 sp, * ch 5, sk 1 dc, 1 dc in next ch-3 sp, 1 dc in each of next 3 dc, 1 dc in next ch-3 sp, repeat from * across and end 1 dc in each of last 2 dc, 1 dc in turning ch of previous row, ch 3, turn. Repeat rows 2 through 7 for pattern.

(111)
Multiple of 3 ch plus 2:**Row 1:** With MC, ch 1, 1 sc in 2nd ch from hk, * 1 sc in next ch, repeat from * across, ch 1, turn. **Row 2:** With MC, * 1 sc in next st, repeat from * across, turn. **Row 3:** With CC, ch 1, * 1 sc in each of next 2 sc, sk 1 sc, yo, insert hk from right to left under sc 1 row below skipped sc, yo and draw through, (yo and draw through 2 lps on hk) twice (dc around post made), repeat from * across and end 1 sc in each of last 2 sc, ch 1, turn. **Row 4:** With CC, * 1 sc in next st, repeat from * across, turn. **Row 5:** With MC, ch 1, * 1 sc in each of next 2 sc, 1 dc around post of sc 1 row below last sc worked, sk 1 sc, repeat from * across and end 1 sc in each of last 2 sc, ch 1, turn. Repeat rows 2 through 5 for pattern.

(112)

Multiple of 3 ch plus 1: **Row 1:** With MC, ch 1, 1 sc in 2nd ch from hk, * ch 2, sk 2 ch, 1 sc in next ch, repeat from * across, turn. **Row 2:** With CC, ch 3, * sk 1 sc, 3 dc in next ch-2 sp, ch 1, repeat from * across and end ch 1, 1 dc in last sc. Take lp off hook and return to beg of row. **Row 3:** With MC, 1 sc in turning ch at beg of row, * ch 2, sk 3 dc, 1 sc in next ch-1 sp, repeat from * across, pull CC lp of last row through last lp on hk, turn. Repeat rows 2 and 3 for pattern.

(113)

Multiple of 8 ch: **Row 1:** With MC, ch 2, 1 dc in 3rd ch from hk, * 1 dc in each of next 2 ch, yo, insert hk in next ch, yo and draw through, yo and draw through 2 lps on hk, drop MC, with CC yo and draw through last 2 lps on hk, 1 dc in each of next 3 ch, yo, insert hk in next ch, yo and draw through, yo and draw through 2 lps on hk, drop CC, with MC yo and draw through last 2 lps on hk, 1 dc in next ch, repeat from * across and end with MC, yo and draw through last 2 lps on hk, ch 2, turn. **Row 2:** * With MC, 1 dc in each of 1st 3 dc, yo, insert hk in next dc, yo and draw through, yo and draw through 2 lps on hk, drop MC, with CC yo and draw through last 2 lps on hk, 1 dc in each of next 3 dc, yo, insert hk in next dc, yo and draw through, yo and draw through 2 lps on hk, drop CC, with MC yo and draw through last 2 lps on hk, repeat from * across, ch 2, turn. Repeat row 2 for pattern.

(114)

Multiple of 4 ch plus 1: **Row 1:** With MC, ch 1, 1 sc in 2nd ch from hk, * insert hk in same ch, yo and draw through, drop MC, with CC yo and draw through 2 lps on hk, sk 1 ch, 1 sc in next ch, insert hk in same ch, yo and draw through, drop CC, with MC yo and draw through 2 lps on hk, sk 1 ch, 1 sc in next ch, repeat from * across and end 2 MC sc in last ch, turn. **Rows 2 and 3:** With CC, ch 1, * sk 1 st, (1 sc, 1 hdc) in next sc, repeat from * across, turn. **Rows 4 and 5:** Carrying yarn across wrong side of work, with MC, ch 1, * sk 1 st, 1 sc in next st, insert hk in same st, yo and draw through, drop MC, with CC yo and draw through 2 lps on hk, sk 1 st, 1 sc in next st, insert hk in same st, yo and draw through, drop CC, with MC yo and draw through 2 lps on hk, repeat from * across and end sk 1 st, 2 MC sc in last st, turn. Repeat rows 2 through 5 for pattern.

(115)

Multiple of 6 ch plus 1: **Row 1:** With MC, ch 1, insert hk in 2nd ch from hk, * yo and draw through, drop MC, with CC yo and draw through 2 lps on hk, 1 sc in each of next 4 ch, insert hk in next ch, yo and draw through, drop CC, with MC yo and draw through 2 lps on hk, insert hk in next ch, repeat from * across and end 1 MC sc in last ch, ch 1, turn. **Rows 2 and 4:** Carrying yarn across wrong side of work, * with MC 1 sc in next sc, insert hk in next sc, yo and draw through, drop MC, with CC yo and draw through 2 lps on hk, 1 sc in each of next 2 sc, insert hk in next sc, yo and draw through, drop CC, with MC yo and draw through 2 lps on hk, 1 sc in next sc, repeat from * across and end 1 MC sc in last sc, ch 1, turn. **Row 3:** With MC, * 1 sc in each of next 2 sc, insert hk in next sc, yo and draw through, drop MC, with CC yo and draw through 2 lps on hk, insert hk in next sc, yo and draw through, drop CC, with MC yo and draw through 2 lps on hk, 1 sc in each of next 2 sc, repeat from * across

and end 1 MC sc in last sc, ch 1, turn. **Row 5:**
With MC, * insert hk in next sc, yo and draw
through, drop MC, with CC yo and draw through
2 lps on hk, 1 sc in each of next 4 sc, insert hk in
next sc, yo and draw through, drop CC, with MC
yo and draw through 2 lps on hk, repeat from
* across and end 1 MC sc in last sc, ch 1, turn.
Repeat rows 2 through 5 for pattern.

(116)
Multiple of 7 ch plus 8: **Row 1:** With MC, ch 1,
1 sc in 2nd ch from hk, * sk 2 ch, 3 dc in next ch,
ch 1, 3 dc in next ch, sk 2 ch, 1 sc in next ch,
repeat from * across, turn. **Row 2:** With CC,
ch 3, sk 1 sc, * (yo, insert hk in next dc, yo and
draw through) 3 times, yo and draw through 6 lps
on hk, yo and draw through last 2 lps on hk
(cluster made), ch 2, 1 sc in next ch-1 sp, ch 2, 1
cluster over next 3 dc, 1 dc in next sc, repeat
from * across, ch 3, turn. **Row 3:** With CC, 3 dc
in 1st dc, * sk (1 cluster, ch-2), 1 sc in next sc, sk
(ch-2, 1 cluster), (3 dc, ch 1, 3 dc) in next dc,
repeat from * across and end 4 dc in turning ch
of previous row, turn. **Row 4:** With MC, ch 1,
1 sc in 1st dc, * ch 2, 1 cluster over next 3 dc,
1 dc in next sc, 1 cluster over next 3 dc, ch 2,
1 sc in next ch-1 sp, repeat from * across and end
1 sc in turning ch of previous row, ch 1, turn.
Row 5: With MC, 1 sc in 1st sc, * sk (ch-2, 1
cluster), (3 dc, ch 1, 3 dc) in next dc, sk (1 cluster,
ch-2), 1 sc in next sc, repeat from * across, turn.
Repeat rows 2 through 5 for pattern.

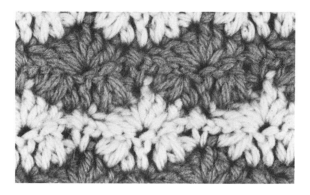

(117)
Multiple of 18 ch: **Row 1:** With MC, ch 1, 1 sc in
2nd ch from hk, * 1 sc in next ch, repeat from
* across, ch 1, turn. **Row 2:** With MC, 2 sc in
1st sc, * 1 sc in each of next 6 sc, (insert hk in
next sc, yo and draw through) twice, yo and
draw through 3 lps on hk (1 dec made), 1 dec
over next 2 sc, 1 sc in each of next 6 sc, (2 sc in
next sc) twice, repeat from * across and end 1 sc
in each of last 7 sc, insert hk in last sc worked, yo

and draw through, drop MC, with CC yo and draw through 2 lps on hk, ch 1, turn. **Row 3:** With CC, 2 sc in 1st sc, * 1 sc in each of next 6 sc, (1 dec over next 2 sts) twice, 1 sc in each of next 6 sc, (2 sc in next sc) twice, repeat from * across and end 2 sc in last sc, ch 1, turn. **Row 4:** With CC, 2 sc in 1st sc, * 1 sc in each of next 6 sc, (1 dec over next 2 sts) twice, 1 sc in each of next 6 sc, (2 sc in next sc) twice, repeat from * across and end 1 sc in each of last 7 sc, insert hk in last sc worked, drop CC, with MC yo and draw through 2 lps on hk, ch 1, turn. **Row 5:** With MC, 2 sc in 1st sc, * 1 sc in each of next 6 sc, (1 dec over next 2 sc) twice, 1 sc in each of next 6 sc, (2 sc in next sc) twice, repeat from * across and end 2 sc in last sc, ch 1, turn. Repeat rows 2 through 5 for pattern.

(118)

Multiple of 6 ch plus 1: **Row 1 (wrong side):** With MC, ch 1, 1 sc in 2nd ch from hk, * sk 2 ch, 6 dc in next ch (shell made), sk 2 ch, 1 sc in next ch, repeat from * across. Take lp off hk and return to beg of row. **Row 2:** Attach CC to 1st sc, ch 3, 3 dc in same sc, * sk 3 dc, 1 sc in sp between last dc and next dc, sk 3 dc, 1 shell in next sc, repeat from * across and end 3 dc in last sc, yo, insert hk in same sc, yo and draw through, yo and draw through 2 lps on hk, drop CC, pick up MC lp and draw through last 2 lps on hk, ch 1, turn. Fasten off CC. **Row 3:** With MC, 1 sc in 1st dc, * keeping all lps on hk (insert hk horizontally from right to left over base of next st, yo and draw through) 7 times, yo and draw through 8 lps on hk (reverse shell made), ch 3, 1 sc in sp before next dc, repeat from * across and end 1 sc in turning ch of previous row, ch 1, turn. **Row 4:** With MC, 1 sc in 1st sc, * sk ch-3, 1 shell in eye of next reverse shell, 1 sc in next sc, repeat from * across. Take lp off hk and return to beg of row. Repeat rows 2 through 4 for pattern.

(119)

Multiple of 2 ch plus 1: **Row 1:** With MC, ch 1, (1 sc, 1 hdc) in 2nd ch from hk, * sk 1 ch, (1 sc, 1 hdc) in next ch, repeat from * across and end insert hk in last ch, yo and draw through, drop MC, with CC yo and draw through 2 lps on hk, ch 1, turn. **Row 2:** Carrying MC along top of work and working sts over MC strand, with CC (1 sc, 1 hdc) in 1st sc, * sk 1 hdc, (1 sc, 1 hdc) in next sc, repeat from * across and end insert hk in last sc, yo and draw through, drop CC, with MC yo and draw through 2 lps on hk, ch 1, turn. **Row 3:** Carrying CC along top of work and working sts over CC strand, with MC (1 sc, 1 hdc) in 1st sc, * sk 1 hdc, (1 sc, 1 hdc) in next sc, repeat from * across and end insert hk in last sc, yo and draw through, drop MC, with CC yo and draw through 2 lps on hk, ch 1, turn. Repeat rows 2 and 3 for pattern.

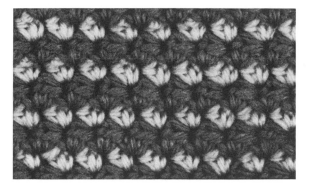

(120)

Multiple of 8 ch plus 4: **Row 1:** With MC, ch 1, 1 sc in 2nd ch from hk, * 1 sc in each of next 2 ch, insert hk in next ch, yo and draw through, drop MC, with CC yo and draw through 2 lps on hk, 1 sc in each of next 3 ch, insert hk in next ch, yo and draw through, drop CC, with MC yo and draw through 2 lps on hk, 1 sc in next ch, repeat from * across and end with MC 1 sc in each of last 4 ch, turn. **Rows 2, 3, 4 and 9:** With MC, ch 1, * 1 sc in each of next 3 sc, insert hk in next sc, yo and draw through, drop MC, with CC yo and draw through 2 lps on hk, 1 sc in each of next 3 sc, insert hk in next sc, yo and draw through, drop CC, with MC yo and draw through 2 lps on hk, repeat from * across and end with MC 1 sc in each of last 4 sc, turn. **Rows 5, 6, 7 and 8:** With CC, ch 1, * 1 sc in each of next 3 sc, insert hk in next sc, yo and draw through, drop CC, with MC yo and draw through 2 lps on hk, 1 sc in each of next 3 sc, insert hk in next sc, yo and draw through, drop MC, with CC yo and draw through 2 lps on hk, repeat from * across and end with CC 1 sc in each of last 4 sc, turn. Repeat rows 2 through 9 for pattern.

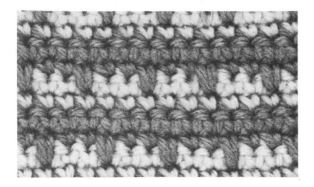

(121)

Multiple of 3 ch plus 2: **Row 1:** With MC, ch 1, 1 sc in 2nd ch from hk, * 1 sc in next ch, repeat from * across, turn. **Rows 2, 5, 6 and 9:** With MC, ch 1, * 1 sc in next sc, repeat from * across, turn. **Row 3:** With CC, ch 1, * 1 sc in each of next 2 sc, sk 1 sc, 1 long sc in st 1 row below skipped st, repeat from * across and end 1 sc in each of last 2 sc, ch 1, turn. **Rows 4 and 8:** With CC, * 1 sc in next st, repeat from * across, turn. **Row 7:** With CC, ch 1, * 1 sc in next sc, sk 1 sc, 1 long sc in st 1 row below skipped st, 1 sc in next sc, repeat from * across and end 1 long sc in st 1 row below last sc, ch 1, turn. Repeat rows 2 through 9 for pattern.

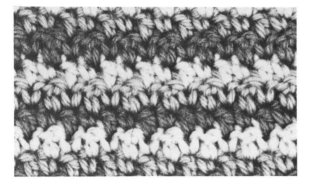

(122)

Multiple of 2 ch plus 1: **Row 1:** With color A, ch 1, 1 sc in 2nd ch from hk, * 1 dc in next ch, 1 sc in next ch, repeat from * across, turn. **Row 2:** With color B, ch 2, * 1 sc in next sc, 1 sc in next dc, repeat from * across and end 1 dc in last sc, turn. **Row 3:** With color C, ch 1, * 1 sc in next dc, 1 dc in next sc, repeat from * across and end 1 sc in last dc, turn. Repeat rows 2 and 3 for pattern, alternating colors A, B, and C on every row.

(123)

Multiple of 4 ch plus 2: **Row 1:** With color A, ch 2, 1 dc in 3rd ch from hk, 1 dc in next ch, * ch 2, sk 2 ch, 1 dc in each of next 2 ch, repeat from * across, turn. **Row 2:** With color B, ch 3, * sk 2 dc, 1 dc in each of 2 skipped ch of foundation ch, ch 2, repeat from * across and end 1 dc in turning ch of previous row, turn. **Row 3:** With color C, ch 2, sk 1 dc, * 1 dc in each of next 2 dc under next ch-2 sp, ch 2, sk 2 dc, repeat from * across and end 1 dc in each of next 2 dc under turning ch of previous row, turn. **Row 4:**

With color A, ch 3, * sk 2 dc, 1 dc in each of next 2 dc under next ch-2 sp, ch 2, repeat from * across and end 1 dc in last dc under turning ch of previous row, turn. Repeat rows 3 and 4 for pattern, alternating colors A, B, and C on every row.

(124)

Multiple of 11 ch plus 9: **Row 1:** With color A, ch 1, 1 sc in 2nd ch from hk, 1 sc in each of next 3 ch, * 3 sc in next ch, 1 sc in each of next 4 ch, sk 2 ch, 1 sc in each of next 4 ch, repeat from * across and end 3 sc in next ch, 1 sc in each of last 4 ch, turn. **Row 2:** Working through back lps of sts only, with color A, ch 1, sk 1 sc, * 1 sc in each of next 4 sc, 3 sc in next sc, 1 sc in each of next 4 sc, sk 2 sc, repeat from * across to within last 5 sts and end 1 sc in each of next 3 sc, sk 1 sc, 1 sc through both lps of last sc, turn. Repeat row 2 for pattern, alternating 2 rows color B, 2 rows color C, and 2 rows color A.

(125)

Multiple of 6 ch plus 3: **Row 1:** With color A, ch 2, (3 dc, ch 1, 3 dc) in 3rd ch from hk, * sk 2 ch, 1 sc in next ch, sk 2 ch, (3 dc, ch 1, 3 dc) in next ch (shell made), repeat from * across and end 1 sc in last ch, turn. **Row 2:** With color B, ch 3, 2 dc in 1st sc, * sk 3 dc, 1 sc in next ch-1 sp, sk 3 dc, 1 shell in next sc, repeat from * across and end 3 dc in turning ch of previous row, turn. **Row 3:** With color C, ch 2, * sk 3 dc, 1 shell in next sc, sk 3 dc, 1 sc in next ch-1 sp, repeat from * across and end sk 2 dc, 1 sc in turning ch of previous row, turn. Repeat rows 2 and 3 for pattern, alternating colors A, B, and C on every row.

7. AFGHAN STITCH, OR TUNISIAN CROCHET

In an earlier chapter we referred to the art of crochet as a many-faceted one and mentioned the afghan stitch, among others, as a type of work that was just a little different from simple straight crochet, for which many patterns with accompanying directions have appeared in Chapter 6. Now we would like to tell you more about this interesting kind of stitch, and to describe how it is worked, to offer you photographs of some attractive afghan stitch patterns with directions for making them, and to speak of the various design possibilities that can be inspired by this type of work.

Sometimes referred to as "Tunisian Crochet," the afghan stitch has a woven look and was originally called "Tricot Crochet," by which name it is still known in Europe. *Tricot* is the French word for "knit," and it was first called by this name because of the woven-textured look which so closely resembles knitting. It is interesting that it is also because of the woven-type texture of this stitch that early settlers in America felt it particularly adaptable for the making of warm, utilitarian blankets or "afghans," and that is how the name "afghan stitch" came into being. Incidentally, the word *afghan* means a native of Afghanistan and our use of the word probably comes from the fact that those Mideasterners used small, brightly colored throw

rugs somewhat similar to our afghans.

While the afghan stitch is still widely used for making beautiful warm blankets and throws, it is also used today for many other intriguing new things. Contemporary crochet, which introduced large needles and looser gauges and radically changed the kind of work that people were doing, also affected the close-knit, small, woven afghan stitch. Designers saw many new possibilities for using it with the new looser gauge and adapted it to making all sorts of home accessories, including throw pillows, wall hangings, and placemats and coasters—and beyond these, to the area of good modern fashion design. Coats, jackets, dresses, belts, and practically every other type of clothing is now being made with it, and some of the designs are very unusual and quite stunning. New stitches have been developed too, several of which are shown below with directions for working them, and here again as in any other crochet designing, your choice of a pattern, a stitch, yarn, a hook and a gauge gives you free rein to make whatever it is that you want to make for yourself.

The afghan hook, a cross between a knitting needle and a crochet hook, is an elongated straight one with a hook at one end (to be used in the same manner as any other crochet hook), and a small knob on the opposite end. The reason for the extra length and the knob is that, unlike any other type of crochet, an afghan-stitch row is always worked in two parts, and on the first part all the stitches are picked up and held on the needle. Consequently there needs to be sufficient length to accommodate all these stitches and the knob is needed to secure them on the hook and to prevent them from slipping off. Because this is such an unusual stitch, worked on a different kind of hook and in a different manner from any other kind of crochet, we have an illustration just below here, placed separately from all our stitch illustrations appearing in the Crocheter's Guide, and showing how to work the basic afghan stitch. It also shows how the row is always worked in two parts, the first part consisting of picking up as many stitches as there are on the piece of work, working from right to left (**A**), and the second part completing the row by working from left to right (the work is never turned) and crocheting the stitches off the hook one by one (**B**). The illustration also shows how the 2nd row of this basic stitch is worked by inserting the afghan hook through the vertical bars of the first row (**C**), and how on the second half of that second row all loops are worked off in the same manner as on the second half of the first row (**D**).

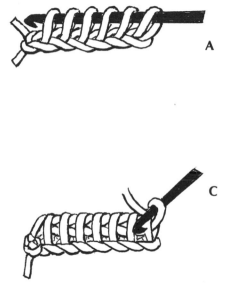

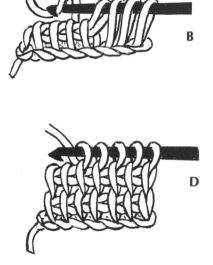

One of the most important things about the basic little afghan stitch which we have not yet mentioned, the one which perhaps has been the main reason for this very simple stitch to have maintained its popularity through the centuries, is its quality of texture which lends itself so perfectly to the use of cross-stitch embroidery worked over it. The woven, even boxlike, effect of the finished basic afghan stitch is perfect for this type of embellishment. Through the years one of the greatest pleasures of needlework enthusiasts has been to produce squares and strips and large solid pieces of basic afghan-stitch crochet, and always they are impatient to complete these pieces in order to be able to go on to embroidering them. The possibilities for beautiful cross-stitch embroidery patterns on this type of work are limitless. Besides the beautiful afghans you might by now be thinking of making with birds nesting in a lovely flower garden, or hounds and hunters at a chase, think also of a tailored dress for yourself with your own monogram spelled out in two or three colors along the length of one side of the skirt, a man's ski jacket with a bold geometric pattern embroidered along the yoke, or a child's jumper alive with Peter Hunt hearts and flowers! Cross-stitches are usually worked with the same weight yarn as that which was used for the basic piece, and in one or many contrast colors, and it is indeed exciting to see a single rose, a small nosegay, or a large floral bouquet blossom into a thing of almost lifelike beauty even as one crosses one little stitch over another onto the basic simple woven background.

Any charted pattern can be used for this type of work, since each little box stitch on your crocheted piece has the same effect as a square on a piece of graph paper, and by following any chart you need only to count square for box to be able to work out your design. By the same token you can also make a chart of your own by tracing a design onto a piece of graph paper, filling in the squares and then copying the design onto your crochet work. Since we've illustrated here the technique of crocheting the basic afghan stitch, we want now to illustrate for you the best method for working cross-stitch embroidery over it.

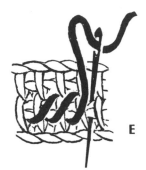

E

F

Each vertical bar of the afghan stitch counts as 1 stitch. Following desired chart for embroidery design and working from left to right, join yarn on wrong side of work in small bottom space that occurs after the vertical bar, bring needle through to right side, work across next vertical bar into top space occurring after that bar, then draw needle through bottom hole directly below **(E).** When the necessary number of stitches have been worked in this manner, complete the stitch by forming a cross from right to left **(F).** To avoid puckering, do not pull the yarn too tightly.

The first photograph in this section depicts a swatch worked in basic afghan stitch. Following that is a charted graph, and just below the graph is a photograph of the same basic afghan-stitch swatch, cross-stitch embroidered according to the chart. We show these photographs in this order so that you can see immediately how the simple box-like stitch takes on a very interesting look when re-embroidered. In Chapter 8 there are a number of other charts, any of which you might want to duplicate on your own basic afghan-stitch work. Interesting textured afghan stitches are also shown in this chapter, with directions, and for methods of increasing and decreasing when working with the afghan stitch, refer to the Crocheter's Guide in Chapter 4.

Note: The final row before fastening off on any piece of afghan-stitch work is done with a row of slip stitch through the vertical bars of the last row.

(A–1)

Multiple of any number of ch: **Row 1:** 1st Half:
Ch 1, insert hk in 2nd ch from hk, yo and draw
through, * insert hk in next ch, yo and draw
through, repeat from * across. 2nd Half: Yo and
draw through 1st lp on hk, * yo and draw through
2 lps on hk, repeat from * across. **Row 2:** 1st
Half: Ch 1, sk 1st vertical bar, * insert hk from
right to left under top strand of next vertical bar,
yo and draw through, repeat from * across and
end insert hk under both strands of last vertical
bar, yo and draw through. 2nd Half: Yo and draw
through 1st lp on hk, * yo and draw through 2 lps
on hk, repeat from * across. Repeat row 2 for
pattern.

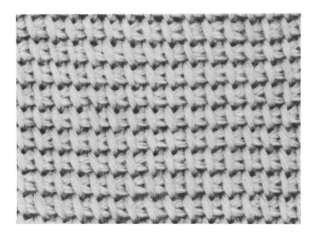

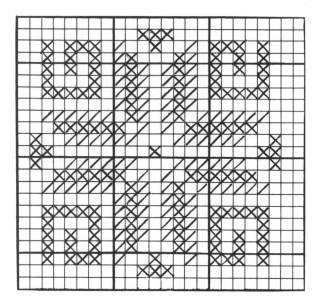

Afghan Stitch Chart

(A–2)
Work pattern #A–1. Embroider with cross-stitch according to chart above.

(A–3)

Multiple of any number of ch. **Row 1:** 1st Half: Ch 1, insert hk in 2nd ch from hk, yo and draw through, * insert hk in next ch, yo and draw through, repeat from * across. 2nd Half: Yo and draw through 1st lp on hk, * yo and draw through 2 lps on hk, repeat from * across. **Row 2:** 1st Half: Ch 1, sk 1st vertical bar, * insert hk in next vertical bar, yo and draw through, repeat from * across. 2nd Half: Yo and draw through 1st lp on hk, * yo and draw through 2 lps on hk, repeat from * across. Repeat row 2 for pattern.

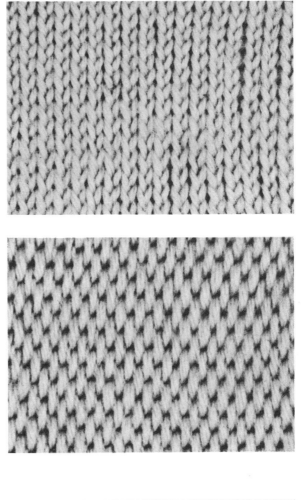

(A–4)

Multiple of any number of ch. **Row 1:** 1st Half: Ch 1, insert hk in 2nd ch from hk, yo and draw through, * insert hk in next ch, yo and draw through, repeat from * across. 2nd Half: Yo and draw through 1st lp on hk, * yo and draw through 2 lps on hk, repeat from * across. **Row 2:** 1st Half: Ch 1, sk 1st vertical bar, * insert hk in sp before next vertical bar, yo and draw through, repeat from * across. 2nd Half: Yo and draw through 1st lp on hk, * yo and draw through 2 lps on hk, repeat from * across. Repeat row 2 for pattern.

(A–5)

Multiple of 2 ch plus 1: **Row 1:** 1st Half: Ch 1, insert hk in 2nd ch from hk, yo and draw through, * insert hk in next ch, yo and draw through, repeat from * across. 2nd Half: Yo and draw through 1st lp on hk, * yo and draw through 2 lps on hk, repeat from * across. **Row 2:** 1st Half: Ch 1, sk 2 vertical bars, * insert hk from right to left under top strand of next vertical bar, yo and draw through, insert hk from right to left under top strand of last skipped vertical bar, yo and draw through, sk 1 unworked vertical bar, repeat from * across. 2nd Half: Yo and draw through 1st lp on hk, * yo and draw through 2 lps on hk, repeat from * across. Repeat row 2 for pattern.

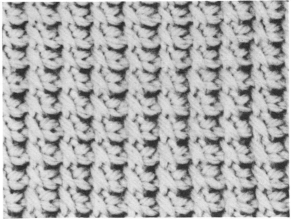

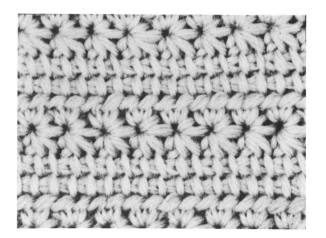

(A–6)

Multiple of 2 ch plus 1. **Row 1:** 1st Half: Ch 1, insert hk in 2nd ch from hk, yo and draw through, * insert hk in next ch, yo and draw through, repeat from * across. 2nd Half: Yo and draw through 1st lp on hk, * yo and draw through 2 lps on hk, repeat from * across. **Rows 2 and 3:** 1st Half: Ch 1, sk 1st vertical bar, * insert hk from right to left under top strand of next vertical bar, yo and draw through, repeat from * across and end insert hk under both strands of last vertical bar, yo and draw through. 2nd Half: Yo and draw through 1st lp on hk, * yo and draw through 2 lps on hk, repeat from * across. **Row 4:** Ch 2, insert hk in 2nd ch from hk, yo and draw through, insert hk from right to left under top strand of 1st vertical bar, yo and draw through, (insert hk from right to left under top strand of next vertical bar, yo and draw through) twice, yo and draw through 5 lps on hk, * ch 1 (eye made), insert hk in eye just made, yo and draw through, insert hk under top strand of last vertical bar worked, yo and draw through, (insert hk under top strand of next vertical bar, yo and draw through) twice, yo and draw through 5 lps on hk (cluster made), repeat from * across, ch 3, turn. **Row 5:** * 2 hdc in next cluster, repeat from * across, turn. **Row 6:** 1st Half: Ch 1, * insert hk in next hdc, yo and draw through, repeat from * across. 2nd Half: Yo and draw through 1st lp on hk, * yo and draw through 2 lps on hk, repeat from * across. Repeat rows 3 through 6 for pattern.

(A–7)

Multiple of 2 ch plus 1: **Row 1:** 1st Half: Ch 1, insert hk in 2nd ch from hk, yo and draw through, * insert hk in next ch, yo and draw through, repeat from * across. 2nd Half: Yo and draw through 1st lp on hk, * yo and draw through 2 lps on hk, repeat from * across. **Row 2:** 1st Half: Ch 1, sk 1st vertical bar, * yo, insert hk under top strand of next 2 vertical bars, yo and draw through, repeat from * across. 2nd Half: Yo and draw through 1st lp on hk, * yo and draw through 2 lps on hk, repeat from * across. **Row 3:** 1st Half: Ch 1, sk 1st vertical bar, * yo, sk yo of previous row, insert hk under top strand of next vertical bar, yo and draw through, repeat from * across. 2nd Half: Yo and draw through 1st lp on hk, * yo and draw through 2 lps on hk, repeat from * across. Repeat row 3 for pattern.

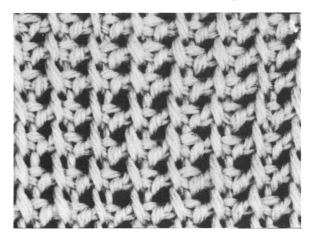

(A–8)

Multiple of 3 ch: **Row 1:** 1st Half: Ch 1, insert hk in 2nd ch from hk, yo and draw through, * insert hk in next ch, yo and draw through, repeat from * across. 2nd Half: Yo and draw through 1st lp on hk, * yo and draw through 2 lps on hk, repeat from * across. **Rows 2 and 3:** 1st Half: Ch 1, sk 1st vertical bar, * insert hk under top strand of next vertical bar, yo and draw through, repeat from * across and end insert hk under both strands of last vertical bar, yo and draw through. 2nd Half: Yo and draw through 1st lp on hk, * yo and draw through 2 lps on hk, repeat from * across. **Row 4:** 1st Half: Ch 1, sk 1st vertical bar, * 4 dc under top strand of next vertical bar, take lp off hk, insert hk in 1st dc of 4-dc group, draw lp of 4th dc through, 1 dc in each of next 2 vertical bars, repeat from * across and end 1 dc in last vertical bar, turn. **Row 5:** * 1 sl st in next st, repeat from * across, turn. **Row 6:** 1st Half: Ch 1, * insert hk in next sl st, yo and draw through, repeat from * across. 2nd Half: Yo and draw through 1st lp on hk, * yo and draw through 2 lps on hk, repeat from * across. Repeat rows 2 through 6 for pattern.

(A–9)

Multiple of 2 ch plus 1: **Row 1:** 1st Half: Ch 1, insert hk in 2nd ch from hk, yo and draw through, * insert hk in next ch, yo and draw through, repeat from * across. 2nd Half: Yo and draw through 1st lp on hk, * yo and draw through 2 lps on hk, repeat from * across. **Row 2:** 1st Half: Ch 1, sk 1st vertical bar, * yo, insert hk under top strand of next 2 vertical bars, yo and draw through, repeat from * across. 2nd Half: Yo and draw through 1st lp on hk, * yo and draw through 2 lps on hk, repeat from * across. **Row 3:** 1st Half: Ch 1, sk 1st vertical bar, * yo, insert hk under yo of previous row and top strand of next vertical bar, yo and draw through, repeat from * across. 2nd Half: Yo and draw through 1st lp on hk, * yo and draw through 2 lps on hk, repeat from * across. Repeat row 3 for pattern.

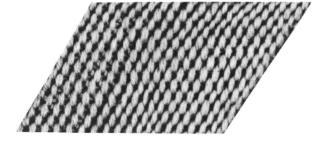

(A–10)

Multiple of any number of ch. **Row 1:** 1st Half: Ch 1, insert hk in 2nd ch from hk, yo and draw through, * insert hk in next ch, yo and draw through, repeat from * across. 2nd Half: Yo and draw through 1st lp on hk, * yo and draw through 2 lps on hk, repeat from * across. **Row 2:** 1st Half: Ch 1, sk 1st vertical bar, * insert hk from right to left under both strands of next vertical bar, yo and draw through, repeat from * across. 2nd Half: Yo and draw through 1st lp on hk, * yo and draw through 2 lps on hk, repeat from * across. Repeat row 2 for pattern.

8. CHARTED DESIGNS

In Chapter 7 we described the very popular use of cross-stitch embroidery on basic afghan-stitch crochet work, and told how the patterns on the squares of a charted design could be easily translated onto the woven boxes of the afghan stitch. In Chapter 9 we will describe and work a little with filet crochet, a type of handwork which has also been a long-standing favorite of many needlework enthusiasts, totally different from the basic afghan stitch, both in the method of working it and in the ultimate purpose for which it is generally used, but bearing the one similarity of always being worked in a series of blocks or boxes, these again particularly suitable for working in charted designs from the squares on a piece of graph paper. Because of this similarity between the two stitches, we want to show here, between the two chapters on these two very different stitches, a group of interesting charted designs, the patterns of which can be translated into either the cross-stitch embroidery designs on the basic afghan-stitch work you are doing, or onto the space-and-block pattern of your filet crochet work.

All of the charts below are planned for the use of just one contrast color, and the patterns include some florals, some stylized designs, and a few geometrics. Needing only to know that each square on a chart counts as a block or box on your crochet work, you can do many things to alter or adapt any of the patterns to fit in with the particular design you have in mind. Flowers can be worked in two or three colors, snowflakes can be simplified or elaborated on, narrow border designs can be repeated again and again to give a general overall effect, and more than one pattern can be used on a single piece of work. For example, Charts numbered 1, 4, and 6 could be beautifully blended together to create a charming afghan design, and Charts numbered 3 and 9 could combine into a handsome ski-sweater pattern. Any of the narrower designs or any part of any of them, worked together with your 3 initials from one of the alphabet charts, would make a very effective monogram on a jacket or skirt, and Chart 7 repeated many times over on your filet mesh tablecloth would make that piece of work a true thing of beauty. Your own imagination can play in many directions when working with charted designs, and your method of working either with those patterns we show or others that you may choose to use would be always the same.

Buy a pad or a large sheet of graph paper, then choose a design you want to use, either from our patterns, some other group of patterns, or one you decide to draft yourself. Count off the number of blocks or squares that are in that portion of your crochet work that you want to cover, then mark off your design to fit onto as many squares of graph paper as the number of blocks or squares on your work. Should the design be an uncharted one that you've decided to trace onto graph paper, then fill in the squares within the boundaries of the outline tracing, and treat it as any other charted design. Counting then the boxes or blocks on your work as

the squares on your graph, work in your pattern in whichever medium you choose. You will find that as the design begins to appear on your work, you will be eager to go on and see more and more of it develop. When you are finished you will feel that you have been through an exciting, pleasurable experience and have created a beautiful work of art of your own.

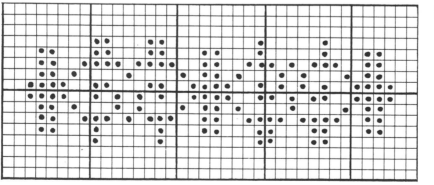

1

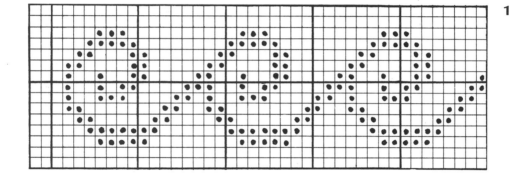

2

3

4

5

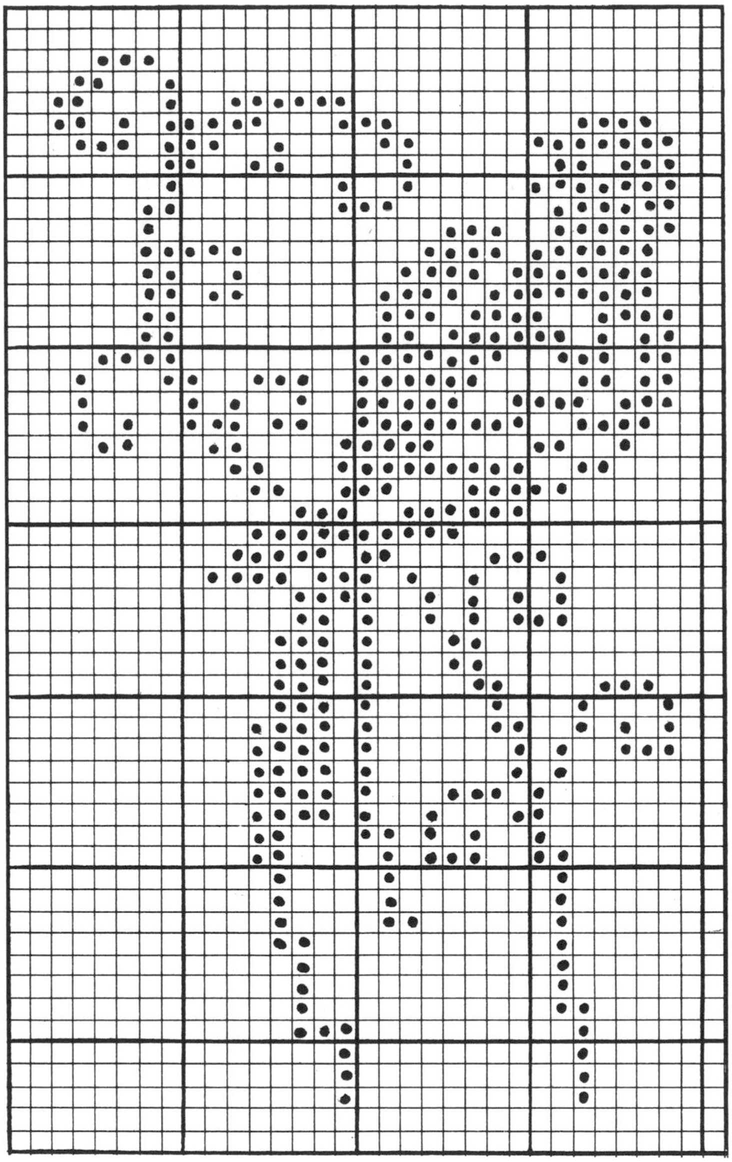

6

7

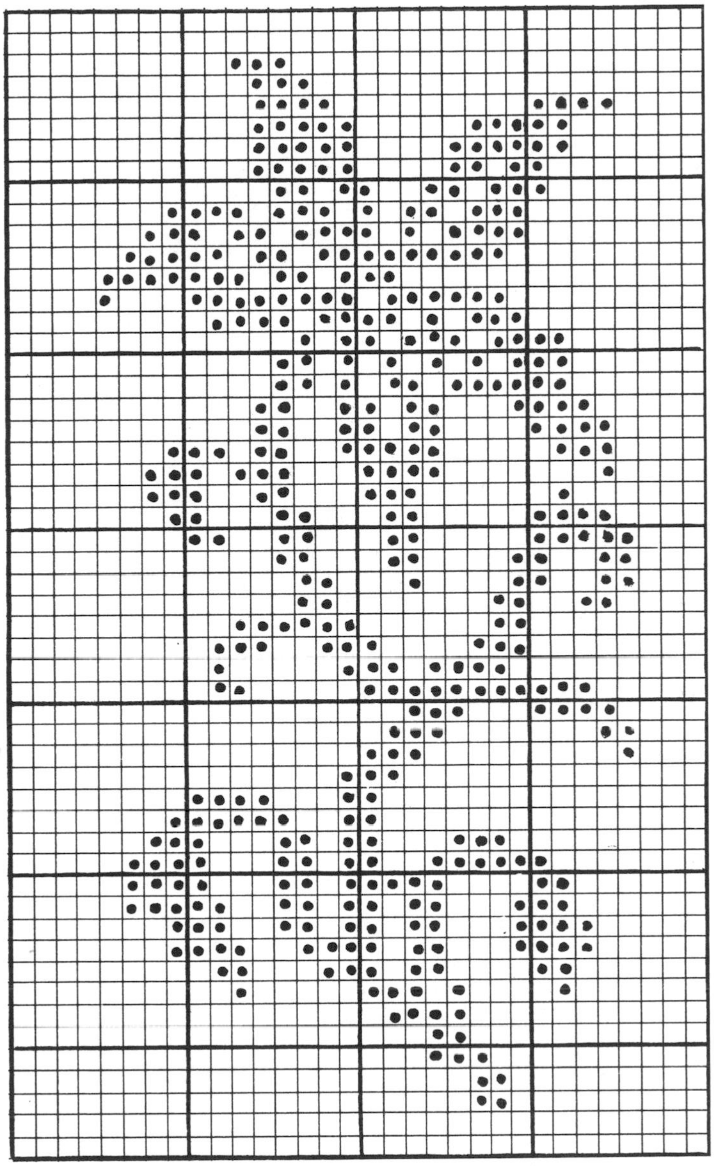

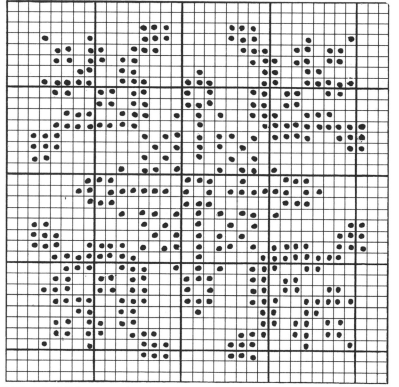

8

9

10

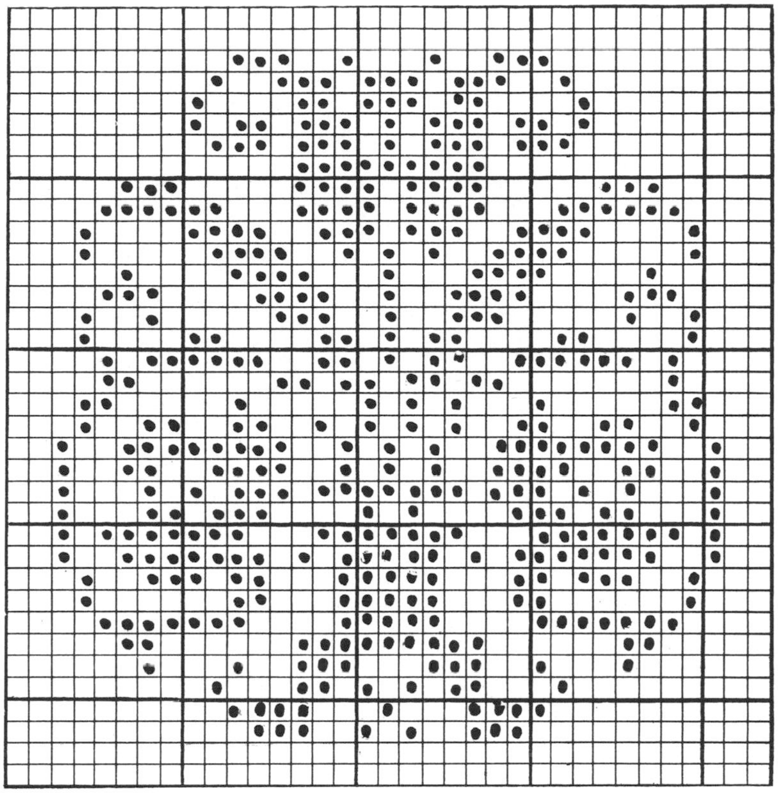

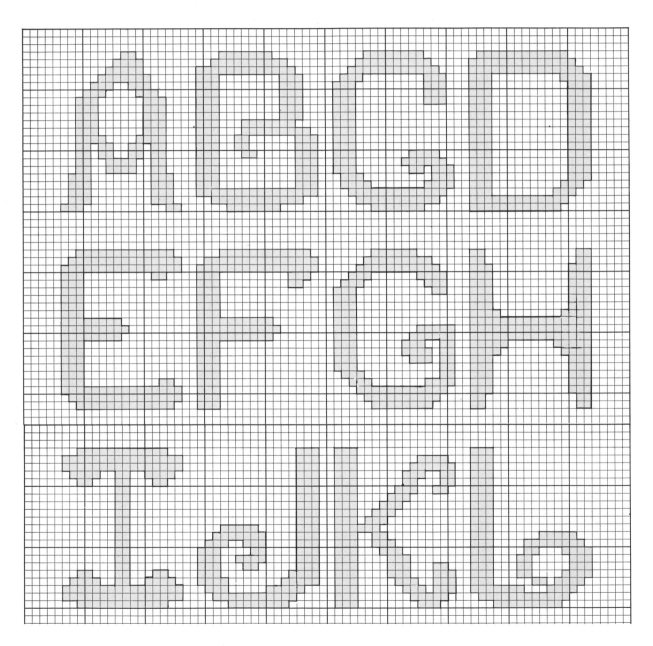

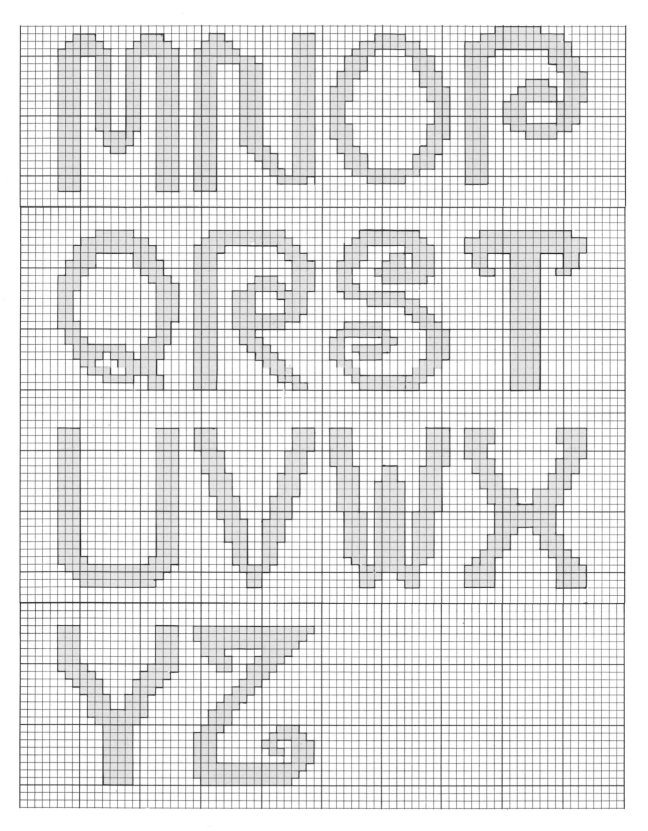

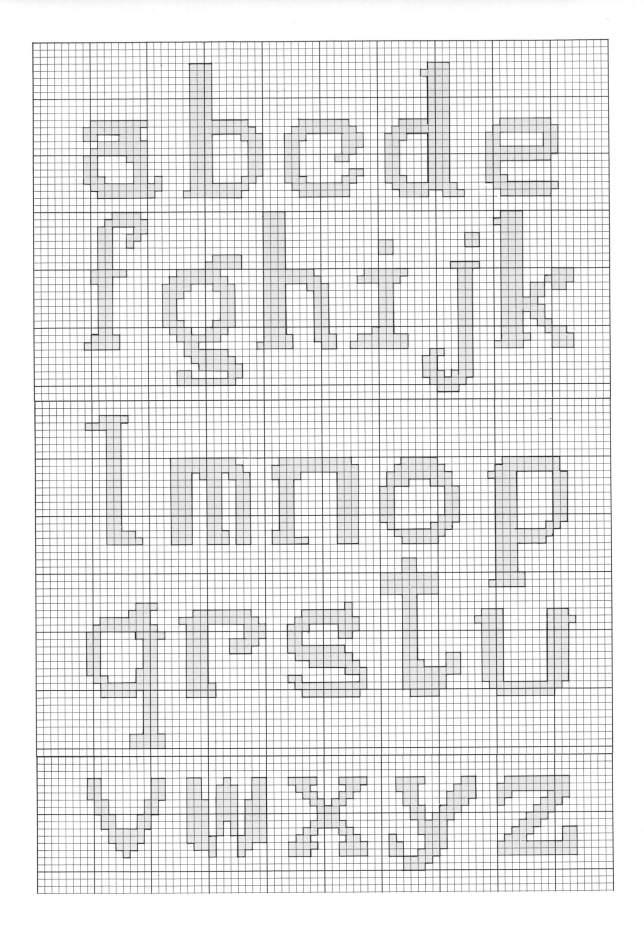

9. FILET CROCHET

As the basic little, wovenlike boxes of the afghan stitch are so very right for the embroidered designs that are usually cross-stitched over them, so the square little boxes of basic filet crochet are also worked almost always with the thought in mind that some type of design will be worked into them. It is not embroidered in this case, but done in a manner which we will describe below, and done in such a way that any of the charted designs shown in Chapter 8, or any other design one chooses, can be used.

There are many types of filet open-mesh stitches, some of which are shown in the chapter on pattern stitches. When we speak of "filet crochet" in this chapter, however, we are referring to the very basic and original filet stitch, worked into a series of square open boxes or spaces with the use of double crochet stitches and 2 chain in between each of the double crochets used. It is this particular stitch that seldom remains finished in its simple basic form of square open spaces, but rather is usually worked in an arrangement of spaces and blocks. The spaces form the background and the blocks the design of the pattern to be filled in, these blocks being made by working a double crochet into the double crochets and the 2 chain between them on the previous row; the specific ones to be

worked are determined by the design being used.

The original and still very popular use of filet crochet is for dainty and lovely tablecloths, bedspreads, coverlets, placemats, and other types of fine household linen, and often too as insets on pieces of woven material. Patterns traditionally have been all-over ones such as a several-times-over repeat of the snowflake design shown below, although often, too, filet work has been done in a stylized series of blocks and spaces, such as those shown below our snowflake pattern.

More often than not this type of crochet is worked with fine thread and a small crochet hook, this being a rather unusual exception to the art of contemporary crochet today, where heavier yarn and larger needles are preferred. The reason for the customary use of the finer thread with this particular stitch is that the double crochet and the 2 chain between form a fairly large space, even at a very tight gauge, and since each space represents a box on the graph paper from which you are working your design, the use of a heavier gauge automatically limits the number of spaces within which you can work out a pattern of sufficient interest. Though we've called this type of fine work one of the unusual exceptions to the new trend of contemporary crochet, we should certainly make mention now of the fact that even this stitch has not been completely untouched by the influence of the heavier gauge being used these days. Within very recent years there are those who have adapted the little spaces and blocks to larger spaces and blocks, to be used for fashion items of clothing such as beach jackets, sweaters, and skirts, both long and short. Usually a stylized pattern of some type is worked into these garments made on the heavier gauge, since stylized designs generally have an all-over effect, and it does not really matter how few or many spaces there are to work with.

There is another rather odd new use for filet crochet that we'd like to tell you about now, and this again is an exception to a general rule. It is one of the few instances when plain open-mesh filet is used with no blocked pattern in it at all. It has been found that this plain open-mesh work forms an ideal background for heavy all-over fringed designs such as one would use for high-pile throw rugs, cosy warm blankets, and heavy furlike winter coats. One works these textures by knotting several strands of cut yarn under each chain-2 space of the open mesh piece, the number and length of the strands depending on the pattern or design one wants to work with. This stitch is good for use as

a fringing background because of the regularity and evenness of the boxes, the ease with which one can draw cut yarn or fringe through the spaces, and beyond this its flexibility, washability and easy care —in contrast to other backings such as canvas, for instance, which is generally hard and stiff and a little more difficult to work with. When filet is used for this purpose it is generally worked with a cotton yarn of some type (no matter what material is used for the actual fringing), since cotton has little "give," and for this reason will better hold the shape of the finished fringed garment.

Shown below is the basic filet stitch, and directly below that a piece of filet crochet worked with the exact design that was used in Chapter 7 for the embroidery on the basic afghan stitch, following the same chart except that in this instance the design is worked in one color only, as all filet designs are worked. Our purpose in showing the same design is to give an example of how charted designs adapt very well, though quite differently, to each of the two media, and to show the different effects that can be achieved. There are no charts for the stylized patterns also shown in this chapter, since these are self-explanatory, and the work actually serves as its own graph.

(F–1)

Multiple of 3 ch plus 1: **Row 1:** Ch 5, 1 dc in 6th ch from hk, * sk 2 ch, repeat from * across and end 1 dc in last ch, ch 5, turn. **Row 2:** Sk 1st dc, * 1 dc in next dc, ch 2, repeat from * across and end 1 dc in last dc, ch 5, turn. Repeat row 2 for pattern.

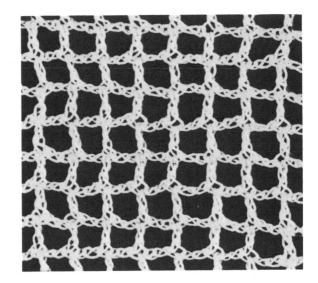

(F–2)

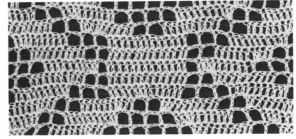

(F–3)

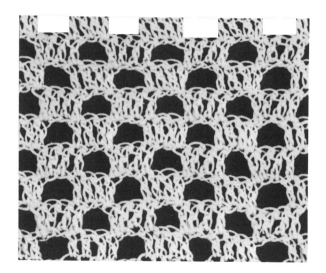

(F–4)

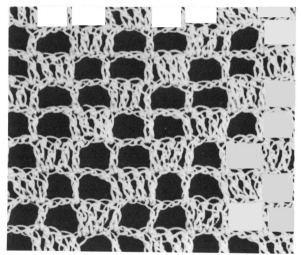

(F–5)

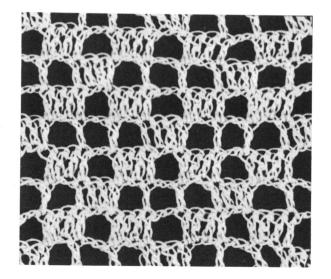

(F–6)

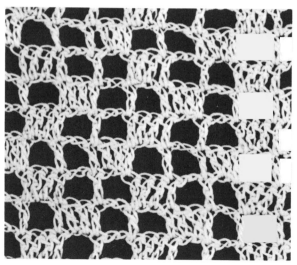

(F–7)

10. MOTIFS

We think that there is more opportunity for creative design when working with motifs than there is in almost any other type of crochet. A motif is a relatively small finished piece of work, and more often than not it is made with the thought in mind that it will be joined to several other motifs to form a much larger piece of some kind. With a number of these little pieces you can make an afghan, a tablecloth, a stole, a skirt, or absolutely anything else you might want to make. The choice is limitless, and whatever it is you have decided on will determine the number, style, and size of the motifs you will want to use.

It is fun to design in this way, and almost like playing a game or putting together the pieces of a jigsaw puzzle. The popular size of a motif today is anywhere between 2″ and 12″, and it is most often made in a round, square, hexagonal, octagonal, or diamond shape. Some motifs are referred to as "blocks" or "granny squares," and "patchwork" is the name often given to this type of crocheting that involves the putting together of several small pieces to achieve one whole.

It is interesting to note here that the standard dictionary definition of "patchwork" is "something made of pieces of different materials, shapes, and colors," and that one of the very reasons for the long and enduring popularity of this type of work is that it has always offered to the crocheter the opportunity of using to good advantage the many bits and pieces of yarn left over from other projects and generally relegated to the scrapbag to serve no purpose at all. Actually, since a motif is a relatively small bit of work finished unto itself, the interest of a large piece composed of many of these smaller ones in different colors and textures is so fascinating that it is often the inclination of many who do this type of work to buy small amounts of several different colors of yarn, and to vary their stitches and motif patterns in order to be able to get the patched effect that many others can get working with their bag of leftovers and the help of a little imagination.

For the purpose of better photography we have made all of our motifs shown below here in just one color, and we have used a medium-weight crochet cotton and a No. E aluminum hook in making them. You can make your own as we did, or you can work the same motifs in any number of other variations. You can use light-, medium- or heavy-weight cotton, wool, or synthetic yarn, working always with the proper-sized hook to accommodate to whatever weight you have chosen; or make each motif in two, three, or four different colors, changing them on the different rounds as it pleases you; or make fewer or more rounds than the number we have shown on each motif. Experimenting in this way can be a lot of fun, and you will find that sometimes in the course of doing it you are creating your own completely new and original motifs. For example, if you were to work our perfectly square 6-round motif No. M6 through Rnd 3 only, you would have crocheted a beautiful star with all sorts of design possibilities of its own.

Truly your imagination has absolutely free play on what you want to do and how you want to work with any of the many beautiful motifs shown below. The single one worked with medium weight wool and a No. J hook to a size of approximately 6" that serves as a lovely trim on the front of a simple sweater or blouse can, if worked a hundred times over with two or three colors, become part of a charming afghan, or again, if worked several times over and in a solid color with crochet cotton and a relatively fine hook, it can become one of the many pieces making up the whole of a lovely place-mat set.

The actual working up of a composite piece made with many motifs is a very interesting procedure, and by and large involves the same simple basic mathematical calculations as those used in all other types of crochet designing. If you are making something in a square or rectangular shape such as a scarf, an afghan, or a tablecloth, you decide first on what width and length you want your piece to be, and then divide that figure by the width and length of 4 of the motifs you are going to use, put together with the joining you have chosen. By doing this you know at once just how many motifs you need in order to achieve the right measurement. If your joined motifs multiply into exactly the size you want, you are ready to start. If however they do not, there is no problem since the complete flexibility of this type of work is so enormous that should your composite whole be smaller or larger than the size you want your piece to be, you can adjust to the right proportion by changing your joining and using one that covers more or less space, depending on whether your piece needs to be larger or smaller than the size you are reaching with your original joining; or by adding rows to or subtracting them from your individual motifs, or even by planning your work to be ended with a crocheted border added around the entire outer edge of your finished piece in order to bring it to a proper size.

By the same token, should the piece you are making be a shaped one, such as a sweater, a tunic, or one of the vests that are popular these days, you would check the measurements for the size garment you want to make in order to determine the number of motifs you need to accommodate to the width and length of it; should any adjustment be necessary, again change the type of joining you are using or the number of rows on your individual motifs, or the size of the hook and the weight of your yarn, which would be another way of making your motifs smaller or larger. Other interesting notes to remember in the making of garments with motifs is that very often the combining of both small and large ones is a fairly simple way of bringing about a good shaping, and also that motifs can be made in a series of straight pieces, and then the motif-assembled garment finished by adding a neckband, sleeve bottoms, and perhaps a front edging with rows of single or double crochet. One good general rule to know, no matter how you make or vary your shaped motif garment, is that you will find it easier to work with small rather than large individual motifs, since by using the smaller ones you have more leeway in placing them in such a way as to be able to achieve a good shaping of, for example, a shoulder or an armhole.

We've mentioned how the choice of one type of joining over another can alter the size of a finished piece of motif work. The one you use can also affect the appearance of the garment too. There are many different ways in which motifs can be connected to each other, and often the method of joining is in itself a fascinating part of this kind of work. At the end of this chapter we will show you a few methods of joining which are just a little different from the more routine ones of either sewing or weaving the motifs together, or joining them with a row of slip stitch or single crochet on the right or wrong side of the work. Your own choice of a joining, whether it be one of ours or one you've improvised yourself, will of course depend largely on what you are making and on the type of motifs you have chosen to use for it. You yourself, placing a few of the small pieces side by side, one next to the other and experimenting a bit, will be best able to judge which suits you best. The particular ones we show below are given only as an example of the kind of interest that can be added to putting together several small pieces to make one large whole. They are adjustable to different sizes and shapes of motifs, and if you prefer any of these especially, you might see if they adjust to the ones you are using. If they do not, then by looking at and studying them, perhaps you will be able to change them so that you can use them with the motifs you've chosen to work with.

For an explanation of all abbreviations and symbols appearing in the directions given below, refer to the beginning of Chapter 6 on pattern stitches, and for guide rules on crocheting and designing, refer to Chapters 4 and 12.

(Motifs begin on page 116.)

Motifs

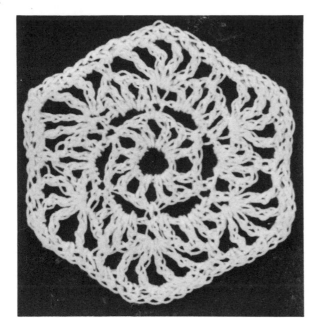

(M-1)

Ch 8, j with sl st to form a ring. **Rnd 1:** Ch 4 (counts as 1 dc), * 1 dc in center of ring, ch 1, repeat from * 10 times, j with sl st to 3rd ch of starting ch-4 — 12 dc made. **Rnd 2:** 1 sc in 1st ch-1 sp, ch 4, *sk (1 dc, ch-1 sp, 1 dc), 1 sc in next ch-1 sp, ch 4, repeat from * 4 times, j with sl st to 1st sc —6 ch-4 sps made. **Rnd 3:** 1 sc in same sc as joining, * ch 1, (1 dc, ch 1) 4 times in next ch-4 sp, 1 sc in next sc, repeat from * 4 times and end ch 1, (1 dc, ch 1) 4 times in next ch-4 sp, j with sl st to 1st sc. **Rnd 4:** Ch 5, 1 tr in same sc as joining, ch 1, *sk (ch-1 sp, 1 dc) twice, 1 sc in next ch-1 sp, ch 1, sk (1 dc, ch-1 sp) twice, (1 tr, ch 1) 4 times in next sc, repeat from * 4 times and end sk (ch-1 sp, 1 dc) twice, 1 sc in next ch-1 sp, ch 1, (1 tr, ch 1) twice in same sc as joining, j with sl st to 4th ch of starting ch-5. **Rnd 5:** Sl st in each of next 2 ch-1 sps, sl st in next sc, 1 sc in next ch-1 sp, ch 1, 1 sc in next ch-1 sp, * ch 1, (1 sc, ch 1, 1 sc) in next ch-1 sp, (ch 1, 1 sc in next ch-1 sp) 4 times, repeat from * 4 times and end ch 1, (1 sc, ch 1, 1 sc) in next ch-1 sp, (ch 1, 1 sc in next ch-1 sp) twice, j with sl st to 1st sc. F.O.

(M-2)

Ch 5, turn. **Row 1:** 2 dc in 5th ch from hk, ch 3, 3 dc in same ch, turn. **Row 2:** 1 sl st in each of 1st 3 dc, (1 sl st, ch 3, 2 dc) in next ch-3 sp, (ch 2, 3 dc in same ch-3 sp) twice, turn. **Row 3:** 1 sl st in each of 1st 3 dc, (1 sl st, ch 3, 2 dc, ch 2, 3 dc) in next ch-2 sp, sk 3 dc, (3 dc, ch 2, 3 dc) in next ch-2 sp (shell made), turn. **Row 4:** 1 sl st in each of 1st 3 dc, (1 sl st, ch 3, 2 dc, ch 2, 3 dc) in next ch-2 sp, sk 3 dc, 1 dc in sp before next dc, sk 3 dc, 1 shell in next ch-2 sp, turn. **Row 5:** 1 sl st in each of 1st 3 dc, (1 sl st, ch 3, 2 dc, ch 2, 3 dc) in next ch-2 sp, sk 3 dc, (1 dc, ch 3, 1 dc) in next dc, sk 3 dc, 1 shell in next ch-2 sp, turn. **Row 6:** 1 sl st in each of 1st 3 dc, (1 sl st, ch 3, 2 dc, ch 2, 3 dc) in next ch-2 sp, ch 1, sk 4 dc, 9 dc in next ch-3 sp, ch 1, sk 4 dc, 1 shell in next ch-2 sp, turn. **Row 7:** 1 sl st in each of 1st 3 dc, (1 sl st, ch 3, 2 dc, ch 2, 3 dc) in next ch-2 sp, ch 1, sk (3 dc, ch-1), 1 dc in each of next 9 dc, ch 1, sk (ch-1, 3 dc) 1 shell in next ch-2 sp, turn. **Row 8:** 1 sl st in each of 1st 3 dc, (1 sl st, ch 3, 2 dc, ch 2, 3 dc) in next ch-2 sp, ch 1, sk (3 dc, ch-1), * insert hk in sp between next 2 dc, yo and draw through, (yo, insert hk in same sp, yo and draw through) twice, yo and draw through 6 lps on hk (puff st made), ch 2, repeat from * 7 times, sk (ch-1, 3 dc), 1 shell in next ch-2 sp, turn. **Rows 9, 10, 11, 12, 13, 14 and 15:** 1 sl st in each of 1st 3 dc, (1 sl st, ch 3, 2 dc, ch 2, 3 dc) in next ch-2 sp, ch 1, sk (3 dc, ch-1), (1 puff st, ch 2) in each ch-2 sp between 2 puff sts of previous row, sk (last puff st, ch-2, 3 dc), 1 shell in next ch-2 sp, turn—1 less puff st on each row. **Row 16:** 1 sl st in each of 1st 3 dc, (1 sl st, ch 3, 2 dc, ch 2, 3 dc) in next ch-2 sp, sk (3 dc, ch-1, 1 puff st, ch-2, 3 dc), 1 shell in next ch-2 sp, turn. **Row 17:** 1 sl st in each of 1st 3 dc, (1 sl st, ch 3, 2 dc) in next ch-2 sp, sk 6 dc, 3 dc in next ch-2 sp. F.O.

(M-3)

Ch 4, j with sl st to form a ring. **Rnd 1:** * 1 sc in center of ring, ch 3, repeat from * 5 times, j with sl st to 1st sc—6 ch-3 sps made. **Rnd 2:** * 1 sc in next ch-3 sp, (ch 1, 1 dc in same ch-3 sp) twice, ch 1, 1 sc in same ch-3 sp, repeat from * 5 times, j with sl st to 1st sc, turn—6 petals made. **Rnd 3:** With wrong side facing, 1 sc around base of 1st sc of rnd 1, * ch 5, 1 sc around base of next sc of rnd 1, repeat from * 4 times, ch 5, j with sl st to 1st sc, turn—6 ch-5 sps made. **Rnd 4:** With right side facing, * 1 sc in next ch-5 sp, (ch 1, 1 dc in same sp) 3 times, ch 1, 1 sc in same sp, repeat from * 5 times, j with sl st to 1st sc, turn—6 petals made. **Rnd 5:** Repeat rnd 3, working around base of sc on rnd 3, turn. **Rnd 6:** With right side facing, * 1 sc in next ch-5 sp, (ch 1, 1 dc in same sp) 5 times, ch 1, 1 sc in same sp, repeat from * 5 times, j with sl st to 1st sc, turn. **Rnd 7:** Repeat rnd 3, working around base of sc on rnd 5, turn. **Rnd 8:** With right side facing, * 1 sc in next ch-5 sp, (ch 1, 1 dc in same sp) 7 times, ch 1, 1 sc in same sp, repeat from * 5 times, j with sl st to 1st sc. F.O.

(M-4)

Ch 10, j with sl st to form a ring. **Rnd 1:** Ch 3, 4 dc in center of ring, take lp off hk, insert hk in 3rd ch of starting ch-3, draw lp of 4th dc through, * ch 3, 5 dc in center of ring, take lp off hk, insert hk in 1st dc of 5-dc group, draw lp of 5th dc through (popcorn made), repeat from * 6 times, ch 2, j with sl st to top of 1st popcorn—8 popcorns made. **Rnds 2 and 4:** (1 sl st, ch 6, 1 dc) in next ch-3 sp, * ch 3, (1 dc, ch 3, 1 dc) in next ch-3 sp, repeat from * around, ch 3, j with sl st to 3rd ch of starting ch-6. **Rnds 3 and 5:** (1 sl st, ch 3, 4 dc) in next ch-3 sp, take lp off hk, insert hk in 3rd ch of starting ch-3, draw lp of 4th dc through, * ch 3, 1 popcorn in next ch-3 sp, repeat from * around, ch 3, j with sl st to top of 1st popcorn. **Rnd 6:** 1 sl st in next ch-3 sp, * ch 8, sk next ch-3 sp, 1 sc in next ch-3 sp, repeat from

* around, ch 8, j with sl st to starting sl st. **Rnd 7:** Ch 3, * (1 popcorn, ch 2) 3 times in each of next 2 ch-8 sps, 8 tr in each of next 2 ch-8 sps, ch 2, repeat from * around, j with sl st to top of 1st popcorn. **Rnd 8:** (1 sl st, ch 3, 1 popcorn) in next ch-2 sp, * (ch 2, 1 popcorn in next ch-2 sp) 4 times, ch 5, sk 1 popcorn, 1 sc in next tr, (ch 5, sk 1 tr, 1 sc in next tr) twice, ch 5, sk 1 tr, 1 tr in each of next 4 tr, (ch 5, sk 1 tr, 1 sc in next tr) 3 times, ch 5, sk 1 popcorn, 1 popcorn in next ch-2 sp, repeat from * around and end ch 5, j with sl st to top of 1st popcorn. **Rnd 9:** (1 sl st, ch 3, 1 popcorn) in next ch-2 sp, * (ch 2, 1 popcorn in next ch-2 sp) 3 times, sk 1 popcorn, (ch 5, 1 sc in next ch-5 sp) 3 times, ch 5, sk next ch-5 sp, 1 tr in next tr, (ch 2, 1 tr in next tr) 3 times, ch 5, sk next ch-5 sp, 1 sc in next ch-5 sp, (ch 5, 1 sc in next ch-5 sp) twice, ch 5, sk 1 popcorn, 1 popcorn in next ch-2 sp, repeat from * around and end ch 5, j with sl st to top of 1st popcorn. **Rnd 10:** (1 sl st, ch 3, 1 popcorn) in next ch-2 sp, * (ch 2, 1 popcorn in next ch-2 sp) twice, sk 1 popcorn, (ch 5, 1 sc in next ch-5 sp) 3 times, ch 5, sk next ch-5 sp, 2 dc in next tr, (ch 3, 2 dc in next tr) 3 times, ch 5, sk next ch-5 sp, 1 sc in next ch-5 sp, (ch 5, 1 sc in next ch-5 sp) twice, ch 5, sk 1 popcorn, 1 popcorn in next ch-2 sp, repeat from * around and end ch 5, j with sl st to top of 1st popcorn. **Rnd 11:** (1 sl st, ch 3, 1 popcorn) in next ch-2 sp, * ch 2, 1 popcorn in next ch-2 sp, sk 1 popcorn, (ch 5, 1 sc in next ch-5 sp) 3 times, ch 5, sk next ch-5 sp, (1 dc in each of next 2 dc, ch 4) twice, 1 popcorn in next ch-3 sp, (ch 4, 1 dc in each of next 2 dc) twice, ch 5, sk next ch-5 sp, 1 sc in next ch-5 sp, (ch 5, 1 sc in next ch-5 sp) twice, ch 5, sk 1 popcorn, 1 popcorn in next ch-2 sp, repeat from * around and end ch 5, j with sl st to top of 1st popcorn. **Rnd 12:** (1 sl st, ch 3, 1 popcorn) in next ch-2 sp, * sk 1 popcorn, (ch 5, 1 sc in next ch-5 sp) 3 times, ch 5, sk next ch-5 sp, (1 dc in each of next 2 dc, ch 4) twice, 1 popcorn in next ch-4 sp, ch 2, sk 1 popcorn, 1 popcorn in next ch-4 sp, (ch 4, 1 dc in each of next 2 dc) twice, ch 5, sk next ch-5 sp, 1 sc in next ch-5 sp, (ch 5, 1 sc in next

ch-5 sp) twice, ch 5, sk 1 popcorn, 1 popcorn in next ch-2 sp, repeat from * around and end ch 5, j with sl st to top of 1st popcorn. **Rnd 13:** (1 sl st, 1 sc) in next ch-5 sp, ch 5, 1 sc in next ch-5 sp, * ch 7, 1 sc in next ch-5 sp, ch 5, sk next ch-5 sp, (1 dc in each of next 2 dc, ch 4) twice, 1 popcorn in next ch-4 sp, ch 2, 1 popcorn in next ch-2 sp, ch 2, 1 popcorn in next ch-4 sp, (ch 4, 1 dc in each of next 2 dc) twice, ch 5, sk next ch-5 sp, 1 sc in next ch-5 sp, ch 7, 1 sc in next ch-5 sp, (ch 5, 1 sc in next ch-5 sp) 3 times, repeat from * around and end ch 5, j with sl st to 1st sc. F.O.

(M-5)

Ch 6, j with sl st to form a ring. **Rnd 1:** Ch 3, (3 dc in center of ring, ch 1) 3 times, 2 dc in center of ring, j with sl st to 2nd ch of starting ch-3. **Rnd 2:** Ch 3, 3 dc in 1st ch-1 sp (last ch of starting ch-3 of previous rnd), ch 1, * (3 dc, ch 1, 3 dc) in next ch-1 sp, ch 1, repeat from * twice and end 2 dc in starting sp, j with sl st to 2nd ch of starting ch-3. **Rnd 3:** Ch 3, 3 dc in 1st ch-1 sp, ch 1, * 3 dc in next ch-1 sp, ch 1, (3 dc, ch 1, 3 dc) in next ch-1 sp (corner), ch 1, repeat from * twice and end 3 dc in next ch-1 sp, ch 1, 2 dc in starting sp, j with sl st to 2nd ch of starting ch-3. **Rnd 4:** Ch 3, 3 dc in 1st ch-1 sp, ch 1, * (3 dc in next ch-1 sp, ch 1) twice, (3 dc, ch 1, 3 dc) in next corner ch-1 sp, ch 1, repeat from * twice and end (3 dc in next ch-1 sp, ch 1) twice, 2 dc in starting sp, j with sl st to 2nd ch of starting ch-3. **Rnd 5:** Ch 3, 3 dc in 1st ch-1 sp, ch 1, * (3 dc in next ch-1 sp, ch 1) 3 times, (3 dc, ch 1, 3 dc) in next corner ch-1 sp, ch 1, repeat from * twice and end (3 dc in next ch-1 sp, ch 1) 3 times, 2 dc in starting sp, j with sl st to 2nd ch of starting ch-3. F.O.

(M-6)

Ch 5, j with sl st to form a ring. **Rnd 1:** Ch 6 (counts as 1 dc and ch 3), * 1 dc in center of ring, ch 3, repeat from * 6 times, j with sl st to 3rd ch of starting ch-6 —8 dc made. **Rnd 2:** Ch 3 (counts as 1 dc), * 4 dc in next ch-3 sp, 1 dc in next dc, repeat from * around and end 4 dc in last ch-3 sp, j with sl st to 3rd ch of starting ch-3 —40 dc made. **Rnd 3:** * Ch 6, 1 sc in 2nd ch from hk, 1 hdc in next ch, 1 dc in next ch, 1 tr in next ch, 1 dbl tr in last ch, sk 5 dc, 1 long sc in dc 1 row below next dc, repeat from * 7 times. F.O. **Rnd 4:** Attach yarn to turning ch of any star point, ch 4, (1 tr, ch 3, 2 tr) in same ch, * ch 6, 1 sc in turning ch of next star point, ch 6, (2 tr, ch 3, 2 tr) in turning ch of next star point (corner made), repeat from * twice and end ch 6, 1 sc in next star point, ch 6, j with sl st to 4th ch of starting ch-4. **Rnd 5:** Ch 3 (counts as 1 dc), 1 dc in next tr, * 5 dc in ch-3 sp (corner made), 1 dc in each of next 2 tr, 6 dc in next ch-6 sp, 1 dc in next sc, 6 dc in next ch-6 sp, 1 dc in each of next 2 tr, repeat from * twice and end 5 dc in next ch-3 sp (corner made), 1 dc in each of next 2 tr, 6 dc in next ch-6 sp, j with sl st to 3rd ch of starting ch-3—88 dc made. **Rnd 6:** Ch 4, sk 1 dc, (1 dc, ch 3, 1 dc) in next dc (corner made), * (ch 1, sk 1 dc, 1 dc in next dc) 10 times, ch 1, sk 1 dc, (1 dc, ch 3, 1 dc) in next dc, repeat from * twice, and end (ch 1, sk 1 dc, 1 dc in next dc) 8 times, ch 1, j with sl st to 3rd ch of starting ch-4. F.O.

(M-7)

Ch 8, j with sl st to form a ring. **Rnd 1:** Ch 3, (counts as 1 dc), 17 dc in center of ring, j with sl st to 3rd ch of starting ch-3—18 dc made. **Rnd 2:** * Ch 5, sk 2 dc, 1 sc in next dc, repeat from * 5 times. **Rnd 3:** Ch 3 (counts as 1 dc), * 8 dc in next ch-5 sp, repeat from * around, j with sl st to 3rd ch of starting ch-3—49 dc made. **Rnd 4:** Working through back lps of sts only, ch 3 (counts as 1 dc), 1 dc in joining sp, * sk 1 dc, (ch 1, 1 dc in next dc) 5 times, ch 1, sk 1 dc, 2 dc in next dc, repeat from * 4 times and end sk 1 dc, (ch 1, 1 dc in next dc) 5 times, ch 1, j with sl st to 2nd ch of starting ch-3. **Rnd 5:** Ch 6 (counts as 1 dc and ch 3), 1 dc in joining sp (1st corner), sk 1 dc, * (ch 1, 1 dc in next dc) 6 times, ch 1, (1 dc, ch 3, 1 dc) in next dc (corner made), repeat from * 4 times and end sk 1 dc, (ch 1, 1 dc in next dc) 6 times, ch 1, j with sl st to 3rd ch of starting ch-6. **Rnd 6:** Ch 6, 1 dc in joining sp, * (ch 1, sk 1 dc, 1 dc in next ch-1 sp) 7 times, ch 1, (1 dc, ch 3, 1 dc) in corner ch-3 sp, repeat from * 4 times and end (ch 1, sk 1 dc, 1 dc in next ch-1 sp) 7 times, ch 1, j with sl st to 3rd ch of starting ch-6. F.O.

(M-8)

Ch 4, j with sl st to form a ring. **Rnd 1:** Ch 3 (counts as 1 dc), 11 dc in center of ring, j with sl st to 3rd ch of starting ch-3—12 dc made. **Rnd 2:** Ch 3 (counts as 1 dc), 1 dc in joining sp, * 2 dc through back lp only of next dc, repeat from * around, j with sl st to 3rd ch of starting ch-3—24 dc made. **Rnd 3:** Ch 6, * sk 1 dc, 1 dc through back lp only of next dc, ch 3, repeat from * around, j with sl st to 3rd ch of starting ch-6—12 ch-3 sps made. **Rnd 4:** Ch 3, (1 tr, 2 dbl tr, 1 tr, 1 dc) in next ch-3 sp, * (1 dc, 1 tr, 2 dbl tr, 1 tr, 1 dc) in next ch-3 sp, repeat from * around, j with sl st to 3rd ch of starting ch-3. F.O.

(M-9)

Ch 7, j with sl st to form a ring. **Rnd 1:** Ch 5 (counts as 1 dc and ch 2), * 1 dc in center of ring, ch 2, repeat from * 10 times, j with sl st to 3rd ch of starting ch-5—12 dc made. **Rnd 2:** Ch 3, 3 dc in joining sp, take lp off hk, insert hk in 3rd ch of starting ch-3, draw lp of 3rd dc through, * ch 3, 4 dc in next dc, take lp off hk, insert hk in 1st dc of 4-dc group, draw lp of 4th dc through (popcorn made), repeat from * around, ch 3, j with sl st to top of 1st popcorn. **Rnd 3:** Ch 6, 1 dc in 4th ch from hk, * 1 dc in top of next popcorn, ch 4, 1 dc in 4th ch from hk (picot made), repeat from * around, j with sl st to 2nd ch of starting ch-6. **Rnd 4:** Ch 3, 2 dc in joining sp, * ch 5, sk 1 picot, 3 dc in next dc, repeat from * around, ch 5, j with sl st to 3rd ch of starting ch-3. **Rnd 5:** Ch 5, * sk 1 dc, 1 dc in next dc, ch 2, sk 2 ch, 1 dc in next ch, ch 2, sk 2 ch, 1 dc in next dc, ch 2, repeat from * around and end ch 2, sk 2 ch, j with sl st to 3rd ch of starting ch-5. **Rnd 6:** Repeat rnd 2. F.O.

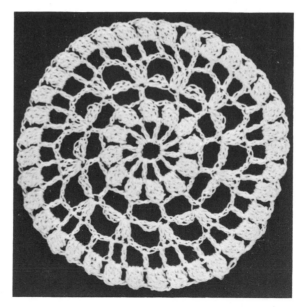

(M-10)

Ch 6, j with sl st to form a ring. **Rnd 1:** Ch 2 (counts as 1 dc), 15 dc in center of ring, j with sl st to 2nd ch of starting ch-2—16 dc made. **Rnd 2:** Ch 4, * 1 dc in next dc, ch 2, repeat from * around, j with sl st to 2nd ch of starting ch-4. **Rnd 3:** Ch 2, (1 dc, ch 3, 2 dc) in next ch-2 sp, * (ch 2, 1 sc in next ch-2 sp) 3 times, ch 2, (2 dc, ch 3, 2 dc) in next ch-2 sp (corner made), repeat from * twice and end (ch 2, 1 sc in next ch-2 sp) 3 times, ch 2, join with sl st to 2nd ch of starting ch-2. **Rnd 4:** 1 sl st in next dc, 1 sl st in next corner sp, ch 2, (1 dc, ch 3, 2 dc) in same corner sp, * (ch 2, 1 sc in next ch-2 sp) 4 times, ch 2, (2 dc, ch 3, 2 dc) in next corner sp, repeat from * twice and end (ch 2, 1 sc in next ch-2 sp) 4 times, ch 2, j with sl st to 2nd ch of starting ch-2. **Rnd 5:** 1 sl st in next dc, 1 sl st in next corner sp, ch 2, (1 dc, ch 4, 2 dc) in same corner sp, * (ch 1, 2 dc in next ch-2 sp) 5 times, ch 1, (2 dc, ch 4,

2 dc) in next corner sp, repeat from * twice and end (ch 1, 2 dc in next ch-2 sp) 5 times, ch 1, j with sl st to 2nd ch of starting ch-2. F.O.

(M-11)

Ch 6, j with sl st to form a ring. **Rnd 1:** Ch 3, 1 dc in center of ring, * ch 2, (yo, insert hk in center of ring, yo and draw through, yo and draw through 2 lps on hk) twice, yo and draw through last 3 lps on hk, repeat from * 6 times and end ch 2, j with sl st to 3rd ch of starting ch-3, turn. **Rnd 2:** Ch 3, 2 dc in 1st ch-2 sp, * ch 2, 3 dc in next ch-2 sp, repeat from * 6 times and end ch 2, j with sl st to 3rd ch of starting ch-3. **Rnd 3:** * 1 sc in next dc, sk 1 dc, ch 1, [yo twice, insert hk in next ch-2 sp, yo and draw through, (yo and draw through 2 lps on hk) twice] 3 times, yo and draw through last 4 lps on hk, ch 1, sk 1 dc, repeat from * 7 times, j with sl st to 1st sc. **Rnd 4:** Ch 1, * sk ch-1, 3 sc in top of next st, sk ch-1, (3 dc, ch 2, 3 dc) in next sc (corner made), sk ch-1, 3 sc in top of next st, sk ch-1, 1 sc in next sc, repeat from * 3 times, j with sl st to 1st sc. **Rnd 5:** Ch 2, work 1 dc in each st and 3 dc in each corner ch-2 sp around, j with sl st to 2nd ch of starting ch-2. F.O.

(M-12)

Ch 6, j with sl st to form a ring. **Rnd 1:** Ch 4, [yo twice, insert hk in center of ring, yo and draw through, (yo and draw through 2 lps on hk) twice] twice, yo and draw through last 3 lps on hk, * ch 5, [yo twice, insert hk in center of ring, yo and draw through, (yo and draw through 2 lps on hk) twice] 3 times, yo and draw through last 4 lps on hk (cluster made), repeat from * 6 times, and end ch 2, 1 dc in top of 1st cluster. **Rnd 2:** Ch 3, 1 sc in same cluster as last dc worked, * ch 5, (1 sc, ch 3, 1 sc) in next ch-5 sp, repeat from * 6 times and end ch 2, 1 dc in 1st dc. **Rnd 3:** Ch 3, 1 sc in same dc as last dc worked, * ch 9, (1 sc, ch 3, 1 sc) in next ch-5 sp, repeat from * 6 times. **Rnd 4:** Ch 6, (1 cluster, ch 5) twice in 5th ch of next ch-9, 1 cluster in same ch, * ch 6, sk 4 ch of next ch-9, (1 sc, ch 5, 1 sc) in next ch, ch 6, sk 4 ch of next ch-9, (1 cluster, ch 5) twice in next ch, 1 cluster in same ch, repeat from * twice and end sk 4 ch of next ch-9, (1 sc, ch 5, 1 sc) in next ch, ch 2, j with sl st to 1st ch of starting ch-6. F.O.

(M-13)

Ch 8, j with sl st to form a ring. **Rnd 1:** Ch 6 (counts as 1 dc and ch 3), * 1 dc in center of ring, ch 3, repeat from * 6 times, j with sl st to 3rd ch of starting ch-6. **Rnd 2:** Ch 2, 3 dc in next ch-3 sp, ch 2, * 4 dc in next ch-3 sp, ch 2, repeat from * around, j with sl st to 2nd ch of starting ch-2. **Rnd 3:** 1 sl st in each of next 3 dc, ch 2, 5 dc in next ch-2 sp, ch 1, * 6 dc in next ch-2 sp, ch 3, 6 dc in next ch-2 sp, ch 1, repeat from * twice and end 6 dc in next ch-2 sp, ch 3, j with sl st to 2nd ch of starting ch-2. **Rnd 4:** Ch 5, sk 2 dc, * 1 sc in sp before next dc, ch 3, 1 sc in next ch-1 sp, ch 3, sk 3 dc, 1 sc in sp before next dc, ch 3, (2 dc, ch 3, 2 dc) in next ch-3 sp, ch 3, sk 3 dc, repeat from * twice and end 1 sc in sp before next dc, ch 3, 1 sc in next ch-1 sp, ch 3, sk 3 dc, 1 sc in sp before next dc, ch 3, (2 dc, ch 3, 1 dc) in next ch-3 sp, j with sl st to 2nd ch of starting ch-5. F.O.

(M-14)

Ch 10, j with sl st to form a ring. **Rnd 1:** Ch 10, * 4 tr in center of ring, ch 7, repeat from * twice and end 3 tr in center of ring, j with sl st to 3rd ch of starting ch-10. **Rnd 2:** Ch 3, * 1 tr in each of next 3 ch, ch 7, sk 1 ch, 1 tr in each of next 3 ch, 1 tr in each of next 4 tr, repeat from * twice and end 1 tr in each of next 3 ch, ch 7, sk 1 ch, 1 tr in each of next 3 ch, 1 tr in each of next 3 tr, j with sl st to 3rd ch of starting ch-3. **Rnd 3:** Ch 3, * 1 tr in each of next 3 tr, 1 tr in each of next 3 ch, ch 7, sk 1 ch, 1 tr in each of next 3 ch, 1 tr in each of next 7 tr, repeat from * twice and end 1 tr in each of next 3 tr, 1 tr in each of next 3 ch, ch 7, sk 1 ch, 1 tr in each of next 3 ch, 1 tr in each of next 6 tr, j with sl st to 3rd ch of starting ch-3. F.O.

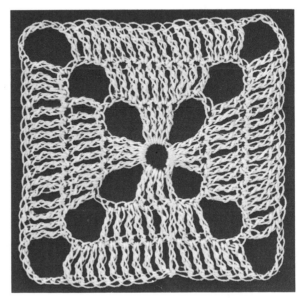

(M-15)

Rnd 1: Ch 5, 1 tr in 5th ch from hk, * ch 4, [yo twice, insert hk in same ch, yo and draw through, (yo and draw through 2 lps on hk) twice] twice, yo and draw through last 3 lps on hk (2-tr cluster made), repeat from * 6 times and end ch 4, j with sl st to 4th ch of 1st ch-5—8 ch-4 sps made.
Rnd 2: Sl st in next ch-4 sp, ch 4, 1 2-tr cluster in same ch-4 sp, ch 4, [yo twice, insert hk in same ch-4 sp, yo and draw through, (yo and draw through 2 lps on hk) twice] 3 times, yo and draw through last 4 lps on hk (3-tr cluster made), * ch 11, sk next ch-4 sp, (1 3-tr cluster, ch 4, 1 3-tr cluster) in next ch-4 sp, repeat from * twice and end ch 11, j with sl st to top of 1st 2-tr cluster. **Rnd 3:** Sl st in next ch-4 sp, ch 4, 1 dc in same ch-4 sp, * ch 6, 15 sc in next ch-11 sp, ch 6, (1 dc, ch 1, 1 dc) in next ch-4 sp, repeat from * twice and end ch 6, 15 sc in next ch-11 sp, ch 6, j with sl st to 3rd ch of starting ch-4. F.O.

(M-16)

Ch 5, j with sl st to form a ring. **Rnd 1:** Ch 3, 15 dc in center of ring, j with sl st to 3rd ch of starting ch-3. **Rnd 2:** 1 sc in joining sp, * ch 8, insert hk in 2nd ch from hk, yo and draw through, (insert hk in next ch, yo and draw through) 6 times, yo and draw through 8 lps on hk, ch 1 (shell made), sk 1 dc, 1 sc in next dc, repeat from * 6 times and end 1 shell, sk 1 dc, j with sl st to 1st sc—8 shells made. F.O. **Rnd 3:** Attach yarn in sp between 4th and 5th lps of any shell, ch 1, 1 sc in same sp, * ch 7, 1 sc in sp between 4th and 5th lps of next shell, ch 4, 1 sc in sp between 4th and 5th lps of next shell, repeat from * twice and end ch 7, 1 sc in sp between 4th and 5th lps of next shell, ch 4, j with sl st to 1st sc. **Rnd 4:** Ch 1, 1 sc in joining sp, * 1 sc in each of next 3 ch, 3 sc in next ch (corner made), 1 sc in each of next 3 ch, 1 sc in next sc, 1 sc in each of next 4 ch, 1 sc in next sc, repeat from * twice and end 1 sc in each of next 3 ch, 3 sc in next ch, 1 sc in each of next 3 ch, 1 sc in next sc,

1 sc in each of next 4 ch, j with sl st to 1st sc.
Rnd 5: 1 sc in each sc and 3 sc in each center
corner sc around. F.O.

(M-17)
Ch 6, j with sl st to form a ring. **Rnd 1:** Ch 4,
23 tr in center of ring, j with sl st to 4th ch of
starting ch-4. **Rnd 2:** Ch 5, (yo, insert hk
horizontally from right to left under ch-4 of
previous rnd, yo and draw up a long lp) 5 times,
yo and draw through 11 lps on hk, ch 1, * sk 1 tr,
(2 dc, 1 tr, 2 dc) in next tr, sk 1 tr, (yo, insert hk
horizontally from right to left under next tr, yo
and draw up a long lp) 5 times, yo and draw
through 11 lps on hk, ch 1 (puff st made), repeat
from * around and end sk 1 tr, (2 dc, 1 tr, 2 dc) in
next tr, sk 1 tr, j with sl st to top of 1st puff st—6
puff sts made. **Rnd 3:** * 1 sc in each of next 2 dc,
3 sc in next tr (corner made), 1 sc in each of next
2 dc, 1 sc in top of next puff st, repeat from
* around, j with sl st to 1st sc. F.O.

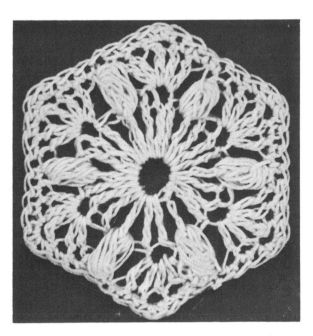

(M-18)
Ch 7, j with sl st to form a ring. **Rnd 1:** Ch 5,
* 1 hdc in center of ring, ch 2, repeat from * 7
times, j with sl st to 3rd ch of starting ch-5.
Rnd 2: Ch 3, 1 hdc in joining sp, * ch 3, 2 hdc in
next hdc, repeat from * around and end ch 3, j
with sl st to 3rd ch of starting ch-3. **Rnd 3:** 1 sl st
in next hdc, 1 sl st in next ch-3 sp, * ch 7, 1 sc in
next ch-3 sp, repeat from * around and end ch 7,
j with sl st to starting ch-3 sp. **Rnd 4:** 1 sl st in
next ch-7 sp, ch 3, 4 hdc in same sp, * ch 3,
5 hdc in next ch-7 sp, repeat from * around and
end ch 3, j with sl st to 3rd ch of starting ch-3.
Rnd 5: Ch 3, 1 hdc in each of next 2 hdc, * ch 3,
sk 2 hdc, 4 hdc in next ch-3 sp, 1 hdc in each of
next 3 hdc, repeat from * around and end ch 3,
sk 2 hdc, 4 hdc in next ch-3 sp, j with sl st to
3rd ch of starting ch-3. **Rnd 6:** Ch 6, * sk 2 hdc,
4 hdc in next ch-3 sp, 1 hdc in each of next
5 hdc, ch 3, repeat from * around and end

sk 2 hdc, 4 hdc in next ch-3 sp, 1 hdc in each of next 4 hdc, j with sl st to 3rd ch of starting ch-6. **Rnd 7:** 1 sl st in next ch-3 sp, ch 3, 3 hdc in same sp, * 1 hdc in each of next 7 hdc, ch 3, sk 2 hdc, 4 hdc in next ch-3 sp, repeat from * around and end 1 hdc in each of next 7 hdc, ch 3, sk 2 hdc, j with sl st to 3rd ch of starting ch-3. **Rnd 8:** Ch 3, 1 hdc in each of next 8 hdc, * ch 3, sk 2 hdc, 4 hdc in next ch-3 sp, 1 hdc in each of next 9 hdc, repeat from * around and end ch 3, sk 2 hdc, 4 hdc in next ch-3 sp, j with sl st to 3rd ch of starting ch-3. **Rnd 9:** Ch 3, 1 hdc in each of next 6 hdc, * ch 3, sk 2 hdc, 4 hdc in next ch-3 sp, 1 hdc in each of next 11 hdc, repeat from * around and end ch 3, sk 2 hdc, 4 hdc in next ch-3 sp, 1 hdc in each of next 4 hdc, j with sl st to 3rd ch of starting ch-3. **Rnd 10:** Ch 3, 1 hdc in each of next 4 hdc, * ch 3, sk 2 hdc, 1 hdc in next ch-3 sp, ch 3, 1 hdc in each of next 13 hdc, repeat from * around and end ch 3, sk 2 hdc, 1 hdc in next ch-3 sp, ch 3, 1 hdc in each of next 8 hdc, j with sl st to 3rd ch of starting ch-3. F.O. **Rnd 11:** Attach yarn to 1st hdc of any hdc-group, ch 3, 1 hdc in each of next 10 hdc, * ch 4, sk 2 hdc, 1 sc in next ch-3 sp, 1 sc in next hdc, 1 sc in next ch-3 sp, ch 4, 1 hdc in each of next 11 hdc, repeat from * around and end ch 4, sk 2 hdc, 1 sc in next ch-3 sp, 1 sc in next hdc, 1 sc in next ch-3 sp, ch 4, j with sl st to 3rd ch of starting ch-3. **Rnd 12:** Ch 3, 1 hdc in each of next 8 hdc, * ch 6, 1 hdc in each of next 3 sc, ch 6, 1 hdc in each of next 9 hdc, repeat from * around and end ch 6, 1 hdc in each of next 3 sc, ch 6, j with sl st to 3rd ch of starting ch-3. **Rnd 13:** Ch 3, 1 hdc in each of next 6 hdc, * ch 5, 1 hdc in next ch-6 sp, ch 5, sk 1 hdc, 1 sc in next hdc, ch 5, sk 1 hdc, 1 hdc in next ch-6 sp, ch 5, 1 hdc in each of next 7 hdc, repeat from * around and end ch 5, 1 hdc in next ch-6 sp, ch 5, sk 1 hdc, 1 dc in next hdc, ch 5, sk 1 hdc, 1 hdc in next ch-6 sp, ch 5, j with sl st to 3rd ch of starting ch-3. **Rnd 14:** Ch 3, 1 hdc in each of next 4 hdc, * ch 5, 1 sc in next ch-5 sp, 1 sc in next hdc, 1 sc in next ch-5 sp, ch 6, 1 sc in next ch-5 sp, 1 sc in next hdc, 1 sc in next ch-5 sp,

ch 5, 1 hdc in each of next 5 hdc, repeat from
* around and end ch 5, 1 sc in next ch-5 sp, 1 sc
in next hdc, 1 sc in next ch-5 sp, ch 6, 1 sc in
next ch-5 sp, 1 sc in next hdc, 1 sc in next
ch-5 sp, ch 5, j with sl st to 3rd ch of starting
ch-3. **Rnd 15:** Ch 3, 1 hdc in next 2 hdc, * ch 6,
1 hdc in each of next 3 sc, ch 5, 1 sc in next
ch-6 sp, ch 5, 1 hdc in each of next 3 sc, ch 6,
1 hdc in each of next 3 hdc, repeat from * around
and end ch 6, 1 hdc in each of next 3 sc, ch 5,
1 sc in next ch-6 sp, ch 5, 1 hdc in each of next
3 sc, ch 6, j with sl st to 3rd ch of starting ch-3.
Rnd 16: Ch 3, 1 hdc in next hdc, * ch 5, 1 sc in
next ch-6 sp, ch 5, sk 1 hdc, 1 sc in next hdc,
ch 5, 1 hdc in next sc, ch 5, sk 1 hdc, 1 sc in next
hdc, ch 5, 1 sc in next ch-6 sp, ch 5, (yo, insert hk
in next hdc, yo and draw through, yo and draw
through 2 lps on hk) twice, yo and draw through
last 3 lps on hk, repeat from * around and end
ch 5, 1 sc in next ch-6 sp, ch 5, sk 1 hdc, 1 sc in
next hdc, ch 5, 1 hdc in next sc, ch 5, sk 1 hdc,
1 sc in next hdc, ch 5, 1 sc in next ch-6 sp, ch 5, j
with sl st to 3rd ch of starting ch-3. F.O.

(M-19)
Rnd 1: Ch 2, 8 sc in 2nd ch from hk, j with sl st
to 1st sc. **Rnd 2:** Ch 5, sk 1 sc, 1 sc in next sc,
(ch 4, sk 1 sc, 1 sc in next sc) twice, ch 4, j with sl
st to 1st ch of starting ch-5. **Rnd 3:** 1 sl st in next
ch-4 sp, ch 4, 6 tr in next ch-4 sp, (ch 2, 7 tr in
next ch-4 sp) 3 times, ch 2, j with sl st to 4th ch
of starting ch-4. **Rnd 4:** Ch 3, 1 dc in joining sp,
(1 dc in each of next 2 tr, 2 dc in next tr) twice,
ch 3, * (2 dc in next tr, 1 dc in each of next 2 tr)
twice, 2 dc in next tr, ch 3, repeat from * around,
j with sl st to 3rd ch of starting ch-3. **Rnd 5:** Ch 4,
1 tr in joining sp, 1 tr in next dc, 2 tr in next dc,
1 tr in next dc, 4 tr in each of next 2 dc, (1 tr in
next dc, 2 tr in next dc) twice, ch 2, turn. **Rnd 6:**
1 dc in next tr, 1 tr in each of next 4 tr, 1 dc in
next tr, ch 2, sk 2 tr, 1 dc in next tr, 1 tr in each
of next 4 tr, 1 dc in next tr, ch 2, sk 4 tr, 1 sl st in
next tr. F.O. With right side facing, work rnds 5
and 6 over each of remaining 3 groups of dc's.

(M-20)

Ch 6, j with sl st to form a ring. **Rnd 1:** Ch 2, (yo, insert hk in center of ring, yo and draw through, yo and draw through 1 lp on hk, yo and draw through 2 lps on hk) twice, yo and draw through last 3 lps on hk, * ch 5, (yo, insert hk in center of ring, yo and draw through, yo and draw through 1 lp on hk, yo and draw through 2 lps on hk) 3 times, yo and draw through last 4 lps on hk (cluster made), ch 2, 1 cluster, repeat from * twice and end ch 5, 1 cluster, ch 2, j with sl st to 2nd ch of starting ch-2. **Rnd 2:** 1 sl st in next st, 1 sl st in next ch-5 sp, ch 2, (yo, insert hk in same ch-5 sp, yo and draw through, yo and draw through 1 lp on hk, yo and draw through 2 lps on hk) twice, yo and draw through last 3 lps on hk, * ch 2, 1 cluster in same ch-5 sp, ch 2, 3 dc in next ch-2 sp, ch 2, 1 cluster in next ch-5 sp, repeat from * twice and end ch 2, 1 cluster in same ch-5 sp, ch 2, 3 dc in next ch-2 sp, ch 2, j with sl st to 2nd ch of starting ch-2. **Rnds 3, 4, and 5:** 1 sl st in next st, 1 sl st in next ch-2 sp, ch 2, (yo, insert hk in same ch-5 sp, yo and draw through, yo and draw through 1 lp on hk, yo and draw through 2 lps on hk) twice, yo and draw through last 3 lps on hk, * ch 2, 1 cluster in same ch-2 sp, ch 2, 2 dc in next ch-2 sp, 1 dc in each dc of next dc-group, 2 dc in next ch-2 sp, ch 2, 1 cluster in next ch-2 sp, repeat from * twice and end ch 2, 1 cluster in same ch-2 sp, ch 2, 2 dc in next ch-2 sp, 1 dc in each dc of next dc-group, 2 dc in next ch-2 sp, ch 2, j with sl st to 2nd ch of starting ch-2. F.O.

(M-21)

Ch 6, j with sl st to form a ring. **Rnd 1:** Ch 1,
12 sc in center of ring, j with sl st to 1st sc.
Rnd 2: Ch 4, 2 tr in joining sp, * ch 3, sk 1 sc, 3 tr
in next sc, repeat from * around and end ch 3, j
with sl st to 4th ch of starting ch-4. **Rnd 3:** Ch 4,
1 tr in joining sp, * 1 tr in next tr, 2 tr in next tr,
ch 6, 1 sc in 4th ch from hk (picot made), ch 2,
2 tr in next tr, repeat from * around and end 1 tr
in next tr, 2 tr in next tr, 1 picot, ch 2, j with sl st
to 4th ch of starting ch-4. **Rnd 4:** Ch 4, 1 tr in
joining sp, * 1 tr in each of next 3 tr, 2 tr in next
tr, ch 9, sk 1 picot, 2 tr in next tr, repeat from
* around and end 1 tr in each of next 3 tr, 2 tr in
next tr, ch 9, sk 1 picot, j with sl st to 4th ch of
starting ch-4. **Rnd 5:** Ch 4, yo twice, insert hk in
joining sp, yo and draw through, (yo and draw
through 2 lps on hk) twice, [yo twice, insert hk in
next tr, yo and draw through, (yo and draw
through 2 lps on hk) twice] twice, yo and draw
through last 4 lps on hk, * ch 5, 1 sl st in next tr,
ch 5, [yo twice, insert hk in next tr, yo and draw
through, (yo and draw through 2 lps on hk) twice]
3 times, yo twice, insert hk in same tr, yo and
draw through, (yo and draw through 2 lps on hk)
twice, yo and draw through last 5 lps on hk (left
cluster made), ch 6, sk 4 ch, (1 sc, ch 4, 1 sc) in
next ch, ch 6, sk 4 ch, yo twice, insert hk in next
tr, yo and draw through, (yo and draw through
2 lps on hk) twice, yo twice, insert hk in same tr,
yo and draw through, (yo and draw through 2 lps
on hk) twice, [yo twice, insert hk in next tr, yo
and draw through, (yo and draw through 2 lps on
hk) twice] twice, yo and draw through last 5 lps
on hk, repeat from * 4 times and end ch 5, 1 sl st
in next tr, ch 5, 1 left cluster over next 3 tr, ch 6,
sk 4 ch, (1 sc, ch 4, 1 sc) in next ch, ch 6, sk 4 ch,
j with sl st to top of 1st cluster. F.O.

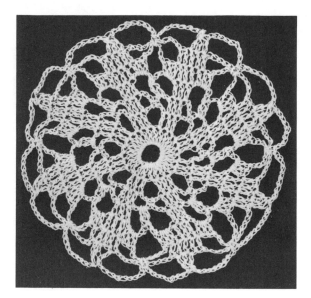

(M-22)

Ch 10, j with sl st to form a ring. **Rnd 1:** Ch 3, 23 dc in center of ring, j with sl st to 3rd ch of starting ch-3. **Rnd 2:** Ch 3, 1 dc in each of next 2 dc, * ch 5, 1 dc in each of next 3 dc, repeat from * around and end ch 5, j with sl st to 3rd ch of starting ch-3. **Rnd 3:** Ch 3, 1 dc in each of next 2 dc, * ch 3, 1 sc in next ch-5 sp, ch 3, 1 dc in each of next 3 dc, repeat from * around and end ch 3, 1 sc in next ch-5 sp, ch 3, j with sl st to 3rd ch of starting ch-3. **Rnd 4:** Ch 3, 1 dc in each of next 2 dc, * ch 5, (yo, insert hk in next ch-3 sp, yo and draw through, yo and draw through 2 lps on hk) twice, yo and draw through last 3 lps on hk, ch 5, 1 dc in each of next 3 dc, repeat from * around and end ch 5, (yo, insert hk in next ch-3 sp, yo and draw through, yo and draw through 2 lps on hk) twice, yo and draw through last 3 lps on hk, ch 5, j with sl st to 3rd ch of starting ch-3. **Rnd 5:** Ch 3, 1 dc in each of next 2 dc, 3 dc in next ch-5 sp, * ch 9, 3 dc in next ch-5 sp, 1 dc in each of next 3 dc, 3 dc in next ch-5 sp, repeat from * around and end ch 9, 3 dc in next ch-5 sp, j with sl st to 3rd ch of starting ch-3. **Rnd 6:** Ch 3, 1 dc in each of next 3 dc, * ch 11, sk (2 dc, ch-9, 2 dc), 1 dc in each of next 5 dc, repeat from * around and end ch 11, sk (2 dc, ch-9, 2 dc), 1 dc in next dc, j with sl st to 3rd ch of starting ch-3. **Rnd 7:** Ch 3, (yo, insert hk in next dc, yo and draw through, yo and draw through 2 lps on hk) twice, yo and draw through last 3 lps on hk, * ch 9, sk 1 dc, 1 sc in ch-9 sp of rnd 5, ch 9, sk 1 dc, (yo, insert hk in next dc, yo and draw through, yo and draw through 2 lps on hk) 3 times, yo and draw through last 4 lps on hk, repeat from * around and end ch 9, sk 1 dc, 1 sc in ch-9 sp of rnd 5, ch 9, j with sl st to top of 1st st. F.O.

(M-23)

Ch 8, j with sl st to form a ring. **Rnd 1:** Ch 1, 24 sc in center of ring, j with sl st to 1st sc.

Rnd 2: Ch 4, [yo twice, insert hk in joining sp, yo and draw through, (yo and draw through 2 lps on hk) twice] twice, yo and draw through last 3 lps on hk (2-tr cluster made), ch 5, [yo twice, insert hk in same sp, yo and draw through, (yo and draw through 2 lps on hk) twice] 3 times, yo and draw through last 4 lps on hk (3-tr cluster made), * sk 3 sc, (1 3-tr cluster, ch 5, 1 3-tr cluster) in next sc, repeat from * around and end sk 3 sc, j with sl st to top of 1st cluster. **Rnd 3:** Ch 4, 1 2-tr cluster in joining sp, * ch 4, 1 2-tr cluster in top of cluster just made, 1 3-tr cluster in top of next cluster of rnd 2, ch 5, 1 3-tr cluster in top of next cluster of rnd 2, repeat from * around and end ch 4, 1 2-tr cluster in top of cluster just made, 1 3-tr cluster in top of next cluster of rnd 2, ch 5, j with sl st to top of 1st cluster. F.O.

(M-24)

Ch 6, j with sl st to form a ring. **Rnd 1:** Ch 1, 12 sc in center of ring, j with sl st to 1st sc.

Rnd 2: Ch 1, * 1 sc in next sc, 2 sc in next sc, repeat from * around, j with sl st to 1st sc—18 sc made. **Rnd 3:** Ch 1, * 1 sc in each of next 2 sc, 2 sc in next sc, repeat from * around, j with sl st to 1st sc—24 sc made. **Rnd 4:** Ch 1, * 1 sc in each of next 3 sc, 2 sc in next sc, repeat from * around, j with sl st to 1st sc—30 sc made.

Rnd 5: Ch 1, * 1 sc in each of next 4 sc, 2 sc in next sc, repeat from * around, j with sl st to 1st sc —36 sc made. **Rnd 6:** Ch 1, * 1 sc in each of next 5 sc, 2 sc in next sc, repeat from * around, j with sl st to 1st sc—42 sc made. **Rnd 7:** Ch 1, * 1 sc in each of next 6 sc, 2 sc in next sc, repeat from * around, j with sl st to 1st sc—48 sc made.

Rnd 8: Ch 4, [yo twice, insert hk in joining sp, yo and draw through, (yo and draw through 2 lps on hk) twice] twice, yo and draw through last 3 lps on hk (2-tr cluster made), * ch 5, sk 2 sc, [yo twice, insert hk in next sc, yo and draw through,

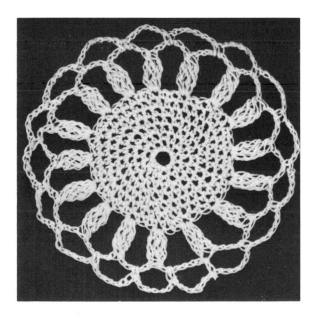

(yo and draw through 2 lps on hk) twice] 3 times, yo and draw through last 4 lps on hk (3-tr cluster made), repeat from * around, and end ch 5, j with sl st to top of 1st cluster. **Rnd 9:** Ch 7, * 1 sc in next ch-5 sp, ch 6, repeat from * around and end 1 sc in last ch-5 sp, j with sl st to 1st ch of starting ch-7. F.O.

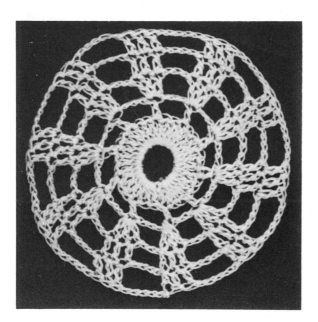

(M-25)
Ch 10, j with sl st to form a ring. **Rnd 1:** Ch 2, 30 dc in center of ring, j with sl st to 1st dc. **Rnd 2:** Ch 5, * sk 2 dc, 1 dc in next dc, ch 3, repeat from * 8 times, j with sl st to 2nd ch of starting ch-5. **Rnd 3:** Ch 2, 2 dc in joining sp, * ch 3, 3 dc in next dc, repeat from * around and end ch 3, j with sl st to 2nd ch of starting ch-2. **Rnd 4:** Ch 2, 1 dc in each of next 2 dc, * ch 4, 1 dc in each of next 3 dc, repeat from * around and end ch 4, j with sl st to 2nd ch of starting ch-2. **Rnd 5:** Ch 2, 1 dc in each of next 2 dc, * ch 5, 1 dc in each of next 3 dc, repeat from * around and end ch 5, j with sl st to 2nd ch of starting ch-2. F.O.

Joinings

(MJ–1)
1st Motif: With right side of motif facing, attach yarn to sp between any 2 dbl tr, * ch 7, 1 sc in sp between next 2 dbl tr, repeat from * around and end 1 sc in joining sp. F.O. *2nd Motif:* With right side facing, attach yarn to sp between any 2 dbl tr, ch 3, holding 1st and 2nd motifs wrong sides tog, 1 sc in any ch-7 sp of 1st motif, ch 3, 1 sc in sp between next 2 dbl tr on 2nd motif, ch 3, 1 sc in next ch-7 sp on 1st motif, ch 3, 1 sc in sp between next 2 dbl tr on 2nd motif (joining made), * ch 7, 1 sc in sp between next 2 dbl tr on 2nd motif, repeat from * around and end 1 sc in joining sp. F.O. *3rd Motif:* With right side facing,

attach yarn to sp between any 2 dbl tr, ch 3, holding 3rd and 1st motifs wrong sides tog, 1 sc in 2nd ch-7 sp to right of joining on 1st motif, ch 3, 1 sc in sp between next 2 dbl tr on 3rd motif, ch 3, 1 sc in next ch-7 sp to right of joining on 1st motif, ch 3, 1 sc in sp between next 2 dbl tr on 3rd motif (joining made), ch 3, holding 3rd and 2nd motifs wrong sides tog, 1 sc in ch-7 sp next to same joining on 2nd motif, ch 3, 1 sc in sp between next 2 dbl tr on 3rd motif, ch 3, 1 sc in next ch-7 sp on 2nd motif, ch 3, 1 sc in sp between next 2 dbl tr on 3rd motif (2nd joining made), * ch 7, 1 sc in sp between next 2 dbl tr on 3rd motif, repeat from * around and end 1 sc in joining sp. F.O. *4th Motif:* With right side facing, attach yarn to any sp between 2 dbl tr, ch 3, holding 4th and 3rd motifs wrong sides tog, 1 sc in 2nd ch-7 sp to right of joining between 2nd and 3rd motifs, ch 3, 1 sc in sp between next 2 dbl tr on 4th motif, ch 3, 1 sc in next ch-7 sp to right of joining on 3rd motif, ch 3, 1 sc in sp between next 2 dbl tr on 4th motif (joining made), ch 3, holding 4th and 2nd motifs wrong sides tog, 1 sc in ch 7 sp next to same joining on 2nd motif, ch 3, 1 sc in sp between next 2 dbl tr on 4th motif, ch 3, 1 sc in next ch-7 sp on 2nd motif, ch 3, 1 sc in sp between next 2 dbl tr on 4th motif (2nd joining made), * ch 7, 1 sc in sp between next 2 dbl tr on 4th motif, repeat from * around and end 1 sc in joining sp. F.O. Follow this method of joining for as many motifs as required to make the desired size and shape of your finished piece, being sure to join additional motifs in one, two, or three places as necessary.

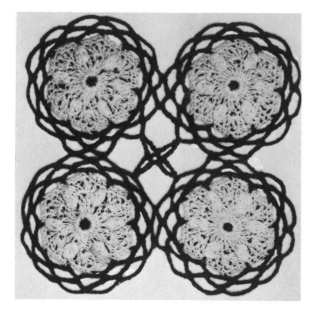

(MJ–2)

1st Motif: **Rnd 1:** With right side facing, attach yarn to 1 sc on any point, * ch 5, sk 3 sc, 1 sc in next sc, repeat from * around and end ch 5, 1 sc in joining sp. **Rnd 2:** 1 sl st in each of next 3 ch, * ch 6, 1 sc in next ch-5 sp, repeat from * around and end ch 6, j with sl st to last sl st. **Rnd 3:** 1 sl st in each of next 3 ch, * ch 7, 1 sc in next ch-6 sp, repeat from * around and end ch 7, j with sl st to last sl st. F.O.—12 ch-7 sps made.

2nd Motif: With right side facing, attach yarn to 1 sc on any point, repeat rnds 1 and 2 of 1st motif. **Rnd 3:** 1 sl st in each of next 3 ch, ch 7, holding 2nd and 1st motifs wrong sides tog and points tog, (1 sc in next ch-6 sp on 2nd motif, ch 3, 1 sc in next ch-7 sp on 1st motif, ch 3) twice, 1 sc in next ch-6 sp on 2nd motif (joining made), * ch 7, 1 sc in next ch-6 sp on 2nd motif, repeat from * around and end ch 7, j with sl st to last sl st. F.O. *3rd Motif:* With right side facing, attach yarn to 1 sc on any point, repeat rnds 1 and 2 of 1st motif. **Rnd 3:** 1 sl st in each of next 3 ch, ch 3, holding 3rd and 1st motifs wrong sides tog and points tog, 1 sc in 3rd ch-7 sp to right of joining on 1st motif, ch 3, 1 sc in next ch-6 sp on 3rd motif, ch 3, 1 sc in 2nd ch-7 sp to right of joining on 1st motif, ch 3, 1 sc in next ch-6 sp on 3rd motif (joining made), * ch 7, 1 sc in next ch-6 sp on 3rd motif, repeat from * around and end ch 7, j with sl st to last sl st. F.O. *4th Motif:* With right side facing, attach yarn to 1 sc on any point, repeat rnds 1 and 2 of 1st motif. **Rnd 3:** 1 sl st in each of next 3 ch, ch 7, 1 sc in next ch-6 sp on 4th motif, ch 3, holding 4th and 3rd motifs wrong sides tog and points tog, 1 sc in 3rd ch-7 sp to right of joining between 3rd and 1st motifs, ch 3, 1 sc in next ch-6 sp on 4th motif, ch 3, 1 sc in 2nd ch-7 sp to right of same joining on 3rd motif, ch 3, 1 sc in next ch-6 sp on 4th motif (joining made), ch 7, 1 sc in next ch-6 sp on 4th motif, ch 3, holding 4th and 2nd motifs wrong sides tog and points tog, 1 sc in 2nd ch-7 sp to left of joining between 2nd and 1st motifs, ch 3, 1 sc in next ch-6 sp on

4th motif, ch 3, 1 sc in 3rd ch-7 sp to left of same joining on 2nd motif, ch 3, 1 sc in next ch-6 sp on 4th motif (2nd joining made), * ch 7, 1 sc in next ch-6 sp on 4th motif, repeat from * around and end ch 7, j with sl st to last sl st. F.O. Follow this method of joining for as many motifs as required to make the desired size and shape of your finished piece, being sure to join additional motifs in one, two or three places as necessary. Work 1 center in any sp between 4 motifs. **Centers:** Ch 4, j with sl st to form a ring, ch 4, 1 sc in free ch-7 sp between joinings on 1 motif, ch 4, sl st in center of ring just made, * ch 4, 1 sc in free ch-7 sp between joinings on next motif, ch 4, sl st in center of ring, repeat from * twice. F.O.

(MJ–3)

1st Motif: **Rnd 1:** With right side facing, attach yarn to any corner sp, ch 3 (counts as 1 dc), 1 dc in same sp, * ch 1, sk 1 cluster, 1 dc in next ch-2 sp, 1 dc in next dc, (ch 1, sk 1 dc, 1 dc in each of next 2 dc) 4 times, ch 1, sk 1 dc, 1 dc in next dc, 1 dc in next ch-2 sp, ch 1, sk 1 cluster, (2 dc, ch 1, 2 dc) in corner sp, repeat from * around and end last repeat 2 dc in same sp as joining, ch 1, j with sl st to 3rd ch of starting ch-3, ch 4, turn. **Rnd 2:** Sk 2 dc, 1 sc in next ch-1 sp, (ch 3, 1 sc in next ch-1 sp) 7 times, * ch 4, sl st in last sc made (corner picot made), (ch 3, 1 sc in next ch-1 sp) 8 times, repeat from * around and end last repeat (ch 3, 1 sc in next ch-1 sp) 7 times, ch 3, j with sl st to 2nd ch of starting ch-4, ch 4, sl st in same ch as last sl st. F.O. *2nd Motif:* With right side facing, attach yarn to any corner sp, repeat rnd 1 of 1st motif. **Rnd 2:** Sk 2 dc, 1 sc in next ch-1 sp, (ch 3, 1 sc in next ch-1 sp) 7 times, holding 2nd and 1st motifs right sides tog, ch 2, sl st in corner picot on 1st motif, ch 2, sl st in last sc made on 2nd motif, (ch 2, sl st in next ch-3 sp on 1st motif, ch 2, 1 sc in next ch-1 sp on 2nd motif) 8 times, ch 2, sl st in corner picot on 1st motif, ch 2, sl st in last sc made on 2nd motif (joining made), (ch 3, 1 sc in next ch-1 sp on 2nd

motif) 8 times, ch 4, sl st in last sc made, (ch 3, 1 sc in next ch-1 sp) 7 times, ch 3, j with sl st to 2nd ch of starting ch-4, sl st in same ch as last sl st. F.O. *3rd Motif:* With right side facing, attach yarn to any corner sp, repeat rnd 1 of 1st motif. **Rnd 2:** Sk 2 dc, 1 sc in next ch-1 sp, (ch 3, 1 sc in next ch-1 sp) 7 times, holding 3rd and 2nd motifs right sides tog, ch 2, sl st in corner picot on 2nd motif, ch 2, sl st in last sc made on 3rd motif, (ch 2, sl st in next ch-3 sp on 2nd motif, ch 2, 1 sc in next ch-1 sp on 3rd motif) 8 times, ch 2, sl st in center of 2 joined corner picots, ch 2, sl st in last sc made on 3rd motif (joining made), (ch 3, 1 sc in next ch-1 sp on 3rd motif) 8 times, ch 4, sl st in last sc made, (ch 3, 1 sc in next ch-1 sp) 7 times, ch 3, j with sl st to 2nd ch of starting ch-4, ch 4, sl st in same ch as last sl st. F.O. *4th Motif:* With right side facing, attach yarn to any corner sp, repeat rnd 1 of 1st motif. **Rnd 2:** Sk 2 dc, 1 sc in next ch-1 sp, (ch 3, 1 sc in next ch-1 sp) 7 times, holding 4th and 3rd motifs right sides tog, ch 2, sl st in corner picot on 3rd motif, ch 2, sl st in last sc made on 4th motif, (ch 2, sl st in next ch-3 sp on 3rd motif, ch 2, 1 sc in next ch-1 sp on 4th motif) 8 times, ch 2, sl st in center of 3 joined corner picots, ch 2, sl st in last sc made on 4th motif (joining made), holding 4th and 1st motifs right sides tog, (ch 2, sl st in next ch-3 sp on 1st motif, ch 2, 1 sc in next ch-1 sp on 4th motif) 8 times, ch 2, sl st in corner picot on 1st motif, ch 2, sl st in last sc made on 4th motif (2nd joining made), (ch 3, 1 sc in next ch-1 sp on 4th motif) 7 times, ch 3, j with sl st to 2nd ch of starting ch-4, ch 4, sl st in same ch as last sl st. F.O. Follow this method of joining for as many motifs as required to make the desired size and shape of your finished piece, being sure to join additional motifs in one, two, or three places as necessary.

11. FRINGES, EDGINGS, AND INSERTIONS

An edging is a type of finishing that is used as a border or as trimming and most times, however it is used, adds embellishment and a beautiful and interesting final touch. A crocheted edging can be worked on almost anything, whether it is a piece of knitted or crocheted work, a manufactured or hand-sewn article of clothing or home decor, or any other thing that you yourself might design with the thought in mind that a special and important part of the finished work will be the edging that is added to it. This final touch can be an easy simple design or a more involved and elegant one, or it can be added with just the knotting of a plain or fancy fringe. The type of edging you choose to use depends, of course, on whatever it is you want to trim, and again on your own good taste and imagination as to how you want to do it.

Some edgings are worked horizontally, others vertically; whichever way they are done, either they can be sewn to whatever it is they are going to trim or, in many instances, particularly when worked horizontally, they can be crocheted right onto the edge where they are to be placed. On crocheted or knitted pieces you can do the edging with a crochet hook, working into only as many stitches as are necessary to achieve a smooth unrippled edge. On fabric perhaps the easier way is to sew your edging onto the material, although another good way of adding a crocheted edge onto a fabric end is to punch a series of evenly spaced holes along the edge of the cloth and then crochet through the holes, counting each hole as though it were a stitch.

While edgings and insertions are both used for trim, they differ in that an edging is used as a border, while an insertion which has the same edge on two sides is set between two pieces of whatever it is that is being trimmed. Placed in this way, it becomes an integral part of the design that is being created. Both types of trim can be worked with crochet cotton and a small hook as ours were made, or with a medium- or heavy-weight yarn and an appropriately-sized larger hook, your choice depending actually on the type of design you are working and the effect you want to achieve.

The beauty of a simple linen tablecloth-and-napkin set can be greatly enhanced with the addition of a lovely hand-crocheted border around the edges, as can a bedspread or coverlet that you've trimmed with an attractive fringe, and a pretty dress becomes even prettier with a lacy edge worked along its hemline. It comes as a bit of a surprise too that this type of crochet work, designed and planned primarily for the purpose of ornamentation and trimming, has also the special added virtue of serving a very functional and practical purpose in that it can frequently be used as an imaginative and decorative way of lengthening things that for one reason or another have become too short. For example, you can make your little girl's slightly outgrown blue velvet party dress 1" or 2" or 3" longer by adding a crocheted edging around the bottom of it, and you can even make it practically a brand-new dress by adding some of that same edging around the neck and sleeve ends; and an inch or two of a metallic-gold crocheted trim worked across the bottom and perhaps up the sides of your elegant damask draperies would make them just long enough to hang right over the new windows they now cover, and would probably make them more stunning than they ever were before.

Designing with insertions can be a lot of fun too, and indeed this type of work offers a fine outlet for any type of creative imagination. Think what an attractive long evening skirt you could make by having strips of black material joined one to the other with crocheted inserts alternated color-wise in bands of brilliant red, strong yellow, and emerald green! There are limitless possibilities such as this for all kinds of original designs, and working with inserts is again like playing the game of putting together the pieces of a jigsaw puzzle, much as we described in our chapter on motifs. We're thinking in terms now of such marvelous things as an afghan crocheted in a series of deep blue squares, in a fairly simple texture, and put together with lacy pale blue inserts; lovely white casement curtains layered in a series of white antique satin strips alternating with white linen crocheted inserts; and a festive stole made up almost entirely of openwork insert strips and joined together with contrast-color crocheted zigzag chains.

We could go on and on with many more ideas, but we feel that perhaps we have already sparked your imagination and that once you've looked at the several photographs of beautiful trimmings that follow here you will be quite ready and eager to start work on some lovely project of your own.

(E-1)

Work 1 row sc along desired edges. Depending on pattern used in piece to be edged, work as many sc as necessary to be sure work lies flat. Always use the same number of sc on parallel sides. For a square corner, work 3 sc in corner st; for a rounded corner, work 1 sc in corner st.

(E-2)

Row 1: Work edging #E-1 along desired edges, ending with a multiple of 3 sts plus 2. **Row 2:** 1 sc in 1st sc, * ch 3, sl st in 3rd ch from hk (picot made), 1 sc in each of next 2 sc, repeat from * across and end 1 sc in last sc. F.O. *Variations:* Use a different number of sc's between picots or a different size picot. To change the size of a picot, ch as many sts as desired, then work a sl st in the ch furthest from hk. If altering this edging, adjust the multiple at end of row 1.

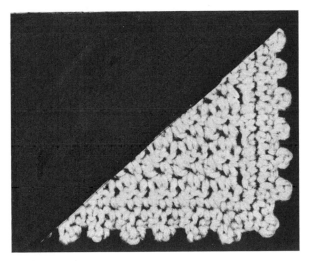

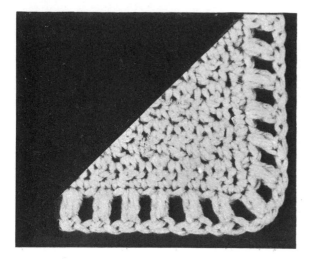

(E-3)

Row 1: Work edging #E-1 along desired edges, ending with a multiple of 2 sts plus 1. **Row 2:** Ch 2, * yo, insert hk in next sc, yo and draw through, yo, insert hk in same sc, yo and draw through, yo and draw through 4 lps on hk, yo and draw through last 2 lps on hk (cluster made), ch 1, sk 1 sc, repeat from * across and end 1 cluster in last sc. F.O. *Variations:* Change the number of ch's between clusters. Always sk the same number of sc as the number you ch. The size of the cluster can also be changed by working the center portion of each cluster (yo, insert hk in same sc, yo and draw through) as many times as desired. In completing a cluster, always yo and draw through 1 less than the number of lps on your hk, then yo and draw through last 2 lps on hk. If altering this edging, adjust the multiple at end of row 1.

(E-4)

Row 1: Work edging #E-1 along desired edges, ending with a multiple of 3 sts. **Row 2:** Ch 5, * sk 2 sc, 1 sc in next sc, ch 4, repeat from * across and end 1 sc in last sc. F.O. *Variations:* Change the number of ch's between sc's, and if desired, change the number of sc's skipped. If altering this edging, adjust the multiple at end of row 1.

(E-5)

Row 1: Work edging #E-1 along desired edges, ending with a multiple of 6 sts plus 1. **Row 2:** Ch 1, * 1 sc in next sc, sk 2 sc, 5 dc in next sc (shell made), sk 2 sc, repeat from * across and end 1 sc in last sc. F.O. *Variations:* Change the number of dc's in each shell, or make the shells with sc's, hdc's or tr's. Adjust the number of sc's you sk to accommodate the type of shell you make, so work lies flat. If altering this edging, adjust the multiple at end of row 1.

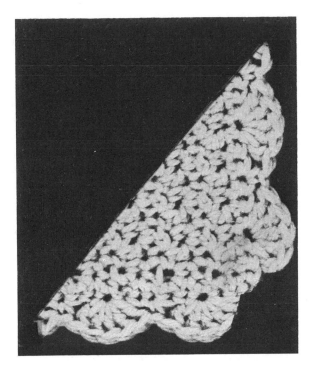

(E-6)

Work edging #E-1 along desired edges. Cut several strands of yarn each to measure twice the desired finished length plus ¼". Holding 3 strands tog, fold them in half, insert hk in 1 st, draw the center fold of the 3 strands through this st forming a lp, draw the 6 ends through the lp just made. Knot 3 strands in this manner through every other st. Trim ends evenly. *Variations:* Change the number of strands you knot through a st, or knot strands through as many sts as desired.

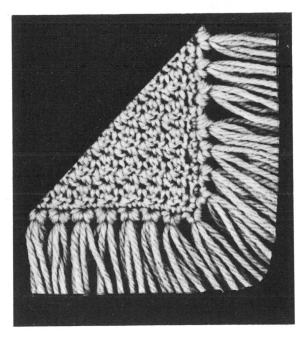

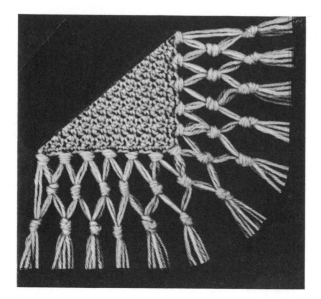

(E-7)

Work edging #E-1 along desired edges. Cut several strands of yarn each to measure twice the desired finished length plus ¼" for each row of knots desired. Work fringe #E-6 along desired edges knotting 4 strands through every 3rd st.

Row 1: Knot 4 strands of 1st fringe to 4 strands of next fringe ¾" below original knot, * knot 4 strands of same fringe to 4 strands of next fringe ¾" below original knot, repeat from * across.

Row 2: Knot loose 4 strands of 1st fringe to 4 strands of next fringe ¾" below last row of knots, * knot 4 strands of same fringe to 4 strands of next fringe ¾" below last row of knots, repeat from * across. Vary in same manner as #E-6, or by having as many rows of knots as desired.

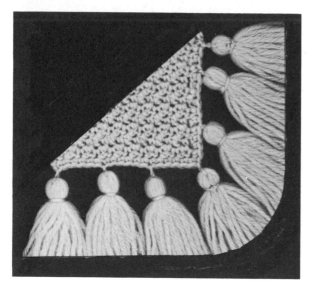

(E-8)

Work edging #E-1 along desired edges. Make 1 tassel for every 6th sc along same edges. **Tassel:** Cut 21 strands of yarn each to measure twice the desired finished length. Cut one 6" length of yarn and tie tightly around center of 20 strands previously cut. Fold strands in half. Take last cut strand and tie tightly around folded strands ¾" down from top. Attach tassel to sc by drawing the top strand through and tying into a knot. Draw ends of knotted strand down through center of tassel. Trim ends evenly. *Variations:* Change the size (number of strands) and/or the length of each tassel, or knot tassels in as many sc as desired.

(E-9)

Work edging #E-1 along desired edges. Make 1 pompon for every 3rd sc along same edges.
Pompon: Cut 20 strands of yarn each to measure twice the desired finished diameter of pompon plus 1″. Cut one 6″ length of yarn and tie tightly around center of strands. Fold strands in half. Trim ends until a ball is formed. Roll ball in palm of hand for fluffiness. Attach pompon to sc by drawing top strand through and tying into a knot. *Variations:* Change the size (number of strands) and/or the length of each pompon, or knot pompons in as many sc as desired.

(E-10)

Work edging #E-1 along desired edges, ch 1, turn. **Row 1:** * Insert hk in next sc, wind yarn over index finger, holding finger 1 ¾″ above work, yo and draw through (pulling yarn from under index finger), drop lp to right side of work, yo and draw through 2 lps on hk, repeat from * across, ch 1, turn. **Row 2:** * 1 sc in next st, repeat from * across, ch 1, turn. Repeat rows 1 and 2 for pattern and end last repeat with row 1.

(E–11)

Beginning at narrow edge, ch 15. **Row 1:** * [yo twice, insert hk in 15th ch from hk, yo and draw through, (yo and draw through 2 lps on hk) twice] 3 times, yo and draw through last 4 lps on hk (3-tr cluster made), ch 4, [yo twice, insert hk in 4th ch from hk, yo and draw through, (yo and draw through 2 lps on hk) twice] twice, yo and draw through last 3 lps on hk (2-tr cluster made),

ch 15, repeat from * until piece measures desired length and end 1 3-tr cluster in 15th ch from hk. **Finishing:** Ch 6, 1 dc in same ch as 1st cluster, * ch 4, 1 dc in same ch as next cluster, repeat from * across top long edge. F.O. Attach yarn to 1st ch-15 sp, ch 2, 18 sc in same sp, * 18 sc in next ch-15 sp, repeat from * across bottom long edge. F.O.

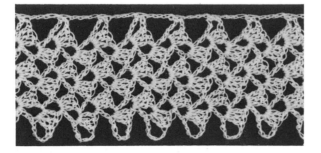

(E-12)
Beginning at narrow edge, ch 11. **Row 1:** (3 dc, ch 2, 1 dc) in 7th ch from hk, * sk 1 ch, (3 dc, ch 2, 1 dc) in next ch, repeat from * once, ch 6, turn. **Row 2:** * (3 dc, ch 2, 1 dc) in next ch-2 sp, repeat from * twice, ch 6, turn. Repeat row 2 for pattern until piece measures desired length and end last repeat ch 5. **Finishing:** * 1 sc in next ch-6 sp (turning ch of previous row), ch 3, repeat from * across 1 long edge. F.O.

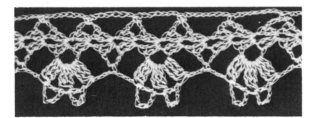

(E-13)
Beginning at narrow edge, ch 6. **Row 1:** (2 dc, ch 2, 2 dc) in 6th ch from hk, ch 5, turn. **Row 2:** (2 dc, ch 2, 2 dc) in ch-2 sp (shell made), ch 5, turn. Repeat row 2 for pattern until piece measures desired length and end with an odd number of ch-5 sps on 1 long edge, and 1 more ch-5 sp on opposite long edge. **Finishing:** Ch 5, yo twice, insert hk in next ch-5 sp (on long edge with odd number of ch-5 sps), yo and draw through, (yo and draw through 2 lps on hk) twice, [yo twice, insert hk in same ch-5 sp, yo and draw through, (yo and draw through 2 lps on hk) twice] twice, yo and draw through last 4 lps on hk (cluster made), * (ch 6, 1 dc in top of last cluster made, 1 cluster in same ch-5 sp) twice, ch 3, 1 sc in next ch-5 sp, ch 3, 1 cluster in next ch-5 sp, repeat from * across 1 long edge and end (ch 6, 1 dc in top of last cluster made, 1 cluster in same ch-5 sp) twice, ch 5, 1 sc at base of 1st shell. F. O. Attach yarn to 1st ch-5 sp on opposite long edge, 1 sc in same ch-5 sp, * ch 7, 1 sc in next ch-5 sp, repeat from * across. F.O.

(E-14)

Beginning at narrow edge, ch 10. **Row 1:** * yo twice, insert hk in 10th ch from hk, yo and draw through, (yo and draw through 2 lps on hk) twice, [yo twice, insert hk in same ch, yo and draw through, (yo and draw through 2 lps on hk) twice] twice, yo and draw through last 4 lps on hk (cluster made), ch 7, 1 cluster in 7th ch from hk, ch 10, repeat from * until piece measures desired length and end last repeat 1 cluster in 10th ch from hk, ch 3, turn. **Finishing:** * 10 dc in next ch-10 sp, 1 sc in next ch-7 sp, repeat from * across 1 long edge and end 10 dc in last ch-10 sp, ch 2, 1 sl st in same ch as 1st cluster. F.O.

(E-15)

Beginning at narrow edge, ch 28. **Row 1:** 1 tr tr in 16th ch from hk, ch 2, sk 2 ch, 1 dbl tr in next ch, ch 2, sk 2 ch, 1 tr in next ch, ch 2, sk 2 ch, 1 dc in next ch, ch 2, sk 2 ch, 1 sc in last ch, ch 1, turn. **Row 2:** * 1 sc in next st, ch 2, sk ch-2, repeat from * 3 times and end 1 sc in last st, ch 1, turn. **Row 3:** 1 sc in 1st sc, ch 2, 1 dc in next sc, ch 2, 1 tr in next sc, ch 2, 1 dbl tr in next sc, ch 2, 1 tr tr in last sc, ch 1, turn. **Row 4:** Repeat row 2, ch 15, turn. **Row 5:** 1 tr tr in 1st sc, ch 2, 1 dbl tr in next sc, ch 2, 1 tr in next sc, ch 2, 1 dc in next sc, ch 2, 1 sc in last sc, ch 1, turn. Repeat rows 2 through 5 for pattern until piece measures desired length. F.O. **Finishing:** Attach yarn to 1st ch-15 sp, ch 3, 2 dc in same sp, * 15 dc in same ch-15 sp, 3 dc in next ch-15 sp, repeat from * across and end 15 dc in same ch-15 sp. F.O.

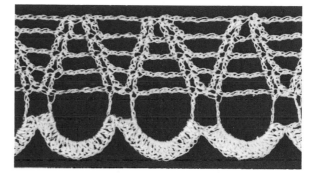

(E-16)

Beginning at narrow edge, ch 4. **Row 1:** 1 dc in 4th ch from hk, ch 5, (yo, insert hk in same ch, yo and draw through, yo and draw through 2 lps on hk) twice, yo and draw through last 3 lps on hk (cluster made), ch 7, turn. **Row 2:** Sk (1 cluster, 2 ch), (1 cluster, ch 5, 1 cluster) in next ch, ch 15, turn. **Row 3:** Sk (1 cluster, 2 ch), (1 cluster, ch 5, 1 cluster) in next ch, ch 7, turn. Repeat rows 2 and 3 for pattern until piece measures desired length and end last repeat with row 3, ch 3, do not turn. **Finishing:** * 9 dc in next ch-7 sp, repeat from * across top long edge, turn. **Next Row:** 1 sl st in each of next 5 dc, 1 sc in same dc as last sl st made, * ch 7, sk 8 dc, 1 sc in next dc, repeat from * across and end 1 sl st in each of last 4 dc. F.O. Attach yarn to 1st ch-15 sp on opposite long edge, ch 3, 6 dc in same sp, * ch 4, 1 sl st in 4th ch from hk (picot made), 7 dc in same ch-15 sp, 7 dc in next ch-15 sp, repeat from * across and end 1 picot, 7 dc in same ch-15 sp. F.O.

(E-17)

Beginning at narrow edge, ch 6. **Row 1:** 1 sc in 3rd ch from hk, ch 2, sk 2 ch, 1 dc in next ch, * (ch 5, 1 dc in last dc made) twice, ch 5, 1 sc in 3rd ch from hk, ch 2, 1 dc in last dc made (picot lp made), repeat from * until piece measures desired length, ch 8, turn. **Finishing:** * Sk next picot lp, 1 sc in next ch-5 sp, ch 3, 1 sc in next ch-5 sp, ch 7, repeat from * across and end sk last picot lp, 1 sc in same ch as 1st dc was made. F. O.

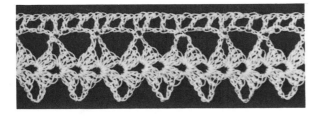

(E-18)

Beginning at narrow edge, ch 8. **Row 1:** (3 dc, ch 2, 3 dc) in 8th ch from hk, ch 5, turn. **Row 2:** (3 dc, ch 2, 3 dc) in ch-2 sp, ch 5, turn. Repeat row 2 for pattern until piece measures desired length and end with an odd number of ch-5 sps on 1 long edge and 1 less on opposite edge.

Finishing: Row 1: Ch 7, 1 sc in next ch-5 sp along top long edge, * ch 5, 1 sc in next ch-5 sp, repeat from * across, ch 4, turn. **Row 2:** Sk (1 sc, 1 ch), * (1 dc in next ch, ch 1, sk 1 ch) twice, 1 dc in next sc, ch 1, sk 1 ch, repeat from * across and end (1 dc in next ch, ch 1, sk 1 ch) twice, 1 dc in 5th ch of turning ch of previous row. F.O.

(E-19)

Beginning at narrow edge, ch 12. **Row 1:** 1 dc in 4th ch from hk, 1 dc in next ch, (1 dc, ch 2, 1 dc) in next ch, ch 2, sk 2 ch, 1 dc in each of next 4 ch, ch 3, turn. **Row 2:** 1 dc in each of next 3 dc, (1 dc in next dc, ch 2) twice, 1 dc in each of next 2 dc, sk 1 dc, 1 dc in 3rd ch of turning ch of previous row, ch 3, turn. **Row 3:** 1 dc in each of next 2 dc, (1 dc, ch 2, 1 dc) in next dc, (ch 2, 1 dc in next dc) twice, 1 dc in each of next 2 dc, sk 1 dc, 1 dc in 3rd ch of turning ch of previous row, ch 3, turn. **Row 4:** 1 dc in each of next 4 dc, (2 dc in next ch-2 sp, 1 dc in next dc) 3 times, 1 dc in each of next 2 dc, 1 dc in 3rd ch of turning ch of previous row, ch 3, turn. **Row 5:** 1 dc in each of next 2 dc, (1 dc, ch 2, 1 dc) in next dc, ch 2, sk 2 dc, 1 dc in each of next 4 dc, ch 3, turn. Repeat rows 2 through 5 for pattern until piece measures desired length and end last repeat with row 4. F.O.

(E-20)

Beginning at narrow edge, ch 11. **Row 1:** (1 dc ch 3, 1 dc) in 11th ch from hk, ch 4, turn. **Row 2:** [Yo twice, insert hk in ch-3 sp, yo and draw through, (yo and draw through 2 lps on hk) twice] twice, yo and draw through last 3 lps on hk, * ch 5, [yo twice, insert hk in same ch-3 sp, yo and draw through, (yo and draw through 2 lps on hk) twice] 3 times, yo and draw through last 4 lps on hk (3-tr cluster made), repeat from * twice and end sk (1 dc, 3 ch), 1 dc in next ch (fan made), ch 10, turn. **Row 3:** (1 dc, ch 3,

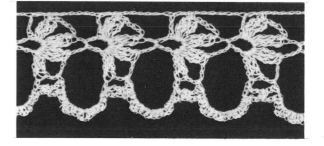

1 dc) in 2nd ch-5 sp, ch 4, turn. Repeat rows 2 and 3 for pattern until piece measures desired length and end last repeat with row 2. F.O. **Finishing:** Attach yarn to top of 1st cluster of 1st fan, * ch 5, 1 sc in next ch-5 sp, ch 10, 1 sc in top of 1st cluster of next fan, repeat from * across bottom long edge and end ch 5, 1 sc in next ch-5 sp, ch 1, turn. **Next Row:** 1 sc in ch-5 sp, * ch 3, 12 sc in next ch-10 sp, ch 3, 1 sc in next ch-5 sp, repeat from * across. F.O.

(E-21)

Multiple of 16 ch plus 12: **Row 1:** Ch 1, 1 sc in 2nd ch from hk, * 1 sc in next ch, repeat from * across, ch 3, turn. **Row 2:** 1 dc in 1st sc, * ch 2, sk 2 sc, 1 dc in each of next 2 sc, repeat from * across, ch 1, turn. **Row 3:** * 4 sc in each of next 2 ch-2 sps, 2 sc in next ch-2 sp, ch 9, turn, sk 7 sc, 1 sc in next sc, turn, 13 sc in ch-9 sp, 2 sc in same ch-2 sp as last 2 sc were made, 4 sc in next ch-2 sp, repeat from * across and end last repeat 2 sc in same ch-2 sp as last 2 sc were made. F.O.

(E-22)

Multiple of 7 ch: **Row 1:** Ch 1, 1 sc in 2nd ch from hk, * 1 sc in next ch, repeat from * across, ch 4, turn. **Row 2:** Yo twice, insert hk in 4th ch from hk, yo and draw through, (yo and draw through 2 lps on hk) twice, [yo twice, insert hk in same ch, yo and draw through, (yo and draw through 2 lps on hk) twice] twice, yo and draw through last 4 lps on hk, ch 7, [yo twice, insert hk in same ch, yo and draw through, (yo and draw through 2 lps on hk) twice] 4 times, yo and draw through last 5 lps on hk (4-tr cluster made), * sk 6 sc, (1 4-tr cluster, ch 7, 1 4-tr cluster) in next sc, repeat from * across, turn. **Row 3:** * 12 sc in next ch-7 sp, repeat from * across. F.O.

(E-23)

Multiple of 10 ch: **Row 1:** Ch 1, 1 sc in 2nd ch from hk, * 1 sc in next ch, repeat from * across, ch 5, turn. **Row 2:** * Sk 4 sc, (1 dc, ch 2, 1 dc) in next sc, ch 5, sk 4 sc, 1 sc in next sc, ch 5, repeat from * across and end 1 sc in last sc. F.O.

(E-24)

Multiple of 7 ch plus 1: **Row 1:** Ch 4, 1 dc in 5th ch from hk, * ch 5, sk 5 ch, 1 dc in next ch, ch 1, 1 dc in next ch, repeat from * across, ch 1, turn. **Row 2:** 1 sc in 1st ch-1 sp, ch 3, 1 sc in next ch-5 sp, * ch 9, 1 sc in same ch-5 sp, ch 3, 1 sc in next ch-1 sp, ch 3, 1 sc in next ch-5 sp, repeat from * across and end last repeat 1 sc in turning ch of previous row, ch 1, turn. **Row 3:** 1 sc in 1st ch-3 sp, * 12 sc in next ch-9 sp, 1 sc in next ch-3 sp, ch 5, 1 sc in next ch-3 sp, repeat from * across and end last repeat 1 sc in last ch-3 sp. F.O.

(E-25)

Multiple of 14 ch plus 4: **Row 1:** Ch 1, 1 sc in 2nd ch from hk, (ch 3, sk 2 ch, 1 sc in next ch) twice, * ch 5, sk 4 ch, 1 sc in next ch, (ch 3, sk 2 ch, 1 sc in next ch) 3 times, repeat from * across and end last repeat (ch 3, sk 2 ch, 1 sc in next ch) twice, ch 1, turn. **Row 2:** 1 sc in 1st ch-3 sp, ch 3, 1 sc in next ch-3 sp, * ch 3, yo twice, insert hk in next ch-5 sp, yo and draw through, (yo and draw through 2 lps on hk) twice, yo twice, insert hk in same ch-5 sp, yo and draw through, (yo and draw through 2 lps on hk) twice, yo and draw through last 3 lps on hk (cluster made), (ch 3, 1 cluster in same ch-5 sp) twice, (ch 3, 1 sc in next ch-3 sp) 3 times, repeat from * across and end last repeat (ch 3, 1 sc in next ch-3 sp) twice. F.O.

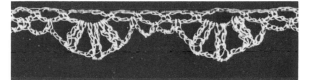

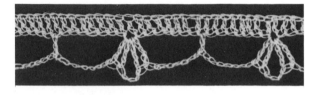

(E-26)

Multiple of 16 ch: **Row 1:** Ch 2, 1 dc in 3rd ch from hk, * 1 dc in next ch, repeat from * across, ch 10, turn. **Row 2:** * Sk 7 dc, (2 tr, ch 3, 2 tr) in next dc (shell made), ch 7, sk 7 dc, 1 dc in next dc, ch 7, repeat from * across and end 1 dc in last dc. F.O.

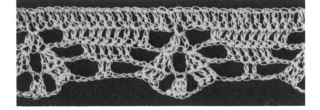

(E-27)

Multiple of 17 ch plus 15: **Row 1:** Ch 3, 1 dc in 4th ch from hk, * 1 dc in next ch, repeat from * across, ch 3, turn. **Row 2:** 1 dc in each of next 4 dc, * ch 3, sk 3 dc, 3 dc in next dc, ch 3, sk 3 dc, 1 dc in each of next 10 dc, repeat from * across and end 1 dc in each of last 4 dc, 1 dc in turning ch of previous row, ch 3, turn. **Row 3:** 1 dc in each of 1st 3 dc, * ch 3, sk (2 dc, ch-3), 3 dc in next dc, ch 3, sk 1 dc, 3 dc in next dc, ch 3, sk (ch-3, 2 dc), 1 dc in each of next 6 dc, repeat from * across and end last repeat 1 dc in each of last 2 dc, 1 dc in turning ch of previous row, ch 6, turn. **Row 4:** Sk (3 dc, ch-3), 1 dc in each of next 3 dc, ch 3, sk 1 ch, 3 dc in next ch, ch 3, sk 1 ch, 1 dc in each of next 3 dc, * ch 3, sk (ch-3, 2 dc), 1 dc in each of next 2 dc, ch 3, sk (2 dc, ch-3), 1 dc in each of next 3 dc, ch 3, sk 1 ch, 3 dc in next ch, ch 3, sk 1 ch, 1 dc in each of next 3 dc, repeat from * across and end ch 3, sk (ch-3, 3 dc), 1 dc in turning ch of previous row. F.O.

(E-28)

Multiple of 7 ch plus 5: **Row 1:** Ch 1, 1 sc in 2nd ch from hk, 1 sc in each of next 2 ch, * ch 4, 1 sc in 4th ch from hk (picot made), 1 sc in each of next 2 ch, ch 9, turn, sk (2 sc, 1 picot, 2 sc just made), 1 sc in next sc, turn, 13 sc in ch-9 sp, 1 sc in each of next 5 ch of foundation chain, repeat from * across and end last repeat 13 sc in last ch-9 sp. F.O.

(E-29)

Multiple of 4 ch plus 1: **Row 1:** Ch 5, 1 dc in 6th ch from hk, * ch 1, sk 1 ch, 1 dc in next ch, repeat from * across, ch 1, turn. **Row 2:** 1 sc in 1st ch-1 sp, * ch 6, sk next ch-1 sp, 1 sc in next ch-1 sp, repeat from * across, ch 3, turn. **Row 3:** 4 dc in 1st ch-6 sp, * ch 1, 4 dc in next ch-6 sp, repeat from * across. F.O.

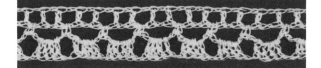

(E-30)

Multiple of 12 ch plus 1: **Row 1:** Ch 5, 1 dc in 6th ch from hk, * ch 1, sk 1 ch, 1 dc in next ch, repeat from * across, ch 2, turn. **Row 2:** 1 dc in next ch-1 sp, ch 3, 1 sc in 3rd ch from hk (picot made), * ch 4, 1 sc in 3rd ch from hk, 1 dc in same ch-1 sp as last dc made, ch 3, sk 2 ch-1 sps, 1 dc in next ch-1 sp, 1 picot, repeat from * across and end ch 4, 1 sc in 3rd ch from hk, 1 dc in same ch-1 sp, ch 3, turn. **Rows 3 and 4:** Sk 1 picot, 1 dc in next ch (between 2 picots), 1 picot, ch 1, 1 picot, 1 dc in same ch as last dc made (shell made), * ch 3, 1 shell in center ch of next shell, repeat from * across. F.O.

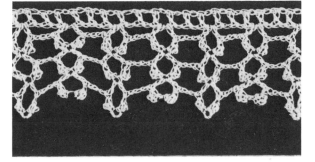

(E-31)

Beginning at narrow edge, ch 4. **Row 1:** 2 dc in 4th ch from hk, (ch 2, 2 dc) in same ch, ch 5, turn. **Row 2:** Sk 2 dc, (2 dc, ch 2, 2 dc) in ch-2 sp, ch 5, turn. Repeat row 2 for pattern until piece measures desired length. **Finishing:** When final row is completed, * ch 5, 1 sc in next ch-5 sp, repeat from * across 1 long edge and end ch 5, 1 sc in 4th ch of foundation ch-4. F.O. Attach yarn to 1st turning ch on opposite long edge, * ch 5, 1 sc in next ch-5 sp, repeat from * across. F.O.

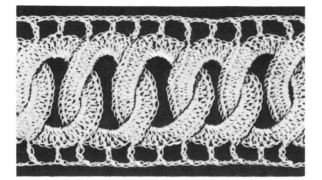

(E-32)

1st ring: Ch 25, j with sl st to form a ring. **Rnd 1:** Ch 3, 49 dc in center of ring, j with sl st to 3rd ch of starting ch-3. F.O. **2nd ring:** Ch 25, insert ch through center of last ring made, j with sl st to form a ring. **Rnd 1:** Ch 3, 49 dc in center of 2nd ring, j with sl st to 3rd ch of starting ch-3. F.O. Continue to make rings in same manner as 2nd ring until piece measures desired length.

Finishing: Attach yarn to any dc on last ring, ch 6, * sk 2 dc, 1 dc in next dc, ch 2, sk 2 dc, yo twice, insert hk in next dc, insert hk through any dc of next ring, yo and draw through both sts, (yo and draw through 2 lps on hk) 3 times, ch 2, sk 2 dc on 2nd ring, 1 dc in next dc, ch 2, repeat from * across 1 long edge, and end sk 2 dc, 1 dc in next dc, ch 2, sk 2 dc, 1 dc in next dc. F.O. Sk 19 dc on last ring, attach yarn and work across opposite long edge in same manner. F.O.

(E-33)

Beginning at narrow edge, ch 11. **Row 1:** 1 sc in 2nd ch from hk, * 1 sc in next ch, repeat from * across, ch 1, turn. **Row 2:** * 1 sc in next sc, repeat from * across, ch 1, turn. **Row 3:** *1 sc in next sc, repeat from * across, ch 6, turn. **Row 4:** Sk 3 sc, * 1 dc in next sc, ch 2, sk 2 sc, repeat from * once and end 1 dc in last sc, ch 1, turn. **Row 5:** * 1 sc in next dc, 2 sc in ch-2 sp, repeat from * once and end 1 sc in next dc, 3 sc in turning ch of previous row, ch 1, turn. Repeat rows 2 through 5 for pattern until piece measures desired length and end last repeat with row 3. F.O.

(E-34)

Beginning at narrow edge, ch 11. **Row 1:** [Yo twice, insert hk in 11th ch from hk, yo and draw through, (yo and draw through 2 lps on hk) twice] 3 times, yo and draw through last 4 lps on hk (cluster made), ch 10, turn. **Row 2:** 1 cluster in 10th ch from hk, ch 10, turn. Repeat row 2 for pattern until piece measures desired length (having an even number of clusters), ch 5.

Finishing: Row 1: * Sk 1 cluster, (1 cluster, ch 3, 1 cluster) in next ch-10 sp, ch 4, repeat from * across 1 long edge, ch 4, turn. **Row 2:** * 1 dc in ch-3 sp, ch 2, (1 dc, ch 2, 1 dc) in ch-4 sp, ch 2, repeat from * across and end (1 dc, ch 2, 1 dc) in turning ch of previous row, ch 7, turn. **Row 3:** Sk (1 dc, ch 2, 1 dc), * 1 sc in next ch-2 sp, ch 5, repeat from * across and end 1 sc in turning ch of previous row. F.O. Attach yarn to 11th ch of foundation ch, ch 5, and repeat rows 1 through 3 of finishing along opposite long edge. F.O.

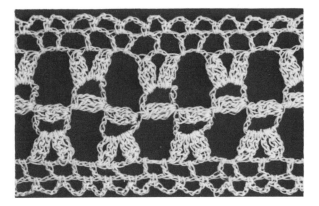

(E-35)

Beginning at narrow edge, ch 5. **Row 1:** * [Yo twice, insert hk in 5th ch from hk, yo and draw through, (yo and draw through 2 lps on hk) twice] 3 times, yo and draw through last 4 lps on hk (cluster made), ch 5, repeat from * for pattern until piece measures desired length (having an even number of clusters) and end last repeat ch 7.

Finishing: Row 1: * [Yo twice, insert hk in same ch as next cluster was made, yo and draw through, (yo and draw through 2 lps on hk) twice] 4 times, yo and draw through last 5 lps on hk, ch 7, 1 sc in same ch as next cluster was made, ch 7, repeat from * around entire piece and end 1 sc in top of last cluster. **Row 2:** 1 sl st in each of next 3 ch, 1 sc in same ch-7 sp, ch 11, * (1 tr in next ch-7 sp) twice, ch 7, repeat from * across 1 long edge and end 1 tr in last ch-7 sp, ch 5, turn. **Row 3:** * Sk 2 sts, 1 dc in next st, ch 2, repeat from * across, leaving last 4 sts free, ch 3, turn. **Row 4:** * 2 dc in next ch-2 sp, 1 dc in next dc, repeat from * across. F.O. Repeat rows 2 through 4 along opposite long edge. F.O.

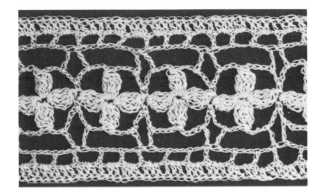

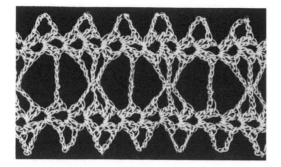

(E-36)

Beginning at narrow edge, ch 16. **Row 1:** (2 dc, ch 2, 2 dc) in 8th ch from hk (shell made), ch 7, sk 7 ch, 1 shell in next ch, ch 7, turn. **Rows 2, 4 and 5:** 1 shell in 1st ch-2 sp, ch 7, 1 shell in next ch-2 sp, ch 7, turn. **Row 3:** 1 shell in 1st ch-2 sp, ch 3, insert hk under last 2 ch-7's, yo and draw through, yo and draw through 2 lps on hk, ch 3, 1 shell in next ch-2 sp, ch 7, turn. Repeat rows 2 through 5 for pattern until piece measures desired length and end last repeat with row 4. F.O.

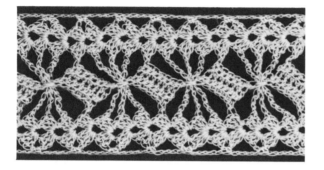

(E-37)

Beginning at narrow edge, ch 16. **Row 1:** (3 dc, ch 2, 3 dc) in 4th ch from hk (shell made), ch 9, sk 11 ch, 1 shell in next ch, ch 2, turn. **Rows 2, 4 and 6:** 1 shell in 1st ch-2 sp, ch 11, 1 shell in next ch-2 sp, ch 2, turn. **Row 3:** 1 shell in 1st ch-2 sp, ch 7, insert hk under ch's of last 3 rows, yo and draw through, yo and draw through 2 lps on hk, ch 1, turn, 1 sc in each of next 7 ch, * ch 1, turn, (1 sc through back lp only of next sc) 7 times, repeat from * 4 times (square made), 1 shell in next ch-2 sp, ch 2, turn. **Row 5:** 1 shell in 1st ch-2 sp, ch 9, 1 shell in next ch-2 sp, ch 2, turn. **Row 7:** 1 shell in 1st ch-2 sp, ch 7, 1 sc in corner of last square made (working over ch's of last 3 rows), ch 1, turn, 1 square over next 7 ch, 1 shell in next ch-2 sp, ch 2, turn. Repeat rows 4 through 7 for pattern until piece measures desired length and end last repeat with row 6 working last row as follows: 1 shell in 1st ch-2 sp, ch 5, 1 sc in corner of last square made (working over ch's of last 3 rows), ch 5, 1 shell in next ch-2 sp. **Finishing:** Ch 5, * 1 sc in next turning ch-2 sp along one long edge, ch 4, repeat from * across. F.O. Attach yarn to 1st ch-2 sp on opposite long edge, repeat last row across. F.O.

(E-38)

Beginning at narrow edge, ch 19. **Row 1:** 1 dbl tr in 10th ch from hk, ch 2, sk 2 ch, 1 tr in next ch, ch 2, sk 2 ch, 1 dc in next ch, ch 2, sk 2 ch, 1 sc in last ch, ch 1, turn. **Row 2:** 1 sc in 1st sc, ch 2, 1 sc in next dc, ch 2, 1 sc in next tr, ch 2, 1 sc in next dbl tr, ch 2, 1 sc in turning ch of previous row, ch 1, turn. **Row 3:** 1 sc in 1st sc, ch 2, 1 dc in next sc, ch 2, 1 tr in next sc, ch 2, 1 dbl tr in next sc, ch 2, 1 tr tr in next sc, ch 1, turn. **Row 4:** 1 sc in next tr tr, ch 2, 1 sc in next dbl tr, ch 2, 1 sc in next tr, ch 2, 1 sc in next dc, ch 2, 1 sc in next sc, ch 7, turn. **Row 5:** Sk 1st sc, 1 dbl tr in next sc, ch 2, ˙1 tr in next sc, ch 2, 1 dc in next sc, ch 2, 1 sc in next sc, ch 1, turn. Repeat rows 2 through 5 for pattern until piece measures desired length and end last repeat with row 3. F.O.

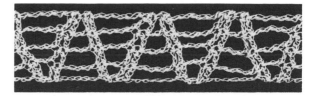

(E-39)

Beginning at narrow edge, ch 8. **Row 1:** (3 dc, ch 2, 3 dc) in 8th ch from hk, ch 5, turn. **Row 2:** (3 dc, ch 2, 3 dc) in ch-2 sp, ch 5, turn. Repeat row 2 for pattern until piece measures desired length. **Finishing: Row 1:** Ch 6, 1 sc in next ch-5 sp along top long edge, * ch 5, 1 sc in next ch-5 sp, repeat from * across, ch 4, turn. **Row 2:** Sk (1 sc, 1 ch), * (1 dc in next ch, ch 1, sk 1 ch) twice, 1 dc in next sc, ch 1, sk 1 ch, repeat from * across and end (1 dc in next ch, ch 1, sk 1 ch) twice. F.O. Attach yarn to opposite long edge and repeat rows 1 and 2 of finishing. F.O.

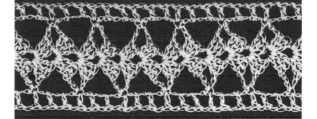

(E-40)

Beginning at narrow edge, ch 8. **Row 1:** 1 sc in 2nd ch from hk, * 1 sc in next ch, repeat from * across, ch 1, turn. **Row 2:** 1 sc in 1st sc, (1 sl st, ch 4, 1 sl st) in next sc (picot made), 1 sc in each of next 3 sc, 1 picot in next sc, 1 sc in last sc, ch 1, turn. **Row 3:** 1 sc in 1st sc, ch 1, sk 1 picot (keep picots in front of ch-1's), 1 sc in each of next 3 sc, ch 1, sk 1 picot, 1 sc in last sc, ch 1, turn. **Row 4:** 1 sc in 1st sc, 1 sc in next ch-1 sp,

1 sc in next sc, 1 picot in next sc, 1 sc in next sc, 1 sc in next ch-1 sp, 1 sc in last sc, ch 1, turn.
Row 5: 1 sc in each of next 3 sc, ch 1, sk 1 picot, 1 sc in each of last 3 sc, ch 1, turn. **Row 6:** 1 sc in 1st sc, 1 picot in next sc, 1 sc in next sc, 1 sc in next ch-1 sp, 1 sc in next sc, 1 picot in next sc, 1 sc in last sc, ch 1, turn. Repeat rows 3 through 6 for pattern until piece measures desired length and end last repeat with row 5. F.O.

12. DESIGNER'S GUIDE

In practically all crafts there are certain rules that should be observed in order to make everything come out just right. So it is, too, for designing anything one wants to crochet. Basic rules for proportion and shaping should be followed or at least employed as guidelines for whatever variation you choose to use in the designing of your own garments. Outlined here alphabetically for easy reference is information about most of the things that will be of greatest value to you in your new venture into the field of crochet and creative designing, and so that we may give you examples, we are going to assume that whatever it is you are making is being worked on a gauge of 3 stitches to 1″ and 7 rows to 2″, knowing by now (after reading the "How to Design" chapter) that if your stitch and row gauge are different, you will need to vary your calculations.

Also given in this chapter in addition to the guideline rules are standard-body-size measurement charts, ranging from infants' size to size 46. Use these as starting points, bearing in mind that if your own measurements vary somewhat from the suggested ones given, you will need to adjust the calculations for your design; and also that allowances beyond the measurements given will have to be made for seaming (see Crocheter's Guide) and for ease of fit for certain types of garments, such as jackets, coats, and other loose-fitting articles of clothing.

A-line Shaping

Regardless of the degree of A-line shaping you want to use in your coat, blouse, dress, or skirt, the basic rule is that the shaping should be gradual rather than jagged. Depending on the styling you are working, A-lines generally vary from 1″ to 3″ in width on each side for a short garment and up to 6″ on longer ones. To work an A-line shaping, for example, if your total decreasing is to be done in an area of 6″ (21 rows), and you are having a 2″ A-line shape on each side, you would need to decrease 6 stitches at each side of work on both the back and front of your garment. Working at the 3-stitch-to-1-inch and 7-rows-to-2-inches gauge, you would decrease 1 stitch at the beginning and end of every fourth row 3 times, then every third row 3 times; and if you are planning a 1″ A-line in an area of 4″ (14 rows), you would decrease 1 stitch at the beginning and end of every fifth row twice, then every fourth row once.

Afghans

Most afghans are rectangular in shape, and usually a minimum of 12″ and a maximum of 20″ longer than they are wide. A minimum width of 48″ and a maximum of 72″, and a minimum length of 58″ and a maximum of 90″ generally fall into the category of most desirable sizes. Since even the smallest of afghans are large pieces, they are practically always worked in sections, either strips, squares, or a series of motifs, and then the sections are joined together to form the total piece by weaving or sewing a thin seam, the use of a row of single crochet or slip stitch along either the right or wrong side of work, or some type of fancy joining, a few of which we show in this book at the end of Chapter 10. Parts of an afghan can also be put together very beautifully with the use of insertions between the parts. Many interesting insertions are shown in Chapter 11. A simple crochet joining on the wrong side of the work makes an inconspicuous seam, and on the right side an exaggerated seam. Often the latter method, when worked in a contrast color, adds much interest to the general pattern of the afghan itself. Whatever method is used, there should be a row of single crochet first around each piece, so that the final joinings are even and lie perfectly flat and smooth, and if more than one color has been used on the afghan, this first row should be worked in color over color for a neater finish.

When an afghan is finally joined and completed, there is usually a border and trim around the entire outer edge. This final finish might be a single crochet border in contrast or self-color, a fringed border, plain or fancy, or a chain-loop crocheted straight or ruffled edging. Whichever finish is used, always there is first a row or two of single crochet, color over color, around the entire edge of the finished piece, squaring out the corners and making the shape of the afghan firm and solid. For further information on how to design, calculate, and final finish all afghans, see "How to Design" (Chapter 5).

Armhole Shaping

The shaping of armholes generally falls into two categories, that for the set-in sleeve and that for the raglan. As in all other shaping, the process must be a gradual one. For regulation armholes, shaping begins at the start of armhole depth and is generally worked by starting on the right side of work and binding off the number of stitches equivalent to between 1″ and 1½ ″ at the beginning of each of the next 2 rows or at the beginning and end of the first row where the shaping begins, and then decreasing 1 stitch at the beginning and end of every other row until the shaping is completed. To determine the number of stitches involved in the complete shaping of both armholes on the back of your garment, you would calculate as follows: Subtract from the total number of stitches the number you will need remaining for the two shoulders and the back of the neck. This will tell you how many stitches you will use in the complete armhole shaping. Let us assume that the back of your garment measures 16″, each of the shoulders measures 4″, and the back of the neck measures 4¼ ″. Calculated to our presumed gauge, you are working on approximately 48 stitches (this figure possibly varying slightly, depending on the multiple of your pattern stitch) at the point where the armhole shaping begins. When you are done with the armhole shaping, you should have remaining the necessary number of stitches to complete both shoulders and the back of neck. In this case it would be 12 + 13 + 12 = 37. Subtract 37 from 48, and you are left with the number of stitches to be bound-off for your armholes. 48 − 37 = 11. Since 11 is not divisible by 2, and you need to divide the remaining stitches by 2 for both of your armholes, you would use a figure which approximates 11 stitches, and is a multiple of 2. In this case we will assume that we have 10 stitches for the shaping of the armholes. Half of 10 for each armhole = 5. You would probably shape your back armholes as follows: Bind off 3 stitches at beginning of the next row, work to within 3 stitches of the end of the row, chain and turn. Work 1 row even, then decrease 1 stitch at beginning and end of every other row twice. Front armholes are always shaped exactly like those on back.

Raglan armholes generally measure approximately 1″ longer than the regulation ones and are decreased gradually, with either a small or no initial bind-off, until no stitches remain. There is no shoulder involved in a raglan, so you need to subtract only the back of neck measurement from the body measurement to determine the shaping of the raglan. With this type of armhole, you need to count your row gauge as well as your stitch gauge. If you are designing a garment the same size as the one worked out above, and the standard armhole measurement on that one is 7″, in this case the armhole would measure 8″. 48 stitches minus 13 (for back of neck) = 35 stitches. In this case we will assume that we have 34 stitches, since again this figure needs to be divisible by 2. Dividing this figure in half (for both armholes), you have 17 stitches for the shaping on each side. Since the armhole is to measure 8″, you would multiply 8 by 7 and divide by 2 (your row gauge) and find that you have 28 rows, with, let us say, a 2-stitch initial bind-off. Raglan shaping at this point is a little more complicated than other sleeve shapings, since you need to know how you can most gradually decrease the necessary number of stitches in the given number of rows, and there is no leeway allowed for not having decreased all your stitches by the time you have reached your full armhole depth. In this case, you would look for the nearest multiple of 17 less 2, for initial bind-off, in 28 rows less 2 for the 8″ armhole. 15 × 2 = 30, which is about as close as you can get with the multiple. You would probably shape your raglan armholes as follows: Bind off 2 stitches at beginning and end of the next row, then decrease 1 stitch every other row 11 times, then every row 4 times. By doing this you will have decreased the 15 stitches in 26 rows, and you will have designed a good-fitting, well-shaped raglan armhole.

Buttonhole Placements

Chapter 4, "Crocheter's Guide," describes how to form buttonholes, but in designing, you should be aware of the generally accepted rules for their placement. On cardigan sweaters the first buttonhole is usually formed when the piece measures 1″ (most garments are worked from the bottom up), the last one 1″ below the start of the neckline (regardless of its shape), and the remaining ones spaced evenly between. On jackets and short coats, the first one usually occurs when your work measures between 8″ and 10″. On longer garments, the placement of the first buttonhole is generally between 12″ and 18″ from the bottom. In all instances, the top one occurs 1″ below the start of neck shaping, except perhaps where very large buttons are being used, and in that case you would probably start that last buttonhole ½″ to 1″ lower to accommodate the extra circumference of the button. Usually buttonholes are placed about ¾″ to 1″ in from the front edge, and on double-breasted garments a space of between 3½″ and 5″ is generally allowed between the two sets of buttonholes.

Capes and Ponchos

These types of garments are usually crocheted from the top down. Shaping is still gradual, although it needs to be calculated carefully, since the top neck and shoulder portion is much smaller than the full bottom width, and increases are needed at the proper places so that the piece grows as necessary to achieve correct measurements from neck to bust to bottom fullness. To clarify, a good-fitting garment of this type with a 12″ circumference for neck opening, a 36″ circumference at the bust, and an 88″ circumference at the bottom might allow 7″ in which you must grade from the top to the bust measurement, and 23″ from that point to the bottom—the total length from top to bottom being, let us say, 30". In a presumed gauge of 3 stitches to 1" and 7 rows to 2", you would start out with 36 stitches at the neck, graduating to 108 stitches in approximately the first 24 rows to the bust, and then to 264 stitches for full width in approximately the next 80 rows. That is as many rows as you need to the bottom of your poncho. However, since in a garment of this type full width occurs often approximately 5" to 6" above the bottom, or in this case 20 rows less than the full 80 rows, your calculations would be: $108 - 36 = 72$, which is the number of stitches you will need to increase in your first 24 rows, and $264 - 108 = 156$, which is the number of stitches you will need to increase in your next 60 rows.

You would probably work your garment in this manner: Chain 36, presuming that that is a multiple of the pattern stitch you've chosen to work with. Work even for ½", then increase 12 stitches, evenly spaced, every fourth row 6 times, making a total of 72 stitches increased in 24 rows. You now have 108 stitches increased in 24 rows, and a bust measurement of 36"; your piece is 7" long. You now need to increase 156 stitches in the next 60 rows to achieve full width at proper length. It would be best now to increase 12 stitches every fourth row 12 times then 6 stitches every sixth row twice. You now have increased the additional 156 stitches in 60 rows, and you have reached full width at a point approximately 5" above the total length of your garment. You would then work even for the remaining 5" to complete your poncho. (*Note:* In working this type of garment the top is usually done in one piece, then the work is divided into either two or four sections soon after the full bust measurement has been reached, and then seamed in the final finish. This is done because the total number of stitches becomes quite large as you work down, and it is unwieldy to work in one piece.)

Cardigans

Cardigans are usually made by working the garment in five parts, and then adding the finish. The back is worked first, then each of the two fronts, and finally the sleeves. Each front is worked to measure half the size of the back, plus whatever stitches need to be added for overlap. For instance, if you have the usual single set of buttonholes, which are generally placed approximately ¾" to 1" in from center front, you would need to add at least 1" to each of your cardigan fronts. If, on the other hand, you are designing your cardigan with a double-breasted set of double buttonholes having, for example, a 5" overlap, you would need to divide that 5" in half and add 2½" to each front. Another rule for the designing of cardigans is that, as an open sweater and very often a casual type of garment meant to be worn over something like a blouse or slipover, it should be made 1" wider all around, and the armholes should be made ½" to 1" deeper than regulation. This will provide the ease of fit necessary for this type of garment.

Coats and Jackets

Rules for cardigans generally apply to coats and jackets as well, with the exception that these garments are always designed to be worn over other clothing and must be calculated with that thought in mind. They are never as tight-fitting as a sweater of any type. Using basic measurements to start with, between 2" and 5" should be allowed for extra width of both body and sleeves, and an extra 1½" to 3" for armhole depth. The placement of buttons and buttonholes also varies a little from that on cardigans. For a knowledge of this, refer to the general information on buttonholes earlier in this chapter.

Gathering

When gathering is included in a design, whether it be for a full dirndl skirt, a peplum, a hat brim, or any other project involving a degree of fullness or ruffle at some point, designers' rules state that average gathering requires double the starting width, moderate gathering one-half again the starting width, and very full gathering three times the starting width. Any of these proportions can be easily achieved in crocheting, and the method is to increase the necessary number of stitches at the point where gathering is to occur. Unlike any other shaping, gathering requires almost an immediate form, rather than the more gradual one that occurs in most other styling. If an average gathering is desired, the number of stitches on the row would be doubled. For a moderate gathering, one-half again the number of starting stitches would be added, and for a very full gathering the number would be tripled. Since most shaping turns out best when it is started on the right side of the work, and most increasing and decreasing is best done on a single crochet row, regardless of the pattern stitch involved in the rest of the design, average gathering would be made by increasing 1 stitch in each single crochet across the first row, and then returning to whatever pattern is being used, and working even. For directions on how to increase, refer to the Crocheter's Guide. For a moderate gathering, increase 1 stitch in every other stitch across the row in the same manner. A triple increase involves a little variation, because by increasing 2 stitches in each stitch across, you would be apt to pull or stretch your original first stitches out of shape, and thus form gaps, or small holes, in your work. In this case, then, where a triple increase is involved, it is best to work it in a double procedure, increasing 1 stitch in every stitch across the first row, and then 1 in every other stitch on the next row. Should the gathering occur first, followed by your straight work, you would decrease at the end of the ruffle in the same manner as you would have increased if it had occurred at the end.

Hat Shaping

Crocheted hats can be worked either from the top down or the bottom up, and they can be made by working in the round, or by working back and forth. The latter method makes for less difficulty in the shaping process when working with a complicated pattern stitch of any type. The top starting point of a hat measures about 1″ or 1½″; and the bottom, 3″ less than the circumference of your head at a point approximately 1″ below the top of your ears. The reason for using 3″ less than the actual measurement is that there is a lot of stretch to crocheted hats, and to fit properly they should be snug to the head. Hats can be made in any type of stitch, ranging from the basic single crochet to a simple rib, or to an interesting textured stitch. Regardless of the pattern involved, however, your increases or decreases, depending on whether you are working from the top down or the bottom up, come out best when done on a single crochet row. The bottom of a hat is generally finished after the rest of the hat is completed, and if there is no brim or peak or other bottom trim, there should be a small hem (on the wrong side of work) or a ribbed edging. Shaping at the top of the crown can be worked either gradually over a space of 3″ or 4″, or more rapidly over a space of 1″ or 2″, this depending on the style of hat you are making.

As an example of how to start crocheting a hat, let us assume that you want to make a basic pull-on type, in a small all-over textured stitch with a multiple of 4, and in our testing gauge of 3 stitches to 1″ and 7 rows to 2″. First you would measure your head at the widest point just below the top of your ears. If your measurement is 21″, which is average adult size, you would plan your hat to measure 18″ at that point. 18 multiplied by your gauge of 3 stitches to 1″ would be 54, to which you need to add 2 more stitches to accommodate to your pattern multiple. If you decide to work from the bottom up, you would chain 56 stitches and work even in your pattern for the length you want, depending on the depth and style of the hat you are making, both of which will tell you if the top shaping should be done gradually in, let us say, 4″, or more rapidly in 2″. If you want a gradual shaping, you would probably work on your 56 stitches until your piece measures 4″ (or approximately 14 rows) less than the desired total depth, then you would change to single crochet and decrease 7 stitches evenly spaced on every other row 7 times, and 1 stitch at the beginning and end of the next row, thus reducing your width to about 1½" in 15 rows. At this point you would break off your yarn, leaving a long thread, and draw the thread tightly through the remaining stitches. On the other hand, if you wanted a rapid shaping to be worked in about 2", you would change to single crochet when your piece measures 2" (or approximately 7 rows) less than the desired depth, and would probably decrease 7 stitches evenly spaced on every row 7 times, 1 stitch at the beginning and end of the next row, and then fasten off as before. In this same manner of shaping, if you were working your hat from the top down, you would reverse the process and chain 5, then increase in the same way that you decreased until you reach 56 stitches, from which point on you would work even. If a brim or other bottom trim is to be added, you would do it now, before sewing the back seam and blocking your hat into shape. By the same token, if a bottom edge is to be put on, you would also do this just before final finishing.

A few more guides on variations in hats follow here. Berets and tams, at their widest point, are usually double the width of the 3" less than your actual head measurement, though they start or end, depending again on whether you are working from bottom up or top down, with the regulation 3" less than actual head measurement, this for your band, which usually measures between 1½" and 2" deep. The increase or decrease in number of stitches between the band and the widest portion of the beret occurs rapidly, as in the other types of gathering described in an earlier paragraph in this chapter, and the increasing or decreasing, depending on which method is being used, begins about 1" above the bottom of the beret fullness.

Stocking caps are worked in the same manner as other hats, except that increasing or decreasing, as the case may be, is worked very gradually in order to span the difference in the number of stitches between the widest part and the 2- or 3-stitch point which drops to the back of the cap in a space of usually between 12" and 15". For example, in our

presumed gauge, the widest portion of your cap would be worked on 56 stitches. In order to drop to the very few stitches you need in the span of 12", or approximately 42 rows, you would probably decrease 1 stitch at the beginning and end of every other row 15 times and 1 stitch at the beginning and end of every row 12 times. Again, if your drop would be 15", or approximately 53 rows, you would decrease 1 stitch at the beginning and end of every other row 27 times.

Straight brims are worked in the same direction as the rest of the hat, whether from the top down or the bottom up. The bottom of the brim is usually between 1½" and 2" wider than the top of it, and the shaping for this occurs within the first 3 or 4 rows beyond the point where the top of the brim meets the bottom of the crown. Extra-firm brims are often worked either with double yarn for body or with a full turn-under hem, shaped in reverse to the top of the brim. A soft ruffled brim is worked, again, either from the top down or bottom up, and the ruffling is achieved in the same manner as all other gathering, described earlier.

In turnover cuffs, except if worked in one of the stitches that are exactly the same on both sides, such as, for example, single crochet or ribbing, the portion of the hat to be cuffed over needs to be worked in reverse to the rest of the hat so that when turned over the pattern stitch will match. This applies whether the hat is worked from the top down or the bottom up, and can best be achieved by working a wrong side row on the right side of work at the turnover point.

Peaks on hats are made like brims, except that they are worked on only the front half of the hat. They are always added after the rest of the hat has been completed and are shaped to a gradual, narrow roundness at the bottom.

Neck Shaping

There are many styles of neck shaping, the most popular being the round neck, the V-neck, the scoop neck, and the boat neck. Round necks, including those with turtleneck collars, and V-necks have the regulation neck and shoulder shaping on the back. A round neck shaping on the front of a sweater occurs 2" below the start of shoulder shaping, and the number of stitches to be calculated in the shaping of the round neck is the number of stitches on the piece of work, less those required for both shoulders. The shaping is usually done by working each side of the neck separately, allowing for a center bind-off, and usually three gradual decreases on either side of the neck opening. For example, if your piece measures 2" less than the depth of the armhole, and you have 45 stitches on your work, and you need a total of 24 stitches remaining for both shoulders, you would shape your neck as follows: Work across 15 stitches, chain and turn. Decrease 1 stitch at start of next row (neck edge) and repeat this decrease every other row twice more, then work even on 12 stitches until piece measures same as back to shoulders, and shape the shoulder as on back. Return now to row where start of neck shaping began, skip center 15 stitches and work across second half of neck and shoulder to correspond to first half, reversing all shaping.

On a V-neck there is the same number of stitches to work with, but the start of the neck shaping occurs much lower and the shaping would be quite different. V-neck shapings can begin at any point, but the average one starts just after the completion of the armhole shaping. For example, as on the round neck, there are 45 stitches on your work, and you need to have 24 for your shoulders. Since in V-neck shapings you count rows, and you have 6", or approximately 21 rows to work with, you would proceed as follows: Work across 22 stitches, chain and turn. Working on these stitches only, at each neck edge decrease 1 stitch every other row 10 times, then work 1 row even. When piece measures same as back to shoulder, shape your shoulder as on back. Return now to row where neck shaping began, skip center stitch, and work second half of neck and shoulder to correspond to first half, reversing all shaping.

Scoop necks are often the same for both front and back, although sometimes the styling might involve the regulation high neck at back and a scoop in the front only. The depth of this type of shaping is a complete variable, entirely up to your own discretion, although the average scoop occurs approximately 2" above the end of the armhole shaping and generally, by virtue of its width, narrows each of the shoulders by about 1½". Assuming that each of the shoulders in this case requires 8 stitches and there are 45 stitches on your work after the armhole shaping has been completed, you would subtract 16 (two shoulders) from 45 and be left with 29, which is the number of stitches to be worked in your neck shaping. You would probably proceed as follows: Work across 13 stitches, chain and turn. Working on these stitches only, decrease 1 stitch at beginning of next row (neck edge), and repeat this decrease every other row 4 times more. Work even now on 8 stitches until piece measures same as back to shoulders, if the back is regulation length, or whatever armhole measurement is required for the size garment you are making if the back is shaped the same as the front. The shoulder bind-off is the same as the back shoulder bind-off. Return now to row where neck shaping began, skip center 19 stitches and work second half of neck and shoulder shaping to correspond to first half, reversing all shaping.

Boat necks are quite simple to make, and there is never a variation between the shaping of the front and back of the garment. A boat neck is high and wide, and narrows the shoulders by the extra 3" or 4" absorbed by its width. In designing the boat neck, work to 2 rows before the start of the shoulder shaping, work across the foreshortened shoulder stitches of one side, chain and turn. Work 1 row even, then bind off for the shoulders as necessary. Return to row where neck shaping began, skip center stitches and work other side to correspond. If you want a narrow ribbed finish around the neck, you would start the shaping about 1" below the start of the shoulders and add your ribbing after the shoulder shaping has been completed.

Shoulder Shaping

The shaping of shoulders is a relatively simple procedure, started usually on the right side of the work after the armhole depth has been reached. The one point to remember is that shoulders should be shaped gradually in order to have the proper form, generally in two steps where a maximum of 18 stitches is involved for each shoulder, and in three steps, where there are more. For example, if there are 18 stitches to be bound off for each shoulder on the back of a garment, you would probably work as follows: When piece measures desired length to shoulders, ending with a wrong-side row, bind off 9 stitches at the beginning of the next row, work to within the last 9 stitches, chain and turn. Repeat this row once more, then slip stitch across remaining stitches for back of neck. If there are 24 stitches, bind off 8 at the beginning of the next row, work to within the last 8, chain and turn. Repeat this row twice more, then slip stitch across remaining stitches for back of neck.

Sleeve Shapings

A regulation long set-in sleeve, usually worked up from the bottom, starts with the wrist measurement and is worked at that measurement for approximately 2" to 3" whether it has a ribbed cuff or one started with the actual pattern stitch itself. When this portion of the sleeve is completed, a series of increases are made at each side of the work and are continued until there are enough stitches for the full width required for the underarm sleeve measurement. From that point on, you work even until the sleeve measures desired length to underarm, and then you shape the cap. To shape a cap, bind off at each end of the next row the same number of stitches as at armhole bind-off on front and back of the garment, then decrease 1 stitch at the beginning and end of every other row until the cap measures 3" less than the total armhole depth. You then bind off the necessary number of stitches at the beginning and end of each of the next 2 or 4 rows so that the number of stitches remaining measures between 1" and 2". These stitches become your final bind-off. This method of shaping the cap of a set-in sleeve always remains the same, regardless of the length or style of the rest of the sleeve.

Raglan sleeves are worked in the same manner as set-in sleeves to the point where the cap shaping begins. In shaping the raglan cap, the initial bind-off is again the same as that on the back and front of the garment; then you begin to decrease 1 stitch or pattern or part of a pattern (see our paragraphs on decreasing in Chapter 4) as often as is necessary so that the shaping conforms as closely as possible to the shape and length of the raglan on the front and back armholes. When piece measures about 2" to 2½" less than the full length of the armhole, count the number of stitches remaining, then decrease either more or less rapidly (depending on the number of stitches involved) so that the cap will measure, when completed, the same as the armhole, and there are remaining the number of stitches equivalent to approximately 1". These stitches become your final bind-off.

Slipovers

Most all slipover sweaters are worked with exactly the same number of stitches on both back and front, which is that number necessary for the bust or chest measurement, divided in half. Except in instances where there is a different pattern stitch styling on the front, both pieces are worked exactly the same to the point where neck shaping begins.

Suggested Standard Body Size Measurements

Baby and Toddler Sizes

SIZES	6 MOS.	1	2	3	4
Chest	19"	20"	21"	22"	23"
Shoulder back	8¾"	9"	9¼"	9¼"	9¾"
Shoulder	2½"	2½"	2½"	2½"	2¾"
Back of neck	3¾"	4"	4¼"	4¼"	4¼"
Armhole depth	4"	4¼"	4½"	4¾"	5"
Waist to underarm	5½"	6"	6"	6½"	6½"
Underarm sleeve length	6½"	7½"	8½"	9½"	10½"
Sleeve width at underarm	6½"	7½"	8"	8½"	9"
Crotch length	6½"	7"	7½"	8"	8½"

Children's Sizes

SIZES	4	6	8	10	12
Chest	23"	24"	26"	28"	30"
Shoulder back	9¾"	10¼"	10¾"	11¼"	12"
Shoulder	2¾"	3"	3¼"	3½"	3¾"
Back of neck	4¼"	4¼"	4¼"	4¼"	4½"
Armhole depth	4½"	5"	5½"	6"	6½"
Waist to underarm	6½"	7"	7½"	7½"	7½"
Underarm sleeve length	10½"	11½"	12½"	13½"	15"
Sleeve width at underarm	9"	9½"	10"	11"	11½"

Junior Sizes

SIZES	9	11	13	15
Bust	31"	33"	35"	37"
Waist	22"	23"	24"	25"
Hip	32"	34"	36"	38"
Shoulder back	11½"	12¼"	13"	13¼"
Shoulder	3¾"	4"	4¼"	4½"
Back of neck	4"	4¼"	4½"	4¾"
Armhole depth	6¾"	7"	7¼"	7½"
Waist to underarm	7"	7½"	7½"	8"
Underarm sleeve length	17"	17"	17½"	17½"
Sleeve width at underarm	11½"	12"	12"	12½"

Women's Sizes

SIZES	10	12	14	16	18	20
Bust	32"	34"	36"	38"	40"	42"
Waist	24"	25"	26"	28"	30"	32"
Hip	33"	35"	37"	39"	41"	43"
Shoulder back	12¼"	13"	13¾"	14½"	15¼"	16"
Shoulder	4"	4¼"	4½"	4¾"	5"	5¼"
Back of neck	4¼"	4½"	4¾"	5"	5¼"	5½"
Armhole depth	7"	7¼"	7½"	7¾"	8"	8¼"
Waist to underarm	7½"	8"	8"	8½"	8½"	8½"
Underarm sleeve length	17½"	18"	18"	18½"	18½"	18½"
Sleeve width at underarm	11½"	12"	12½"	13"	13½"	14"

Boys' Sizes

SIZES	Slipover			Sleeveless		
	SMALL (26–28)	MEDIUM (30–32)	LARGE (34–36)	SMALL (26–28)	MEDIUM (30–32)	LARGE (34–36)
Chest	27"	31"	35"	27"	31"	35"
Shoulder back	11"	12"	13"	10"	11"	12"
Shoulder	3¼"	3¾"	4"	2¾"	3¼"	3½"
Back of neck	4½"	4½"	5"	4½"	4½"	5"
Armhole depth	6½"	7"	7½"	7½"	8"	8½"
Length to underarm	11"	12½"	14"	10½"	11"	12½"
Underarm sleeve length	14"	15½"	17"			
Sleeve width at underarm	11"	11½"	12"			

Men's Sizes

SIZES	Slipover			Sleeveless		
	SMALL (36–38)	MEDIUM (40–42)	LARGE (44–46)	SMALL (36–38)	MEDIUM (40–42)	LARGE (44–46)
Chest	37"	41"	45"	37"	41"	45"
Shoulder back	16"	17"	18"	15"	16"	17"
Shoulder	5"	5½"	6"	4¼"	5"	5½"
Back of neck	6"	6"	6"	6"	6"	6"
Armhole depth	8½"	9"	9½"	9½"	10"	10½"
Length to underarm	15"	15½"	15½"	13"	13½"	13½"
Underarm sleeve length	19"	19¼"	19½"			
Sleeve width at underarm	15"	16"	17"			

Translation of Crochet Terms

AMERICAN		SPANISH	FRENCH	GERMAN	ITALIAN
Beginning	(beg)	comenzar	commencement	anfang oder anschlag	principio
Chain	(ch)	cadeneta	chainette	luftmasche	catena
Decrease	(dec)	disminuir	diminution	abnehmen	diminuire
Double crochet	(dc)	crochet doble	bride	staebchen	doppio crochet
Half double crochet	(hdc)	mitad de doble crochet	demi-bride	halbstaebchen	mezzo doppio crochet
Increase	(inc)	aumentar	augmentation	aufnehmen	aumentare
Loop	(lp)	gacita	bouclé	schlinge	punto lungo sciolto o cappio
Pattern	(pat)	patrón	point	muster	punto
Round	(rnd)	redondo o vuelta	rang	ründe	giro
Single Crochet	(sc)	crochet sencillo	maille serrée	feste masche	crochet
Stitch	(st)	malla	maille	maschc	maglia
Together	(tog)	junto	ensemble	zusammen	insieme
Yarn over	(yo)	hilo sobre la aguja	jeté	umschlag	gettato

INDEX

abbreviations, pattern stitches, 36
afghans
  designing, 28–29
  gauge, 28
  hooks/needles, 27, 90–91
  number of motifs needed, 114
  striping pattern, 29
  working, 160
  yarn, 28
  see also afghan stitch
afghan stitch, 90–98
  charted designs, 99–108
  clothing, 90, 91–92
  embroidery, cross-stitch, and, 91–92, 94, 99–108
  hook, 90–91
  increasing, 17
  multiple
    of any number of ch, 93, 95, 98
    of 2 ch plus 1, 95–98
    of 3 ch, 97
  see also Afghans
A-line shaping, 31, 159
alphabet charts for monograms, 99, 106–8
armholes
  cardigans, 162
  coats and jackets, 162
  ribbing, 17
  shaping, 32, 34, 160–61
    raglan, 161

beret and tam shaping, 164
binding off, 18
blocking, 21
blocks, 22, 113–38
body size measurements
  actual, using, 30
  baby and toddler, 167
  boys, 168
  children, 167
  "ease" of fit, allowance for, 33
  hip and bust, 33
  junior, 167
  men, 168
  women, 168
boys
  body size measurements, suggested standard, 168
  things to crochet for, 8
buttonholes and buttonloops
  forming, 20
  placement, 161

capes and ponchos, 161–62
cardigans, 162
  armholes, 162
  buttonhole placement,
  "ease" of fit, allowance for, 33, 162
  ribbing, 17
casings, waistband, 20

chain
    foundation, 14
    turning, 14, 16
chaining to turn for next row, 16
charted designs
    monograms, 99, 106–8
charting designs, 99–108
children
    body size suggested standard measurements, 167, 168
    boys, things to crochet for, 8
    girls, things to crochet for, 9
    small, things to crochet for, 8
circles
    making, 18–19
    squaring, 19–20
clothing
    afghan stitch, 90, 91–92
    buttonholes and buttonloops forming, 20
      placement, 161
    designing, 29–34
    fashions and fads, contemporary, 6–7
    filet crochet, 110
    fringes, edgings and insertions, 139–58
    gathering, 162–63
    measurements, suggested standard body, 167–68
    motifs, 114–15
    projects, suggested, 8–9
    shaping (see also Shaping), 159–66
    working sequence, 31
cluster pattern stitch, 54, 56, 61–62, 64–65, 74–75
    color, 85
    edging, 142, 145–47, 148, 149–50
    motifs, 124–25, 126, 130, 133–34
coats and jackets, 162
    afghan stitch, 90, 92
    buttonhole placement, 161
    ''ease'' of fit, allowance for, 33, 162
    shaping, see Shaping
colors
    changing, 16
    finishing: color over color, 25
    pattern stitches, 36, 82–89
    striping patterns, 25, 26, 27–28
contemporary crochet, 5–9
    afghan stitch, 90
    designing, own, 10–11
    hook sizes and stitches to inch, 3, 4

Crocheter's Guide, 12–21
    binding off, 18
    blocking, 21
    buttonholes and buttonloops, 20
    chain, foundation, 14
    chaining to turn for next row, 16
    circle, making a, 18–19
    colors, changing, 16
    decreasing, 17–18
    Double Crochet, 15
    foundation chain, 14
    gauge, 13
    Half Double Crochet, 15
    hemlines, forming, 20
    increasing, 17
    left-handed crocheting, 15–16
    practicing, 12
    ribbing, 16–17
    row, chaining to turn for next, 16
    seaming, 20–21
    Single Crochet, 15
    Slip Stitch, 15
    squares and rectangles, working, 19–20
    stitch, 14–15
    Treble Crochet, 15
    waistband casings, 20
    yarn, joining, 16
cross-stitch embroidery
    afghan stitch and, 91–92, 94, 99–108
    designs, charted, 99–108
cross-stitch pattern, 60, 78
cuffs, ribbing, 17
custom-made crocheting, see Designing your own crochets

decreasing, 17–18
de la Blanchardiere, Mlle Riego, 2
Designer's Guide, 159–69
    afghans, 160
    buttonhole placement, 161
    cardigans, 162
    coats and jackets, 162
    gathering, 162–63
    shaping
      A-line, 159
      armhole, 160–61
      hat, 163–64
      neck, 164–65

Designer's Guide *(cont'd)*
    shoulder, 166
    sleeve, 166
  slipovers, 166
designing your own crochets, 10–11
  afghan, 28–29
  body size measurements actual, using, 30
    suggested standard, 167–68
  charted designs, 99–108
  clothing, 29–34
  Crocheter's Guide, 12–21
  Designer's Guide, 159–69
  dress, child's, 30–33
  fringes, edgings, and insertions, 139–40
  hooks, selecting, 24, 27
  how-to of, 22–34
  information sources, 10
  motifs, 113–38
  pillows
    rectangular, 26–27
    round, 26
    square, 23–26
  rug, 27–28
  slipover, woman's, 33–34
  swatches, practice, 24
  yarns, selecting and buying, 24, 27
designs, charted, 99–108
Double Crochet, 15
Double Treble Crochet, 15
dresses
  afghan stitch, 90, 91–92
  body sizes, suggested, standard, 167–68
  child's, designing, 30–33
  finishing *(see also* Finishing), 32
  flounces, 32–33
  fringes, edgings, and insertions, 139–58
  hemlines, 20
  length, 30
  shaping *(see also* Shaping), 31–32, 159

edgings, fringes, and insertions, 139–58
  flounce, 32–33
  patterns, 141–58
    cluster, 142, 145–47, 148, 149–50
    fringes, 139, 143–45
    multiple of 4 ch plus 1, 153
    multiple of 7 ch, 150
    multiple of 7 ch plus 1, 151

    multiple of 7 ch plus 5, 152
    multiple of 10 ch, 151
    multiple of 12 ch plus 1, 153
    multiple of 14 ch plus 4, 151
    multiple of 16 ch, 152
    multiple of 16 ch plus 12, 150
    multiple of 17 ch plus 15, 152
    picot, 141, 148
    pompon, 145
    shell, 143, 146
    tassel, 144
elastic, casings for, 20
embroidery, cross-stitch
  afghan stitch and, 91–92, 94, 99
  designs, charted, 99–108
England, crocheting vogue, 1–2

filet crochet, 109–12
  clothing, 109
  decreasing, 18
  designs, charted, 99–108
  hook, 109
  increasing, 17
  rugs, fringed, 110
  thread, 109
finishing
  afghan, 29
  blocking, 21
  color over color, 25
  dress, 32
  fringes, edgings and insertions, 139–58
  hemlines, forming, 20
  pillows, 25, 26, 27
  rugs, 28
flounce, 32–33
foundation chain, 14
France, crocheting in, 1, 2
fringes, 139, 143–45

gauge, 13–14
  afghans, 28
  establishing, 13
  row gauge, 13–14
  stitch, 13–14
  testing, 13, 14
gifts, things to crochet for, 9
girls
  junior sizes, suggested standard measurements, 107

girls *(cont'd)*
    things to crochet for, 9
granny squares, 113

Half-Double Crochet, 15
hat shaping, 163–64
    berets and tams, 164
    brims, 164
    stocking caps, 164
hemlines
    edging, 139–58
    flounce for, 32–33
    forming, 20
history of crocheting, 1–4
    contemporary, 5–8
home, things to crochet for, 9
    fringes, edgings, and insertions, 139–59
    monograms, 99, 106–8
hooks/needles
    afghan, 27, 90–91
    filet crochet, 109
    pillow-making, 24
    rugs, 27
    seaming, 20, 21
    sizes and stitches to inch, 3, 4, 13

increasing, 17
    circles, 18–19
    gathering, 162–63
infants and babies
    body size measurements, suggested standard, 167
    things to crochet for, 8
insertions, 139–40
Ireland, crocheting in, 2
Italy, crocheting in, 1

jackets and coats, 162
    afghan stitch, 90, 91–92
    armholes, 162
    buttonhole placement, 161
    "ease" of fit, allowance for, 33, 163
    shaping, *see* Shaping
joining
    motifs, 114–15, 134–38
    seaming, 20–21
    yarn, 16
junior body size measurements, suggested standard,
    167

knot pattern stitch, 64

lace and lace-making, history of, 1–2
left-handed crocheters, 15–16
length, row gauge and, 13–14

measurements, body
    actual, 30
    "ease" of fit, allowance for, 33
    hip and bust, 33
    suggested standard, 167–68
men
    body size measurements, suggested standard, 168
    things to crochet for, 8
monograms, 99, 106–8
motifs, 22, 113–38
    joining, 114–15, 134–38
    number needed, 114
    patterns, 116–34
        cluster, 124–25, 126, 130, 133–34
        petal, 118
        picot, 131
        popcorn, 118–20, 123
        puff, 117, 127
        shell, 117, 126–27
    shaping and, 114
    sizes and shapes, 113
    yarn, 113–14

neck
    opening, divide for, 32
    ribbing, 16–17
    shaping, 32, 34, 164–65
        boat neck, 165
        round neck, 165
        scoop neck, 165
        V-neck, 165
needles, *see* Hooks/needles

open-mesh filet, 109–12
Orvieto lace, 1

patchwork, 113–38
pattern stitches, 35–89
    abbreviations and terms, 36
    chain foundation, 14, 36
    cluster, 54, 56, 61–62, 64–65, 74–75
        color, 85

pattern stitches *(cont'd)*
 edging, 142, 145–47, 148, 149–50
 motifs, 124–25, 126, 130, 133–34
color, 36, 82–89
cross stitch, 60, 78
decreasing, 17–18
edging, 141–58
increasing, 17
knot, single and double, 64
multiple, 36
 of any number of ch, 37–38, 50
 of 2 ch, 38–40, 42, 44, 48, 68, 70, 72
 of 2 ch plus 1, 41–42, 44, 46, 49–50, 52, 54,
  59, 75, 87–88
 of 3 ch plus 1, 40, 43, 49, 51, 59, 60, 66–69,
  73, 83
 of 3 ch plus 2, 45, 82, 88
 of 4 ch, 41, 45–46, 49, 50, 59
 of 4 ch plus 1, 54, 63, 65, 67, 70, 71, 73, 84
 of 4 ch plus 2, 48, 88–89
 of 4 ch plus 3, 53, 58, 66, 73–74
 of 5 ch, 64, 74–75
 of 5 ch plus 1, 55–56, 78
 of 6 ch, 43
 of 6 ch plus 1, 51–52, 54–56, 61, 64, 84–86
 of 6 ch plus 2, 69
 of 6 ch plus 3, 77, 89
 of 6 ch plus 4, 53
 of 6 ch plus 5, 70
 of 6 ch plus 7, 60, 78
 of 7 ch plus 1, 80
 of 7 ch plus 4, 58, 72
 of 7 ch plus 5, 69
 of 7 ch plus 8, 61, 85
 of 8 ch, 83
 of 8 ch plus 1, 63
 of 8 ch plus 3, 71
 of 8 ch plus 4, 65, 87
 of 8 ch plus 5, 72
 of 8 ch plus 6, 74
 of 8 ch plus 7, 62
 of 8 ch plus 9, 62
 of 9 ch, 65, 80–81
 of 9 ch plus 1, 52–53
 of 9 ch plus 2, 81–82
 of 9 ch plus 8, 70
 of 10 ch, 43
 of 10 ch plus 5, 48–49
 of 11 ch plus 9, 57, 89
 of 14 ch plus 11, 77
 of 16 ch plus 5, 76
 of 18 ch, 85–86
multiples, edging
 of 4 ch plus 1, 153
 of 7 ch, 150
 of 7 ch plus 1, edging, 151
 of 7 ch plus 5, 152
 of 10 ch, 151
 of 12 ch plus 1, 153
 of 14 ch plus 4, 151
 of 16 ch, 152
 of 16 ch plus 12, 150
 of 17 ch plus 15, edging, 152
petal, 78
 motifs, 118
picot, 58, 67, 71
 edging, 141, 148
 motifs, 131
popcorn, 51, 53, 59, 63, 66–67, 77
 motifs, 118–20, 123
puff, 40, 73
 motifs, 117, 127
selection, 35
shell, 49, 54–57, 61, 63, 65, 67
 color, 86, 89
 edging, 143, 146
 motifs, 117, 126–27
petal pattern stitch, 78
 motifs, 118
picot pattern stitch, 58, 67, 71
 edging, 141, 148
 motifs, 131
pillows, designing
 colors, finishing, 25
 rectangular, 26–27
 round, 26
 square, 23–26
 striping patterns, 25, 26
placemats, 3
pompons, 145
ponchos and capes, 161–62
popcorn pattern stitch, 51, 53, 59, 63, 66–67, 77
 motifs, 118–20, 123
practicing, 12, 24
projects, possible, 8–9
puff pattern stitch, 40, 73

puff pattern stitch (cont'd)
    motifs, 117, 127

raglan
    armholes, 161
    sleeves, 166
Renaissance, crocheting in, 1
ribbing, 16–17
row
    binding off, 18
    chaining to turn for next, 16
    decreasing stitches, 17–18
    gauge, 13–14
    increasing stitches, 17
rug
    designing, 27–28
    filet crochet, fringed, 110
    finishing, 28
    hooks, 27
    yarns, 27

scarf
    designing, 13–14
    motifs, 114
seaming, 20–21
shaping
    A-line, 31, 159
    armhole, 32, 34, 160–61
    back, 31–32
    beret and tam, 164
    binding off, 18
    blocking, 21
    capes and ponchos, 161–62
    front, 32
    gathering, 162–63
    hat, 163–64
    motifs and, 114
    neck, 32, 164–65, 34
    ribbing, 16–17
    row gauge, 13–14
    shoulder, 32, 34, 166
    sleeve, 31, 32, 166
        cap, 32
shell pattern stitch, 49, 54–57, 61, 63, 65, 67
    color, 86, 89
    edging, 143, 146
        motifs, 117, 126–27
shoulder shaping, 32, 34, 166

Single Crochet, 15
sleeve
    ribbing, 16–17
    shaping, 31, 32, 166
        cap, 32
    raglan, 166
slipovers, 166
    stitches, number of, 31
    designing women's, 33–34
Slip Stitch, 15
squares and rectangles, working, 19–20
stitches, 14–15
    afghan, 90–98
    decreasing, 17–18
    Half Double Crochet, 15
    increasing, 17
    pattern, see Pattern stitches
    Single Crochet, 15
    Slip, 15
    to inch (gauge), 13–14
        hook size and, 3, 4, 13
        testing, 13, 14
    Treble Crochet, 15
    Double, 15
    Triple, 15
    Tunisian Crochet, see Afghan stitch
stocking caps, shaping, 164
striping patterns, 25, 26, 27–28
sweaters
    buttonhole placement, 161
    cardigans, 17, 33, 161, 162
    designing, 33–34
    "ease" of fit, allowance for, 33
    filet stitch, 110
    ribbing, 16–17
    slipovers, 166
        stitches, number of, 31
        women's, designing, 33–34
    working sequence, 31

tam and beret shaping, 164
tassels, 144
techniques and terms, 12–21
    pattern stitches, 36
    translation of terms, 169
    see also Crocheter's Guide; specific subjects

throw pillows, designing
    rectangular, 26–27
    round, 26
    square, 23–26
Treble Crochet, 15
    Double, 15
    Triple, 15
trimmings, 139–58
    flounce, 32–33
Triple Treble Crochet, 15
Tunisian Crochet, *see* Afghan stitch
turning chains, 14, 16

waistband
    casing, 20
    ribbing, 17

women
    body size measurements, suggested standard, 168
    things to crochet for, 9
wools, crocheting with, 2–3

yarn
    afghans, 28
    buying, 24
    colors, changing, 16
    gauge and, 13
    hook size and, 3–4, 13
    joining, 16
    motifs, 113–14
    quantities needed, 24
    rugs, 27
    testing, 13, 14

Notes

Notes

73 74 75 76 77 10 9 8 7 6 5 4 3 2 1